Global Shipping in Small Nations

Global Shipping in Small Nations

Nordic Experiences after 1960

Edited by

Stig Tenold
Norwegian School of Economics

Martin Jes Iversen
Copenhagen Business School

and

Even Lange
University of Oslo

palgrave
macmillan

First published 2012 by
PALGRAVE MACMILLAN

Palgrave Macmillan in the UK is an imprint of Macmillan Publishers Limited, registered in England, company number 785998, of Houndmills, Basingstoke, Hampshire RG21 6XS.

Palgrave Macmillan in the US is a division of St Martin's Press LLC, 175 Fifth Avenue, New York, NY 10010.

Palgrave Macmillan is the global academic imprint of the above companies and has companies and representatives throughout the world.

Palgrave® and Macmillan® are registered trademarks in the United States, the United Kingdom, Europe and other countries.

ISBN: 978–0–230–29454–7

This book is printed on paper suitable for recycling and made from fully managed and sustained forest sources. Logging, pulping and manufacturing processes are expected to conform to the environmental regulations of the country of origin.

A catalogue record for this book is available from the British Library.

A catalog record for this book is available from the Library of Congress.

10 9 8 7 6 5 4 3 2 1
21 20 19 18 17 16 15 14 13 12

Printed and bound in Great Britain by
CPI Antony Rowe, Chippenham and Eastbourne

Contents

Tables

Figures

Preface and Acknowledgements

The roots of this book go back to informal co-operation between researchers at the Copenhagen Business School (CBS) and the Norwegian School of Economics (NHH) in 2007. The impetus was a common interest in research on modern Scandinavian maritime history and a desire to remedy the lack of established channels for such research. Among the early projects was a session at the 2008 European Business History Association Conference in Bergen, which also included participants from the University of Oslo (UiO) and the University of Southern Denmark (SDU).

In January 2009, the co-operation became more formalized, and also more 'Nordic'. The Centre for Shipping Economics and Innovation (CENSEI) at CBS organized an exploratory workshop: Nordic Responses to Economic Integration – the Shipping Sector, 1955–2005. The workshop, joined by participants from the Norwegian Shipping History project at the UiO and researchers from Sweden and Finland, was made possible through a grant from NOS-HS (The Joint Committee for Nordic Research Councils for the Humanities and the Social Sciences).

The 2009 workshop was held at Magleås Kursuscenter outside Copenhagen. Fittingly, this early twentieth-century manor had previously been the venue for informal 'consultations' between Nordic shipowners and shipping bureaucrats during the 1980s. After our meeting at Magleås, the co-operation was formalized into the Nordic Shipping Network, which has met on several occasions. The network also organized annual January workshops at Magleås in 2010 and 2011, again facilitated by grants from NOS-HS. The network members have also participated, with paper presentations and discussions, in two international conferences. The first was the conference 'The Global Shipping Industry in the 21st Century: Dynamics and Transformative Capacity', held in the Åland Islands in 2010; the second was the conference 'Shipping Revolutions after the Second World War', held in Uusikaupunki, Finland in 2011.

This book, which gives an overview of the recent shipping history of four Nordic countries, is the first 'physical' outcome from the Nordic Shipping Network. The editors would like to thank all the authors for their contributions, both the book chapters and discussions along the way. In addition, we are grateful for inputs from Agneta

Karlsson, Andreas Nybø, Thomas Roslyng Olesen and Runolfur Smari Steinthorsson, who also participated in the network. While the aforementioned grant from NOS-HS was necessary to get the Nordic Shipping Network off the ground, we would also like to show our appreciation for funding from:

- The Danish Maritime Fund, for support to CENSEI at CBS
- The Norwegian Research Council for the project *Norwegian Transformations in Shipping*, NHH
- The Norwegian Shipowners' Association and the UiO for the *Norwegian Shipping History* project

The editors would like to thank Paula Turner of Palindrome for patient and conscientious copyediting and Taiba Batool and Ellie Shillitoe at Palgrave Macmillan for editorial and practical support.

Contributors

Espen Ekberg is Postdoctoral Fellow at the University of Agder, Norway. He has published books and articles on the history of the consumer co-operative movement in Norway and internationally, as well as on the contemporary history of Norwegian banking. He is currently part of the research project on the history of Norwegian merchant shipping 1814–2014.

Martin Jes Iversen is Associate Professor of Business History at the Copenhagen Business School. He is the author and editor of several articles and books, including *GN Great Nordic – A Company in Transition* (2005) and *Creating Nordic Capitalism – The Business History of a Competitive Periphery* (2008). Iversen is currently studying the strategic development of the major Danish shipping companies, and is also writing a new book on the shipping conglomerate EAC from a long-term perspective (1897–1997).

Yrjö Kaukiainen is Emeritus Professor of European History at the University of Helsinki and a former President of the International Maritime Economic History Association. His research has focussed on the history of shipping in the nineteenth and twentieth centuries and the history of information transmission in the nineteenth century. Recent publications include 'Journey costs, terminal costs and ocean tramp freights: how the price of distance declined from the 1870s to 2000' (*International Journal of Maritime History*, 2006), 'Growth, diversification and globalization: main trends in international shipping since 1850' (*Research in Maritime History*, 2008) and 'The container revolution and liner freights' (*International Journal of Maritime History*, 2009).

Even Lange is Professor of Modern History at the University of Oslo. He is the founder and former director of the Centre for Business History at BI Norwegian Business School. His earlier research focussed on industrial development, banking, consumer co-operatives and economic policy in the nineteenth and twentieth centuries. Lange is currently directing a research project on the history of Norwegian merchant shipping 1814–2014. Among his recent publications are *International Merchant Shipping in the Nineteenth and Twentieth Centuries: The comparative dimension* (edited with Lewis R. Fischer, 2008) and 'The survival of family dynasties in shipping' (*International Journal of Maritime History*, 2009).

Thomas Taro Lennerfors is a research fellow at the Centre for Business Information Ethics and Associate Professor at the School of Commerce, Meiji University, Japan. His research interests are in business, management and technology and their relationship to ethics, philosophy, and culture. Lennerfors has a PhD in Industrial Management from the Royal Institute of Technology in Stockholm, Sweden, and is the author of *Stockholmsrederierna: Ägandet och nätverkens betydelse för tanksjöfartens utveckling i Stockholm 1980–2000* (2009).

Victor D. Norman is Professor of Economics at the Norwegian School of Economics (NHH) and a member of The Norwegian Academy of Science and Letters. He has published books and articles on a variety of topics within economics, including shipping economics and political economy, but his main research area has been international economics. He is the author, with Avinash K. Dixit, of the groundbreaking *Theory of International Trade* (1980). Norman was Minister of Labour and Government Administration in the Norwegian government from 2001 to 2004.

Jari Ojala is Professor of History in the Department of History and Ethnology at the University of Jyväskylä. He specializes in maritime and business history, and his recent publications include, with Jari Eloranta and Heli Valtonen, 'Quantitative methods in business history: an impossible equation?' (*Management & Organizational History*, 2010) and 'Productivity change in eighteenth century Finnish shipping' in *Shipping and Economic Growth 1350–1850*, edited by Richard W. Unger (2011).

René Taudal Poulsen is Associate Professor of Maritime Business Studies at the University of Southern Denmark. A visiting fellow at the Copenhagen Business School in 2011, he has worked within the fields of marine environmental history and maritime business history. He is a member of the Editorial Board of the *International Journal of Maritime History*. His publications include *An Environmental History of North Sea Ling and Cod Fisheries, 1840–1914* (2007) and, with Henrik Sornn-Friese, 'Downfall delayed: Danish shipbuilding and industrial dislocation' (*Business History*, 2011).

Hans Sjögren is Professor of Economic History and Institutional Economics at Linköping University and Adjunct Professor of Financial

History and Business History at Stockholm School of Economics. He has published extensively in the fields of business history and economic history, for example, on corporate governance, financial crises, history of entrepreneurship and innovation and economic crime. Among his books and articles are *Spelet i Saléninvest* (1999), *Den uthålliga kapitalismen: Bolagsstyrningen i Astra, Stora Kopparberg och Swedish Match* (2005), *Creating Nordic Capitalism – The Business History of a Competitive Periphery* (2008) and 'The transformation of Swedish shipping, 1970–2010: markets, regulations, strategies, and know-how' (*Business History Review*, 2011).

Henrik Sornn-Friese is Associate Professor of Industrial Economics at Copenhagen Business School where he is also co-founder and director of the Centre for Shipping Economics and Innovation. He has published in leading international journals such as *Research Policy, Transportation Journal, International Journal of Entrepreneurship and Regional Development, Industry and Innovation, Business History,* and *International Journal of Maritime History*. He is also author of a textbook on economic theories of the firm and several books on shipping and transportation. His works on the Danish maritime cluster have impacted directly on recent Danish maritime policy.

Stig Tenold is Professor of Economic History at the Norwegian School of Economics (NHH) and leader of the project NORTRASHIP (Norwegian Transformations in Shipping). He is the author of *Tankers in Trouble: Norwegian shipping and the crisis of the 1970s and 1980s* (2006) and other books and articles on Norwegian and international maritime history, East-Asian economic development, and business history. Among his current research areas are nineteenth-century sailing patterns, postwar maritime innovation and the concept of 'scenes' in popular music.

1
Global Shipping in Small Nations: Nordic Experiences after 1960

Stig Tenold, Martin Jes Iversen and Even Lange

The period from the second half of the twentieth century to the beginning of the twenty-first has sometimes been called 'the second era of globalization'. Shipping stood at the centre of this process, a position that may be explained in at least three ways. First, the shipping industry was by far the most important carrier of the expanding global trade in goods and raw materials, which made possible the wave of outsourcing and transnationally integrated value chains. Second, the shipping industry was more global in its growth strategies and political and institutional structures than most other industries. Finally, the cyclical movements of modern shipping could be regarded almost as an economic 'Richter scale' measuring the varying amounts of energy released by globalization. The fate of shipping is thus closely linked to the ebb and tide of economic activity and world trade. At the same time, the industry has made important contributions to the development and shape of the world economy through its reactions to the seismic disturbances.

The Nordic countries have played key roles in shipping for more than 150 years, and the shipping companies of those countries have also been able to respond to this recent period of very choppy waters. The purpose of this book is to map and analyse the varieties of strategies followed by shipping companies in the Nordic countries in the turbulent period from the 1960s until today.

The globalization process presented commercial and political players with a series of new challenges and opportunities – not only the rules of the game but also the playing field itself were changed. The manner in which these changes were interpreted, and the domestic responses to these interpretations, had important ramifications for the Nordic countries and their shipping industries. Differing experiences, changing political and institutional frameworks, as well as diverse shipping company strategies, can be used to illuminate the transformations that have taken place in the international shipping industry.

Declining manufacturing employment and loss of markets have been regarded as a threat to the Western economies over the last 20 years. However, a similar transfer of hegemony – reflecting the new dynamics of globalization – has been evident in shipping since the 1960s. A study of the shipping industry is therefore valuable in providing a map of the changing commercial and institutional landscape in a period of globalization. The strategic responses of both countries and companies determine their success in meeting the challenges of the changing international regime.

With shipping as a front-runner in the globalization process, the Nordic experiences may be useful when analysing the interaction between the domestic economy and the international arena. The unequal developments within Nordic shipping raise the fundamental research question behind this book: Why did important parts of Nordic shipping fail to respond effectively to the economic integration process, while others were able to exploit the opportunities presented by global growth? Answering this question would increase our knowledge in a number of areas. It would provide examples of the general dynamics of the shipping industry, as well as of the transformative capabilities of shipping companies and the relationship between institutional settings and business strategies.

Nordic shipping in transition

In the last part of the twentieth century the shipping industry went through a period of turmoil and fundamental changes. This was not unprecedented. Around a century earlier, the shift of technological paradigm – from sail to steam – presented the main industry actors with a set of challenges that were just as profound.[1] Subsequent technological changes have also been important – new methods of propulsion, large increases in vessel size and more advanced methods of cargo storage and handling. Such technological developments have also paved the way for institutional changes. Indeed, shipping became the first 'footloose' industry, where domestic linkages evaporated as the means of production – ships, capital and labour – were increasingly acquired in an international market.

With regard to both technology and institutions, the Nordic countries at times lagged behind the leaders, but were at other times in the forefront of developments. Nevertheless, Nordic shipping companies have throughout these periods maintained their positions as some of the most important providers of seaborne transport services. Indeed, Greece is probably the only country that has positioned itself as a significant global cross-trader comparable to the Nordic countries. Although the Nordic countries are relatively small compared to the international economy as a whole, they make up a considerable part of the fabric of international shipping.

Table 1.1 gives a rough indication of the Nordic countries' shares of the world fleet from 1960 to 2008. Although this is not a perfect or clear-cut measure of their importance in international shipping, it gives a rough indication of the role they play. To put the proportion of the fleet into perspective; the Nordic share of world population varied between 0.7 and 0.4 per cent over the period, while its share of world GDP lay between 1.9 and 1.4 per cent (Maddison, 2008).

The early 1970s marked the end of the post-war 'golden age' in shipping. The Traditional Maritime Nations (TMNs), to which the Nordic countries belonged, were threatened by the rise of new expanding players, including exotic Flags of Convenience (FoCs) such as Liberia and the Bahamas, the fast-growing Asian nations and, in the 1980s, the Eastern bloc countries.[2] Set against a background of rapidly growing

Table 1.1 Nordic shipping's share of world tonnage (grt), 1960–2008 (per cent)

	1960	1970	1980	1990	2000	2008
Denmark	1.75	1.46	1.28	1.22	2.51	2.98
Finland	0.55	0.61	0.60	0.25	0.43	0.28
Iceland	0.02	0.05	0.04	0.04	0.04	0.06
Norway	8.63	8.50	5.24	5.53	7.34	4.32
Sweden	2.89	2.16	1.01	0.66	1.48	0.90
Nordic	13.84	12.79	8.18	7.70	11.79	8.55

Note: Data for 1960–1990, by registration and 1995–2008 by nationality of owner. Because of the flagging-out of ships to foreign registers, the 1990 figure does not precisely represent the actual tonnage controlled by Nordic subjects. The source is Lloyd's Statistical Tables, various years. It should be pointed out that a comparison based on gross registered tonnage is likely to underestimate the Nordic region's importance for the shipping industry due to the relatively high share of advanced vessels in the region; see the statistical overview in Chapter 6 for some discussion of this. That chapter also provides a more detailed presentation of the development of the various Nordic countries.

world trade, Nordic companies played a important role in international shipping until the crisis of the 1970s and 1980s. After the crisis, the experiences of the various countries differed markedly. Denmark and Norway were able to fully or partly recoup their previous positions, while Swedish and Finnish shipping companies saw their shares of the world fleet dwindle.

Our retrospective analysis of the dramatic challenges of the 1970s and 1980s is of course influenced by the present state of the industry. Today the Nordic region encompasses the world's largest container company, several major dry bulk carriers and oil tanker companies, and a substantial number of companies with leading positions within specialized niches. These successful shipping companies are mainly clustered within Norway and Denmark, and even within specific towns such as Bergen, Copenhagen and Oslo. On the other hand, while most Swedish and Finnish shipping companies were apparently unable to take advantage of the new possibilities within shipping, companies from these countries still play significant roles within ro-ro (roll-on roll-off) and passenger shipping. This illustrates an important point: even within the different countries, there was a great variety of experiences. Some companies prospered, others disappeared.

Our focus on the corporate consequences of upheavals within the shipping world is particularly relevant to the understanding of the relationship between economic crises, structural transformation and innovation. It is easy to see that some Nordic shipping companies were able to identify new patterns for growth, while others failed to respond effectively to the challenges. How can these differences be explained?

In his seminal article 'The Creative Response in Economic History', Joseph Schumpeter (1947) argued that unexpected, dramatic, contextual changes will lead to two categories of corporate response. The first is *the adaptive response*, which is expected, well known and in line with conventional practices. The second category is *the creative response*, which refers to the previously unknown, innovative response, characterized by innovation: the introduction of new economic, technological or organizational methods. Our hypothesis is that the fundamental technological, economic and political upheavals at the end of the twenty-first century caused a number of important 'creative responses' within the Nordic shipping industry. A central purpose of this book is to unveil these responses and thus improve our understanding of the well-known creative destruction processes that take place in economic history. The history of Nordic shipping, in the latest age of fundamental transitions, provides a wealth of good examples in this respect.

The Nordic countries are often portrayed as a region with a common economic and societal 'model'.[3] The purpose of this book is not to confirm or further develop the idea of a Nordic model. We believe, however, that the existence of a common tradition implies that the Nordic countries have been subject to similar kinds of challenges. Even in the international maritime literature, there has been a tendency to view Nordic – or, more frequently, Scandinavian – shipowners as a distinct category (Lovett, 1996, p. 103; Jamieson, 2003, p. 47). Indeed, the maritime economist Martin Stopford (1997, p. 155) even suggests that there is a 'Scandinavian strategy', based on minimizing unit costs. The strategy is contrasted with, for example, the Greek approach of 'playing the market'.

But is it justifiable to regard the Nordic countries as a homogenous region? The chapters in this book show that there have been substantial variations in the roles, structures and strategies of the shipping industries in the different Nordic countries. Moreover, as a result of technological and institutional changes in the shipping sector, questions of national or regional dimensions are much more complicated today than they were in 1960.

Increased complexity – an overview

A discussion of the term 'the Nordic shipping industry' reveals increasing complexity along two dimensions as we move from 1960 towards today. First, the industry itself has become more complex. Second, the national aspect of the industry is no longer as straightforward to define as it was half a century ago.

Let us take the Norwegian shipping industry as an example of the dramatic developments that have taken place. In an analysis of 'the Norwegian shipping industry' that takes 1960 as its point of reference, the main source of ambiguity would relate to how the term 'shipping industry' is defined. It would include a heterogeneous combination of participants and activities, including, but not restricted to:

- different markets, with regard to geographical regions and cargoes transported;
- different types of ships, from ferries to supertankers;
- different areas of activity: shipowning, ship operation, management, etc., and
- different functions, from maritime labour, through investors, to shipowners.

Today, the term 'shipping industry' would include the same kind of heterogeneity, though it has become even more multifaceted as a result of the new markets, ship types, activities and functions that have been added since 1960. Indeed, it is no longer clear-cut what a shipping company does, or to whom the term 'shipowner' refers.

However, in a definition of the contemporary 'Norwegian shipping industry', there would probably be just as much ambiguity related to the concept 'Norwegian'. In 1960, the ships were flying the Norwegian flag, were manned primarily by Norwegian crews, were managed by Norwegian owners and were financed by Norwegian equity – but were serving the international market. Today, it is unclear how the 'Norwegian' component should be defined or determined. What kind of links should we look for, and how strong are they? This, of course, poses substantial challenges for anyone interested in evaluating the development over the period. In some ways, our unit of analysis becomes more and more blurred as we move along.

One way to avoid the effects of increasing ambiguity would be to restrict the analysis to ships and companies that comply with the '1960 definition' of Norwegian shipping throughout the period. That would keep the unit of analysis constant, but it would also mean that the correspondence between actual Norwegian shipping activities and the unit of analysis would deteriorate as we progress in time. Indeed, for the last 20 years of the period the unit of analysis would represent only a minor – and relatively unimportant – proportion of shipping in Norway. The object of our study would be precise and consistent, but it would gradually lose relevance.

The alternative is to treat the subject in a more pragmatic manner, by using the unit of analysis that at any given point in time covers the Norwegian shipping industry in the best possible manner. Although this implies that the subject under investigation will not be defined in the same way throughout the period, it should give an adequate representation of Norwegian shipping at various stages of development. Furthermore, some of the dynamics that we are interested in uncovering and investigating are embodied in the manner in which our subject is transformed across time.

The Norwegian example illustrates a transformation that affected all Nordic countries. The two trends above, the increasing complexity of the shipping industry itself and the demise, or weakening, of the national dimension, have been extensively covered in the literature on shipping, though seldom in an explicit or integrated manner. General overviews of the development of shipping in the period from 1960 to 2008 can be found in a number of contemporary sources and in most textbooks on maritime economics.[4] One of the main reasons for the increased supply-side complexity, technological innovation, has also been the subject of a number of studies.[5] With regard to the national dimension, the last fifty years have not been treated as thoroughly as previous periods, though there have been some analyses in 'country-based' shipping histories.[6] The new forms of registry and organization – including FoCs and 'second registers' – have so far received more attention from maritime economists and political scientists than from maritime historians.[7]

An overview of the arena – 'transformation' and 'relocation'

As previously noted, the shipping industry has been at the centre of developments towards an increasingly integrated world economy. It is a global service industry, transporting raw materials and finished goods from one country to another. Furthermore, the supply of shipping services has increasingly been based on the use of capital and labour acquired in international, rather than domestic, markets.

The linkages between integration in the commodity market and the demand for shipping are self-evident and relatively stable. Increasing world trade creates a need for, and enables the employment of, more shipping tonnage. Accordingly, the very strong growth of world trade since 1960 has laid the foundation for a massive expansion of international shipping capacity. The world fleet in 2008, measured in gross registered tonnage (grt), was almost six times as large as that of 1960.[8]

As a result of shipping's role as the main carrier of cross-border trade flows, the correlation between the growth of world trade and that of shipping demand is relatively strong. For shipping companies, however, the short-term fluctuations around this growth trend have particular significance. Indeed, some of the most prosperous periods in the shipping industry occur when 'exogenous' incidents – positive breaks from the long-term freight rate trend – enter the frame. As a result of sudden unexpected events, such as demand shocks caused by wars or canal closures, freight rates might multiply within weeks, and shipowners may earn large amounts of money. Conversely, strong competition in the shipping market implies that negative deviations from the expected trend have serious implications for the profitability of the shipping sector per se, although some owners might be able to take advantage of the deteriorating market. The period since 1960 provides several examples of both of these mechanisms.

Shipping is characterized by strong and irregular cycles, and the period from 1960 to 2008 has seen its share of both golden years and gloom. There was a strong upward trend in transport demand, particularly in the tanker market, from 1960 to 1973. Subsequently, demand stagnation, accompanied by an absolute decline in tanker transports, led to a shipping depression lasting approximately 15 years. The market during the last part of the 1980s and the 1990s was generally good, until freight rates dropped in the wake of the Asian crisis in 1997. The new millennium saw the strongest boom ever in certain market segments – at times referred to as 'the dry bulk supercycle' – before the spectacular bust in the second half of 2008.

Although the growth in demand has been important in providing an expanding 'playing field', Nordic shipowners were forced to adapt to the actions and strategies of the other players. To some extent they were able to influence the changes in the shipping industry – through, for example, technological and institutional innovations – but these actions were primarily a response to developments in the industry per se.

The two main trends in the structural development of the shipping industry may be labelled 'transformation' and 'relocation'. 'Transformation' is neutral in nationality terms, and simply refers to the changes in how the industry solved its main task: transporting goods by sea from one location to another. The term 'relocation' is partly related to transformation, but emphasizes the national (or, indeed, international) aspect, by also considering the nationality of the agents providing various aspects of the service.

The transformation of the shipping industry in the period 1960 to 2008 has been extensive. The key elements in that transformation are larger ships, new ship types, new patterns and centres of gravity in international trade, new businesses and changes in the manner in which seaborne transport is organized: 'Everything that we today consider modern shipping can be traced to concepts developed during the 1960s' (Bakka, 2005, p. 145).

The world fleet in 1960 consisted primarily of general cargo carriers, tankers, some bulk and combination carriers and a relatively small number of specialized vessels. The development trends most apparent up to 2008 were the extremely strong growth of the fleet and the average size of individual vessels, as seen in Figure 1.1, as well as the shifts in the importance of the various ship types.

Figure 1.1 clearly shows that both the world fleet and the average size of ships increased rapidly from 1960 to the second half of the 1970s. Subsequently that growth levelled out. The fleet declined every year

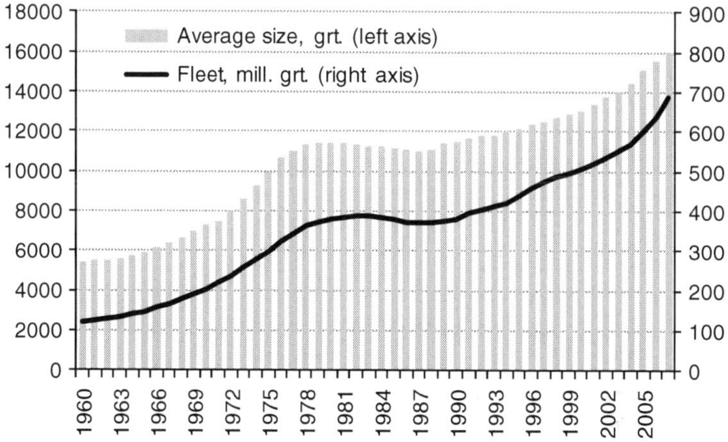

Figure 1.1 World merchant fleet (million grt) and average size of vessels (grt), 1960–2007

Note: Based on data from Lloyd's Register, as adapted by the Institute of Shipping Economics and Logistics, Bremen. Includes all ships larger than 300 grt.

from 1983 to 1986, before commencing on a long period of uninterrupted growth. The average size of ships reached a temporary peak in 1980. In the 20 years after growth resumed in 1987, the average size of the vessels in the world fleet increased by 46 per cent. This pales, however, when compared with the 113 per cent average size growth in the 20 years after 1960.[9]

The strong growth of world trade created a need for more and more shipping capacity and was a precondition for the six-fold expansion of the world fleet. The strong growth in the average size of vessels was a result of improvements in the shipbuilding industry and of the increasing volumes of goods traded by sea, which led to economies of scale in new trades. The shifts in the importance of the different ship types mirror the demand side development of the various segments presented above.

The main technological development in the oil tanker market was the increase in the average size of the vessels, which reached a peak in the late 1970s and has since remained relatively stable. In the non-liquid markets, a move towards larger and larger units was evident, but these segments were also characterized by alternative technological solutions. The dry bulk segment saw the same utilization of economies of scale as the tanker market, but also improved means of handling and storage.

In the general cargo market, two developments stood out. The first was containerization, which represented a new way of organizing transport services. As a result of containerization, and concurrent improvements in the land–sea interface, general cargo carriers have more or less disappeared from the regular liner services. The second development was specialization: flexible general cargo carriers were increasingly replaced by ships targeted at specific commodities such as cars, liquid natural and petroleum gases, forest products, chemicals, cement and tourists.

The process that we have referred to as 'relocation' occurred in parallel with the transformation of the world fleet. On the demand side, the growing importance of Asian economies in international trade was one dominant trend. Japan's emergence as an economic powerhouse in the 1960s and 1970s was significant. The subsequent growth of manufacturing among the Asian tigers and, in particular, China, has had a massive influence on shipping demand.[10]

The most important aspect of the 'relocation', however, is related to the supply of shipping services. The period 1960 to 2008 saw four related processes: the decline of the Traditional Maritime Nations (TMNs), the re-emergence of an international maritime labour market, rapidly growing cross-border investments and, finally, the slicing-up of the shipping value chain. In short – the supply of shipping services was 'internationalized' or 'globalized'.[11] Barton (1999, p. 149) refers to this development as a 'complex trans-nation-state phenomenon, marking a shift from national shipping essentially nationally owned and manned, to globalized shipping via multinational involvement in one ship'.

The 'supply-side relocation' involved a transformation of the fabric of the shipping industry. The domestic anchors of shipping companies – and the companies themselves – changed. Lorange (2009, p. 79) points out that 'the industry is no longer as characterized as it used to be by often relatively small-scale family firms. Publicly traded companies and professional managers have been increasingly replacing the privately held shipping companies and shipowners of the past.'

The first part of the 'relocation' process is the apparent reduction of the TMNs' shipping stronghold – the world fleet was increasingly registered under FoCs and in Emerging Maritime Nations (EMNs), particularly in Asia.[12] Kumar and Hoffmann (2002, p. 35) explain the declining role of the TMNs by a combination of the power of the market forces and 'the political reality of the bargaining table'.[13]

Originally, Greek and American shipowners were the main users of the FoC-institution. As recently as 1970, Cufley (1970, p. 321) claimed that '[o]wnership under the flags of Panama and Liberia was never widely spread amongst the maritime nations. The Governments of most of them prohibited such operations, and still do'. The attitudes of the European countries were, however, changing rapidly. Slightly more than ten years later, almost a quarter of the fleet of the European Community members was flying FoCs.[14]

The share of the world fleet registered in the OECD countries has declined from around two-thirds in 1970 to around 15 per cent in 2008. The main reason for this is the strong growth of the FoC fleets, the tonnage of which amounted to around one-fifth of the world fleet in 1970, but which today make up more than half of international tonnage.[15] Moreover, the fleets of a number of Asian countries have grown considerably. In 2008 almost 18 per cent of the world fleet was registered in China and 'the Asian tigers', up from less than 2 per cent in 1970.

An analysis based on the registration of the vessels provides different results from one based on actual ownership. The relocation becomes less clear-cut – hence the use of the word 'apparent' above – if we look at the actual ownership of the world fleet. However, the decline of the TMNs was nevertheless prominent, though not as dramatic as it was with regard to registration. It is likely that the OECD countries controlled around 80 per cent of the world fleet in 1970.[16] By 2008, the share of the world fleet controlled by the TMNs had declined to slightly more than 60 per cent, and around half of this tonnage was controlled by owners representing the two leading nations, Japan and Greece. Around a quarter of the world fleet was controlled by owners in China and the 'Asian tigers'. In some ways, the 'relocation' of the world fleet may thus be seen as another manifestation of one of the most noteworthy developments in the world economy in the post-war period, that is, Asia's increasingly important role in the world economy.

The second 'relocation' development was the re-emergence of a global market for maritime labour. The reduction of the TMNs' position implied that the dominant role of seafaring labour from these countries declined. The world fleet was increasingly manned by seamen from Asia and non-OECD countries, facilitated by the emergence of a global network of crewing agencies. The fact that FoC vessels could pick their crews from an international pool led to a cost advantage that forced the TMNs to open up for foreign, relatively inexpensive labour as well. Alderton (2004, p. 2) succinctly presents the basis for the formation of a global labour market as 'the industry's increasingly desperate preoccupation with crew costs'.

The third aspect of the 'relocation' pertains to the other main factor of production: capital. The last decades have seen shipping companies increasingly relying on foreign capital, in particular equity from abroad. Restrictions on cross-border capital transactions meant that, until the 1990s, investment funds had primarily come from domestic sources, either retained earnings or domestic equity markets.[17] However, larger vessels and more expensive technological solutions led to higher capital intensity and a greater need for external financing. These funds were increasingly sourced from an international market.[18] International banks, particularly in the United States and Great Britain, were attracted by the apparently high, risk-adjusted returns on shipping investments, and Stokes (1992, p. 23) claims that after the boom of 1967 'there was no stopping the surge of commercial banks wanting to get their piece of the action in shipping finance'.

The borrowing from foreign sources was only the first step, however. Kavussanos and Marcoulis (2005, p. 109) describe the evolution of ship finance from traditional bank borrowing, via charter-backed finance in the first post-war decades, to asset-backed finance and – from the 1990s – to raising funds from the public, either through bonds or shares. The global character of the latter development was to some extent held in check as a result of the various shipping nations' restrictions on foreign shareholding. However, the emergence of an international equity market has paved the way for a large number of cross-border takeovers, mergers and acquisitions (M&As). Cases in point are the Swedish companies Frontline and ICB, taken over by the Norwegian-born shipowner John Fredriksen in 1996 and 1999, respectively, and the old Norwegian company Bergesen, which was acquired by the Hong Kong-controlled company World Wide Shipping in 2003.[19] In the period 1996 to 2000 more than 40 per cent of mergers and acquisitions within shipping were cross-border M&As (Brooks and Ritchie, 2006). Moreover, several European shipping entrepreneurs have companies registered at the New York Stock Exchange, and use the US equity market as the main source of funding. The buyers of such shares, however, come from all over the world.

The three 'relocation' processes identified above paved the way for, and were enhanced by, the fourth process: the slicing-up of the value chain, which dramatically changed the nature of maritime business. This implied that the 'old' shipping companies, enterprises that owned tonnage, employed seafarers and oversaw commercial and technical operations, became far less important. One aspect of this was the rise of specialized 'ship management' companies.[20] According to Mitroussi (2003, p. 78), third-party ship management 'really took off' after the 1973 oil crisis. One of the reasons for this was the takeover of ships from owners in distress by creditors, with little experience within shipping. Subsequently, the influx of companies and investors that were more interested in asset play and dividends than in the actual shipping operations consolidated the role of external ship managers. This introduction of new corporate entities and strategies, including the separation of the ownership from the operation of vessels, fundamentally changed the manner in which shipping services were produced.

Lorange (2009, p. 82) has summed up the changes in the shipping industry, and their relation to the globalization process, as follows: 'with national borders opening up, deregulation in the industry, lower transaction costs, and the growing importance of the capital market, more and more companies are identifying one aspect of the value chain to focus on – e.g., owning ships, using ships, operating ships, or innovating around ships'. This provides a stark contrast to the 'Jacks-of-all-trades', the shipping companies of the past that traditionally controlled all of these activities.

As stated above, the purpose of this book is to analyse the choices and strategies that were formulated and implemented when the shipping sectors in the Nordic countries confronted the fundamental technological, political and economic changes of the last decades of the twentieth century.

First, we aim to map the overall development and substance of the Nordic shipping sector, with emphasis on different regional and national outcomes. These include the important technological and market niches in shipping in the Nordic countries, such as investment and growth within containers, product tankers, reefers, ro-ros, cruisers and supply. Second, we aim to analyse the basis for the development of shipping in the Nordic countries. In this context the chapters will discuss different preconditions for that development, including, for example, competitive structures and institutional and political frameworks.

We believe that such a comparative analysis would not be enhanced by an attempt to identify a system of homogenous Nordic shipping choices and strategies. Instead, we address the question of the basis for the success of Nordic shipping. Was it in fact a success for heterogeneity, with specialization as a result of market integration, technological changes and new political-institutional settings proving to be a good response to the challenges?

Although shipowners in the various Nordic countries were faced by more or less the same set of challenges, we have chosen not to have identical outlines for each chapter. The reason for this is simple: diversity among the various countries suggested that the main concerns, business responses and political considerations varied from country to country. This flexibility has enabled the authors of the different chapters to emphasize the features that they find most important for their particular cases.

The structure of the book

The book consists of chapters focusing on the development of shipping after 1960 in Norway, Denmark, Sweden and Finland. The structure, development and importance of the shipping sector have differed dramatically between these four nations. There are also two more general chapters on Nordic shipping. The first is a statistical overview, which presents data detailing the fleet development of Nordic shipping in general, as well as that of the individual countries, and also discusses the methodological challenges in comparing shipping data across time and countries. The second is a concluding chapter, which uses the knowledge from the previous chapters to look ahead and illuminate the question, 'Is there a future for Nordic shipping?'

In addition to the countries presented in the chapters of this book, there are other Nordic areas with strong links to the maritime industries. In fact, the relationship with the sea is, of necessity, particularly strong in island nations such as the Faroe Islands, Greenland, Iceland and the Åland Islands. All of these cases reflect certain characteristics of shipping in very small nations. In the Faroe Islands, Greenland and Iceland, the maritime dimension – shipping, but even more importantly, fisheries – has constituted a very important part of their national identities. On the other hand, their role in international cross-trades has been very limited. The shipowners of the Åland Islands, however, have a long history of selling their transport services to foreigners. There are very few nations in which international shipping has played such an important role in the local economy – in terms of investments and employment – as in this autonomous region of Finland.

In Chapter 2, Stig Tenold divides the development of Norwegian shipping into three chronological phases. First, the expansion from 1960 to 1973, when Norway's leading international role was cemented by substantial investments in the tanker and dry bulk segments. Second, the shipping crisis from the mid-1970s, which severely affected Norwegian shipping. At the same time, national legislation and rising operational costs led to a massive wave of flagging out, especially in the early 1980s. The final phase follows the introduction of the Norwegian International Ship Register (NIS) in 1987. This period is characterized by a revitalization of the industry, and is marked by a combination of more favourable political conditions and new maritime investments, both in traditional shipping segments and to an even larger extent in specific maritime segments such as offshore supply services, chemical tankers and gas carriers.

The chapter points out an important policy dilemma. On the one hand, until the late 1970s the authorities favoured a restrictive national flag policy in order to maintain Norwegian ownership, crews and investments. On the other, Norwegian shipowners experienced a shipping crisis, which made it increasingly difficult to fulfil this national desire. A dramatic process of flagging out in the early and mid-1980s was followed by the introduction in 1987 of the NIS. This was followed by a strong reflagging, reflecting the fact that high levels of operational costs had been one of the main obstacles for Norwegian shipping during the shipping crisis. In the 1990s and 2000s the more favourable flag policy was followed by a new tax regime. This changed from the pre-1992 system of high formal tax combined with substantial depreciation options (leading to continuous, but not necessarily rational, reinvestments) towards lower tonnage-based taxes. The idea of a 'level playing field' with other shipping countries gradually became the guiding principle of Norwegian tax and flag policies.

The Norwegian shipping company strategies changed in close conjunction with the transformation of the industry on a global level. Until the mid-1980s the structure of Norwegian shipping was quite heterogeneous, with many companies (in 1960, 164 shipping companies owned ships larger than 5000 grt) represented in different segments and registered in several coastal towns. Tenold argues that after 1987 the Norwegian industry moved in two directions. First, investments in specialized segments (in particular offshore) increased. Second, the linkages between the shipping companies and the Norwegian economy were blurred as the 'Norwegian' aspects of ownership, crewing and investments gradually became less clear. The analysis of the individual strategies of the Norwegian shipping firms is divided into four sections: small companies, characterized by a low survival rate in the long term, the medium-sized category, which historically had been most important, the large companies, which proved most likely to survive the crises and, finally, the newcomers.

The chapter is rounded off by four important insights into the experiences of Norwegian shipping from 1960 to 2008. First, Norwegian shipping was marked by cross-trades and was thus at the mercy of the international markets. Second, the problems for Norwegian shipping from the early 1970s were a result of stronger foreign competition as well as lower levels of demand. Third, the political regime played a critical role in the remarkable turnaround of Norwegian shipping after 1987, and, finally, Norwegian shipping is an example of a sector which historically has proven extremely adjustable to fundamental contextual changes.

Chapter 3 presents a success story. Henrik Sornn-Friese, René Taudal Poulsen and Martin Jes Iversen show how specific features linked to shipping company capabilities and the national policy framework characterized the expansive development of Danish shipping through four chronologically distinct periods. Focusing on the markets served, changes in fleet composition and the role of the institutional environment, the authors describe Denmark's distinctive path during the 'sunshine years' of the 1960s, the shipping crises of the 1970s and 1980s, and two intense phases of reframing and impressive growth since then.

The authors emphasize the importance of historical factors and path dependency. Developments in the longer early periods loom large in their explanations of the final growth outcome. Thus, the marked conservatism of Danish shipowners in exploiting the opportunities of the golden 1960s is seen as a precondition for the limited impact of the shipping crises in the following decades. In most other countries, the effects of the crises were devastating. Less vulnerable and less exposed through rapid expansion than most leading maritime nations, Danish actors were able to adjust and survive through turbulent market conditions.

Most of all, it is the particular structure of the population of Danish shipping firms that stands out as the salient explanatory factor behind the *Sonderweg* (special path) separating Denmark's development from those of the other Nordic – and indeed European – countries. Throughout the period the Danish shipping industry consisted of a small group of large firms, leaders in the industry since the late nineteenth century, such as the East Asiatic Company (EAC), A. P. Møller-Maersk and J. Lauritzen. Such a concentrated structure was unusual in the TMNs. Rewarded by their conservatism in the first phase, the five to ten leading firms, representing a major part of the industry, were in most cases able to weather the storm of the second period. The companies then became nuclei for innovation and growth from the late 1980s.

Two important factors seem to have facilitated the crucial role of the old shipping companies. First, they developed strong co-operative skills, both nationally and in an international context. Their co-operative relationships with other shipping companies in the early phases were articulated through a heavy reliance on the relatively stable liner shipping segment, which proved to be among the most profitable in the late 1970s. Second, the development of a co-operative business model – through pool agreements, commercial management contracts with foreign owners and the creative use of bareboat and time chartering – became something of a Danish speciality. This specialized business model accounted for a large part of the exceptionally strong growth of Danish shipping in the twenty-first century.

The establishment of a favourable national institutional framework is the last major factor explaining the expansive development of Danish shipping. From the late 1980s a new and more active national policy approach significantly helped the revival of the shipping sector. Tax and flag-registry regimes were changed along neo-liberal lines to accommodate the needs of globalization. At the same time an industrial policy inspired by Michael Porter's cluster theory, given the label 'the Blue Denmark', seems to have injected vital optimism and energy into the maritime sector, a sharp contrast to the situation in countries such as Sweden.

Illustrated by case studies of major shipping companies such as Maersk, Torm and Norden, Chapter 3 explains how Danish shipping was able to develop the world's largest container shipping company and become leaders in the world of bulk shipping through pools and commercial management. In a nutshell, it tells the story of how the protracted difficulties of the crisis years were overcome by the successful organizational reconfiguration of century-old companies.

Developments in Sweden stand in clear contrast to the Danish success story. In Chapter 4, René Taudal Poulsen, Hans Sjögren and Thomas Taro Lennerfors create a two-dimensional theoretical framework to analyse the decline of the Swedish shipping industry. Combining the influence of four different explanatory factors (markets, regulations, strategies and, finally, know-how and resources), they convincingly show how Swedish shipping fell victim to two periods of decline. The first, in connection with the shipping crises of the 1970s and early 1980s, led to the downfall of the old large companies. A number of new enterprises, partly based on know-how and financial assets that were rescued from the ashes of the defunct companies, expanded rapidly in the latter half of the 1980s and in the 1990s. These new entrants disappeared when they were taken over by foreign interests around the turn of the millennium.

The authors point out that the deteriorating markets in the period 1973 to 1987 can explain why the old structures of Swedish shipping came under heavy strain. However, given that these conditions were just as bad for foreign competitors, they use 'Swedish peculiarities' to illuminate the Swedish case. The regulation of Swedish shipping is the first of these factors. Three policy choices, in particular, reduced Swedish companies' ability to compete in international shipping after 1960: first, the reluctance to allow owners to register ships abroad in the 1970s; second, the failure to introduce an open ship register in the 1980s and finally, the rejection of a tonnage tax regime after the turn of the millennium. In sum, the authors posit that the regulation of shipping in Sweden was far less favourable than the regulatory regimes of countries such as Norway and Denmark.

Despite their emphasis on this unfavourable policy regime, Poulsen, Sjögren and Lennerfors do not acquit the shipping companies of blame. Like shipowners in other countries, the Swedish companies failed to perceive the extent of the structural overcapacity in world shipping markets after 1973. Moreover, for several of the large Swedish companies, a diversified strategy, with loss-making ownership interests in the shipbuilding industry, led to troubles on two fronts. The industry's resurgence from the mid-1980s onwards was primarily due to the appearance of a number of new players. Initially based on the purchase of cheap second-hand tankers and dry bulk carriers and on the operation of these ships under foreign flags, a handful of new companies expanded rapidly, resulting in an all-time high for the Swedish-controlled fleet of more than 20 million dwt by 1998.

The final explanatory factor – know-how and resources – can explain the demise of the new companies that had been responsible for the renaissance of Swedish shipping. The growth of these companies had partly been premised upon the commercial and technical know-how of personnel previously employed in the old shipping conglomerates. Moreover, the companies' financial resources were a combination of 'old' shipping money and new investors. In the long term, however, such know-how and resources were insufficient to ensure a sustainable Swedish shipping industry. This became evident around the turn of the millennium, when the newcomers were subject to more or less hostile takeovers by foreign interests and the companies' headquarters were moved away from Sweden.

There are still isolated 'pockets' of shipping activity in Sweden, and two successful companies – Wallenius and Stena – have shown that it is not impossible for shipowners to have a Swedish base. The two companies followed different strategies, a niche strategy and intra-industry diversification, respectively. For Swedish shipping per se, however, the combination of market forces, unfortunate regulations and failed strategies led to a dramatic deterioration of the country's once prominent role in international shipping.

One of the main lessons from the Swedish experience is the detrimental effects that the regulatory and policy regime can have on the development of national shipping industries. In Chapter 5, Jari Ojala and Yrjö Kaukiainen show that shipping hardly featured on the political agenda in Finland, which again reflects the limited importance of the industry to the Finnish economy. However, the industry was seen to have a very important *indirect* role, as a supporting line of business for the major Finnish export industries and as part of a wider maritime cluster in which shipbuilding played the most prominent part.

Ojala and Kaukiainen ask whether Finland should be considered 'a Nordic exception' as a result of its limited involvement in the international cross-trades. At the same time, they emphasize the crucial linkages between Finnish shipping and the country's imports and exports. Thus, they arrive at the very interesting conclusion that while Finnish shipping after 1960 looks 'modest' in a Nordic perspective, it would still be closer to 'the rule' than to 'the exception' in a global comparison. Indeed, the authors claim that in an international, rather than a Nordic, context, Finland is a rather typical shipping nation.

Several factors explain why shipping in Finland differed from the other Nordic countries. The fundamental reason is the fact that the main market for the shipping companies was carriage of the exports and imports of Finnish industries. This has a number of important implications. First, shipping's role as a 'support industry', rather than a free-standing revenue-generating activity, did not lead to a beneficial institutional environment. Second, the close link to the country's trade was also reflected at the company level. There were relatively few shipping companies in Finland, and the country's shipping industry was dominated by large industrial corporations that had integrated shipowning into their value chain. Finland's rapid transformation from a low-cost to a high-cost country reduced competitiveness in many segments. The shipping companies concentrated on the segments where they had an advantage for institutional or technological reasons. These segments are the transport of passengers in the Baltic and the transport of forest products, such as paper rolls and sawn wood.

Consequently, shipping's role as 'supporting actor' has led to a fleet structure that makes Finland distinctive from an international perspective. Finnish shipping companies are particularly strong within two segments: passenger shipping and ro-ro vessels, both ship types that are well-suited to the lines of business in which Finnish companies are involved. The focus on the home trades is also reflected in the fact that Finnish ships today have been constructed to operate in the difficult conditions of the Baltic, with a large share of the fleet designed to the highest ice classes.

Chapter 6, 'Nordic Shipping – A Statistical Overview', written by Espen Ekberg, provides an important quantitative overview of the sector from 1960 to 2008. The chapter gives a comparative analysis of four countries over almost 50 years. It maps the trends in both individual countries and for Nordic shipping in general. The analyses provide important insights into three overall aspects. First, the changing size of the Nordic fleets. Second, the relative importance of different market segments. Finally, the chapter unveils the important changes in the industry structure of Nordic shipping, including the changing levels of concentration. An appendix supplies an introduction to the statistical sources and various methodological challenges.

The chapters outlined above provide an account of the development of Nordic shipping over the last five decades. In Chapter 7 Victor D. Norman asks the intriguing question, 'Is there a future for Nordic shipping?' The chapter contains an in-depth presentation of the shipping industry and its peculiarities, with an emphasis on the role of independent shipping companies of the kind found in the Nordic countries. Norman provides an unconventional view – seeing shipping more as outsourcing than as a service – and points out that shipping appears to be 'inherently unprofitable'. Furthermore, he discusses 'the survival paradox': the question of why independent shipping has survived – in the Nordic countries and elsewhere – if we accept the suggestion that it is both unprofitable and risky.

Norman's assessment of the future potential of Nordic shipping takes as its point of departure the fact that the Nordic countries no longer have a comparative advantage in shipping of the Heckscher–Ohlin type, based on relative abundance factors. To succeed, Nordic shipping companies have to overcome this handicap, and Norman suggests that this may be done in three ways. First, Nordic owners can base their activities on intermediation; this can be done through the acquisition of low-cost (foreign) crews or cheap capital (for example, through special tax schemes). An alternative is to take advantage of the inefficient asset pricing within shipping, that is, to make money through the timing of sale and purchase of ships. The final alternative is to get the efficiency price premium paid within industrial shipping.

The problem with the three potential strategic avenues that Nordic shipping companies might follow in the future is that they are to some extent self-defeating or mutually exclusive. Although this in principle appears to paint a bleak picture of the future of Nordic shipping – what Norman calls the 'troublesome scenario' – he points out that there are opportunities for Nordic shipping companies to succeed, but that this partly depends on being able to maintain a critical mass of companies at the industry level.

Concluding remarks

Given that the book does not have a conventional 'concluding chapter', we have chosen to present some of the main findings here. The different national experiences presented above, and in more detail in the individual chapters, illustrate the validity of the research question behind the book: Why did important parts of Nordic shipping fail to respond effectively to the economic integration process, while other parts were able to exploit the global growth opportunities?

It is evident that the answers to this question must be sought in the interrelationships between the international market, the domestic policy regime and the strategies of individual businesses. Moreover, to identify the specific responses of the small, open Nordic economies, we may consider the international dimension as more or less exogenous. We are thus left with two parameters – domestic policies and company-specific strategies – that have been particularly important in determining the national trajectories.

How do policy conditions and business strategies relate to each other? Is the relationship characterized by substitutability, complementarity or both? The case of Sweden, where two companies have succeeded despite a policy regime that has been characterized as detrimental, shows that with a sufficiently good strategy, the negative effects of the policies may be neutralized. Similarly, the failures of shipping companies in Norway and Denmark, even in periods of advantageous market conditions, illustrate that a beneficial policy regime alone is insufficient to ensure the profitability of the shipping companies.

This does not mean, however, that policies are unimportant. If we consider the populations of shipping companies in the various Nordic countries, rather than isolated company cases, the potentially important role of shipping policies becomes evident. Given the different policy conditions, it should not come as a surprise that the shipping industry – measured, for example, by the international position of the fleet – has been reduced much more in Sweden than in Denmark or Norway. Shipping policies clearly go some way to explain this difference. The formulation of the policy regime – in particular the role as a supplier of services to the country's trade – can also explain the special development of the Finnish shipping industry.

Although domestic shipping policies create a framework of conditions, benevolent political intentions alone do not enable shipowners to build up sufficient competitive power in the international market. The varying fortunes of EAC and Maersk in Denmark, of Reksten and Bergesen in Norway and of Salén and Stena in Sweden are a testament to this. Corporate strategies are undoubtedly important in determining both failure and success.

Would it have been possible – based on the knowledge available in 1960 – to predict the fates of the individual Nordic shipping companies over the subsequent 50 years? Obviously not. However, with the benefit of hindsight – the knowledge from the various country chapters – we can make more informed 'guesses'. Two elements stand out as crucial in explaining the differences between the companies that responded effectively to the economic integration process and the companies that were unable to exploit the growth opportunities it offered.

The first important element is how the companies reacted when faced with the turbulence of the international market. A useful tool for evaluating these reactions is the distinction between adaptive and creative responses, as presented above. The corporate success stories in this book all involve some kind of innovative approach to the challenges. Technologically based creative responses – the introduction of new ship types and the establishment of specialized niches – have been a common element for most of the surviving Norwegian shipping companies. Commercial and operational innovations – such as the creative use of pools and management contracts – have been a crucial ingredient in the spectacular growth of Danish shipping over the last decade.

Nevertheless, innovation in itself is not enough. Several of the pioneers have disappeared, sometimes eclipsed by more adept followers. Creative responses therefore did not provide a guarantee of survival and success. This brings us to the second element that can explain the fates of the various companies: their choices during 'defining moments'.

One characteristic typical of the leading Nordic shipping companies today is that they have managed to tailor their strategies to the new opportunities presented by the 'second era of globalization'. The way they have been able to do this, however, is easier to identify when we compare it with the companies that were left by the wayside. The chapters therefore devote ample space to the Nordic failures as well.

The companies that lost their once leading positions, or disappeared altogether, generally fall into one of two categories. First, the majority of the companies simply failed to respond to the changing world; while a creative response could not guarantee success, a 'business-as-usual' approach may be regarded as a recipe for decline. Second, for many otherwise successful companies, there have been isolated strategic choices that have led to their demise or decline. The typical example is ill-fated investments, where substantial parts of the company's capital and resources are tied to investments that turn out to be unprofitable.

In this book, we do not give a recipe for future success in the shipping industry. Indeed, we are even reluctant to provide such a recipe for the past. However, the insights from the chapters in this book enable us to say something about the *probability* of success. Given the effects of the policy regime, Swedish companies were more likely to fail than the shipowners in Denmark and Norway. The Danish and Norwegian authorities embraced – albeit reluctantly – the possibilities brought about by the transformation and relocation of the international shipping industry. The Swedes fought against these changes. As a result of the rapid transformation of the international market, companies that had a creative response to the upheavals were more likely to succeed than shipowners that tried to cling to their positions within the 'old' market segments. The consolidation of the shipping industry meant that large companies had a favourable starting point relative to smaller companies.

The Nordic countries, as a group, continue to play an important role in international shipping. Although their share of the international shipping market, in pure tonnage terms, is smaller than it was in 1960, the Nordic presence still constitutes a formidable force in world shipping markets, and in several segments Nordic shipowners have dominant positions. Is this position sustainable in the longer term? In this introduction we have shown that a variety of responses, at both government and company level, have enabled Nordic shipowners, as a group, to maintain their competitive powers from 1960 until today. However, we have also shown that one of the key ingredients in this development is the 'erosion' of the domestic dimension; the leading Nordic companies have been able to stay at the top of their game by becoming 'less Nordic'.

Notes

1. The experiences of the Nordic countries during the transition from sail to steam were addressed in 1980 in a special issue of *Scandinavian Economic History Review*.

2. While the term 'Flags of Convenience' has obvious political connotations, we use it in a neutral manner, reflecting the fact that this was the term used at the time for ships registered in open registers.
3. See, for example, Johnson and Turner (2006)
4. For annual overviews, see, for example, the publications by the Organisation for Economic Cooperation and Development (OECD, 1954–95), the United Nations Conference on Trade and Development (UNCTAD, 1971–2009), or broker reports from, for example, Fearnley & Eger's Chartering Co./ Fearnley's (1960–2009). All of these sources include detailed time series covering the development of shipping demand, the world fleet and freight rates. For presentations with a longer perspective, see, for example, the detailed overviews in Kaukiainen (2008a), Stopford (2009, pp. 35–46 and 118–30) or Wijnolst and Wergeland (2009, pp. 5–176); the discussion of the development to the early 1980s in Beth, Hader and Kappel (1984) or Frankel (1987), or a political economy analysis of the same period in Cafruny (1987). More thematically oriented analyses include the discussions of freight rate developments in Hummels (2007), Kaukiainen (2006, 2009) and Lundgren (1996). The best overview of academic publications on shipping in the last quarter of the twentieth century, though slightly outdated, remains that of Broeze (1998b).
5. Overall surveys of technological development in shipping include Gardiner (1992) and Wijnolst and Wergeland (2009, pp. 177–407). With regard to specific segments, the focus has to a large extent been on containerization and the liner industry; see, for example, Broeze (2002), Talley (2000) and the three books published to commemorate 'the fiftieth anniversary of container shipping', Cudahy (2006), Donovan and Bonney (2006) and Levinson (2006). One source that to a surprisingly limited extent has been mined by maritime historians and economists is the detailed surveys of supply and demand in the various market segments published by shipping analysts such as Drewry and Clarkson.
6. The country that has the best coverage is probably Greece; see Harlaftis (1993, 1996), as well as the more recent Harlaftis and Theotokas (2009). Other contributions that analyse the development of individual countries in this period are Kaukiainen (1993) on Finland, Gibson and Donovan (2000) on the United States, Chida and Davies (1990) on Japan and Jamieson (2003) on the United Kingdom. A new direction in the research on national shipping environments appeared as a result of the theories of 'maritime clusters'. However, most of these contributions give a 'snapshot' presentation of the industries in various countries, rather than an analysis of the long-term dynamics; see, for example, Benito et al. (2003), Wijnolst et al. (2003) or Sornn-Friese (2003).
7. The book by Metaxas (1985) of course misses the developments of the last 25 years, but still provides a good overview of numerous issues related to Flags of Convenience. Mansell (2009, pp. 1–24 and 91–116) discusses the flag state issue and its recent development, whereas Sletmo and Holste (1993) and Thanopoulou (1995) link the flag issue to competitive advantages and market conditions respectively. Organizational changes, in particular the rise of 'ship management' companies, have been addressed by, for example, Mitroussi (2003) and Sletmo (1989), while Theotokas (2007) and Lorange

(2005, 2009) discuss the relationship between shipping company strategies and organization.

8. Based on data from Lloyd's Register, as adapted by the Institute of Shipping Economics and Logistics, Bremen. Includes all ships larger than 300 grt.
9. Calculated on the basis of data from Lloyd's Register, as adapted by the Institute of Shipping Economics and Logistics, Bremen. Includes all ships larger than 300 grt.
10. The term 'Asian tigers' refers to the so-called 'first generation tigers' Hong Kong, Singapore, South Korea and Taiwan and the 'second generation' of Malaysia, Indonesia and Thailand.
11. Alderton and Winchester (2002) and DeSombre (2002, 2006) are examples of research that links the changes in international ship registration directly to the globalization process.
12. For early discussions of FoCs, see Carter (1956), Rochdale (1970) and Osieke (1979).
13. The question of political bargaining is related to the relative bargaining power of cargo-owners and service providers; policies have increasingly been designed to facilitate the movement of goods, regardless of the nationality of the service provider.
14. By 1983, on average 22.7 per cent of the fleets of the ten EC countries were flying Flags of Convenience; data from the Commission of the European Communities (1985), reprinted in Yannopoulos (1988, p. 199).
15. These shares are not indisputable; in particular, the proportions are sensitive to the type of measurement (number of ships, grt or dwt), as well as the definition of the term 'Flags of Convenience'. The data on which the shares are based come from various publications from OECD and UNCTAD.
16. This is based on the share of the OECD-registered tonnage, in addition to the conservative assumption that 80 per cent of the tonnage registered in FoC countries at the time was actually controlled by OECD countries.
17. An exception was, of course, the ships flying FoCs.
18. This is not to say that foreign mortgages were irrelevant before 1960. For example, a substantial part of the Norwegian interwar tanker expansion was facilitated by Swedish banks, and a 1931 article points out that 'It would seem that shipbuilders today to be successful in obtaining orders for the construction of vessels must be financiers rather than builders, as the cost of construction does not count as much as the arranging of the finance for the owner', *Fairplay*, 8 January 1931, p. 108.
19. On the takeovers in Sweden, see Lennerfors (2009, pp. 115–26).
20. See, for example, Spruyt (1994), Panayides and Cullinane (2002), Panayides (2003) or Mitroussi (2003).

2

Boom, Crisis and Internationalized Revitalization: Norwegian Shipping

Stig Tenold

Introduction

The development of Norwegian shipping in the period from 1960 until today has gone through three distinct phases. Massive expansion in the pre-1973 period was followed by decline during the shipping crises of the 1970s and 1980s. The country's shipping industry was revitalized after 1987, following the introduction of the Norwegian International Ship Register. Although the sector has changed tremendously over the period, as a result of innovation, diversification and an increase in internationally sourced factors of production, it remains the case that many of the current service providers have deep roots and long-standing experience within the industry.

The aim of this chapter is to give a broad overview of Norwegian shipping from 1960 to 2008 and point out some of the most important factors that have shaped the development of the industry. The growth, decline and resurgence of Norwegian shipping are explained through the development of four partly related arenas: the international economy (demand), transformations in international shipping (world supply), Norwegian political responses and, finally, strategic adaptation by Norwegian shipowners.

The chapter has three parts. First, some of the main developments in shipping demand and supply over the period 1960 to 2008 are presented. This is followed by an analysis of the Norwegian authorities' responses to the developments at the international level. Finally, the strategies of Norwegian shipping companies are evaluated.

Most of the demand for shipping is purely international. Seaborne transport services are primarily purchased in a world market where the nationality of the transport provider is largely irrelevant. Certain trades and cargoes have been affected by restrictions, but the vast majority of the goods transported in international waters are not influenced by such considerations. Most shippers do not consider the nationality of ships when buying transport services. Consequently the integration of service and commodity markets – the demand side of the globalization process – has been evident throughout the post-war period, and has had a relatively uniform effect on shipowners in different countries.

With regard to the integration of the markets for capital and labour, on the other hand, the policies and regulations enforced by the various shipping nations play a much more important role. Thus in these markets – the supply side of the globalization process – there have been substantial differences between shipowners in different countries. The overall trend has been towards the liberalization of both labour and capital markets, but there are large differences in the speed and degree of integration from one country to another. In general Norway was relatively late in opening up to foreign labour and capital, and Norwegian shipowners' access to investing in shipping companies abroad was also limited during the first decades of our study.

The distinction between the demand and supply sides of the globalization process is used as a backdrop for the analysis that follows. The two sides are, of course, closely related. For example, it will be argued that the depressed demand conditions in the late 1970s and early 1980s, in tandem with supply-side liberalization by important competitors, led the Norwegian authorities to 'globalize' the supply of Norwegian shipping.

Table 2.1 gives a schematic overview of the main trends in the shipping sector in the period 1960 to 2008. Important parameters are overall market conditions (international demand), changes within the shipping industry (international supply), the political framework within Norway and the dominant strategies followed by Norwegian shipping companies. The table therefore provides a template for the subsequent analysis.

This chapter follows the blueprint presented above. We start by sketching demand trends and the transformation of shipping supply at the international level. The Norwegian political responses are then presented, before we look more closely at how Norwegian shipping companies adapted to the situation, given the constraints embedded in the domestic policy.

Table 2.1 Dominant trends in demand, supply, policies and strategies, 1960–2008

Period	Demand	Shipping industry	Political response	Norwegian strategies
1960–73 Boom	Strong growth, in particular oil	Massive investments	Flag regime, limited influence	Economies of scale and innovation
1974–87 Crisis	Collapse (oil) and modest growth	Lower growth and tough competition	Crisis relief and liberalization	Specialization
1988–2008 Revitalization	Recovery and dry bulk supercycle	Further growth and internationalization	The NIS and the taxation issue	Supply-side decoupling

The international economy – shipping demand and supply, 1960–2008

The one thing that – in conceptual terms – remains more or less constant in our unit of analysis is the demand for shipping services, which primarily has been, and mainly still is, international.[1] Consequently one of the main determinants of the development of Norwegian shipping can be considered exogenous: Norwegian owners and authorities can have only a limited effect on demand for their shipping services. It is true that by targeting specific market segments and influencing international regulations it becomes possible to 'nudge' demand in the right direction, but by and large the demand for shipping has to be considered as given. This is particularly relevant for a small country such as Norway, which has traditionally been a relatively insignificant participant in international trade. Third-country shipping has been much more important to Norwegian shipowners than domestically based transport services ever since the 1860s (Brautaset, 2002, pp. 129–67).

The development of demand – in good times and bad – determines the room to manoeuvre for shipowners and other industry participants. The extent to which they are able to adapt successfully to the situation is determined by their own strategies, as well as those of their competitors. This proposition is valid for individual owners as well as for maritime nations. Our analysis looks specifically at demand within three segments: oil transports, dry bulk transports and specialized shipping. Although the backdrop is the same in all instances – demand growing at rates not seen since the pre-1914 period – the basis for the growth, and the growth paths, differed between the segments. Owing to Norway's relatively limited involvement in the liner industry, the development of this part of the shipping market will not be discussed in detail.[2]

Before the oil price increases of the 1970s, the oil transport market was the most vibrant part of the shipping industry. Two factors, in particular, can account for the increase in demand; oil became more important as a source of energy and as an input in production processes, and shifts in the centres of production and consumption increased the average length of voyages and had a positive impact on shipping demand. This was further exacerbated by the closure in 1967 of the Suez Canal, which led to additional increases in sailing distances, as tankers plying some of the most important routes were forced around the Cape of Good Hope.

Until 1973 the double-digit percentages in the growth of the oil market provided respectable profits for a rapidly growing fleet of larger and larger tankers. However, crude oil transport was the market segment that was most severely hit by the subsequent shipping depression, with substantial overcapacity amid falling demand. The market picked up after its nadir in 1983, but growth rates in the subsequent decades were far lower than those witnessed before 1973, as seen in Table 2.2.

The structure of the tanker market changed fundamentally during the crisis. The oil companies scaled down their own investments in tanker capacity, and a growing proportion of the trade was undertaken in the spot market, rather than on medium- or long-term charter contracts. In the early 1970s only around a fifth of the tanker fleet had traded in the spot market but by the late 1990s more than 70 per cent of the fleet was operated on a voyage-by-voyage basis (Stopford, 2009, p. 437). The development partly reflected the reduced dominance of the major oil companies in the oil trading market.

The dry bulk market also saw rapid growth during the 1960s which slowed after the 1973 oil price increase. However, there was no absolute decline in demand of the kind witnessed in the oil tanker market, and there was also increasing variation between the different major dry bulk goods, as seen in Table 2.3. Moreover, whereas the post-crisis growth rates in the oil tanker market were reduced decade by decade,

Table 2.2 Annual growth and decline of oil transport demand, 1962–2008

Period	1962–67	1967–73	1973–83	1983–90	1990–2000	2000–08
Growth	12.4 %	16.3%	–5.9%	3.9%	2.7%	2.2%

Note: Annual compound growth rates of crude oil transports, based on ton-miles. Data calculated on the basis of Fearnley & Eger, *Review*, various issues.

Table 2.3 Growth of dry, bulk transport demand, 1962–2008

Period	1962–73	1973–80	1980–90	1990–2000	2000–2008
Iron ore	16.1%	2.1%	2.0%	2.6%	8.4%
Coal	10.6%	10.7%	6.8%	3.1%	5.7%
All non-oil bulk	10.5%	5.2%	2.4%	3.7%	6.0%

Note: Annual compound growth rates, based on ton-miles. Data calculated on the basis of Fearnley & Eger, *Review*, various issues.

dry bulk growth accelerated in the 1990s and in the first years of the new millennium. In the period 2000 to 2008 the enormous increase in Chinese iron ore imports led to a 'supercycle', with record freight rate levels. The spectacular crash in the market during the second half of 2008 had many of the same characteristics as the oil transport collapse in the early 1970s.

The final segment presented in this brief overview of shipping demand – specialized shipping – is heterogeneous relative to the previous two. The growth of this segment was partly based on trade taken over from general cargo vessels and partly on the transport of commodities that had hitherto not been transported by sea. The low starting points of many specialized subsegments mean that the growth rates are very high. Among the most important specialized shipping segments are gas shipping, reefer transport, chemical tanker transport, open hatch bulk shipping and cruise shipping.

Owing to the variety in the nature of the goods transported by specialized ships, it is difficult to give precise aggregate demand data. However, we may gain an indication of the extent of the growth by looking at the supply of specialized shipping services. The world's fleet of specialized vessels consists of around 8000 ships, corresponding to around one-sixth of the world's cargo ships. Stopford (2009, p. 69) lists thirteen different types of specialized ships, while the overview from 1960 in Cufley (1960, pp. 221–93) contains only three types of vessels referred to as 'specialized': LPG (liquid petroleum gas) carriers, reefers and bulk carriers. However, the latter category is not even counted among the specialized ship types by Stopford.

Norwegian responses I – shipping policies

As a Traditional Maritime Nation (TMN), and one in which shipping played a paramount role in external economic relations and in domestic economic development, Norway was hugely affected by changes in the shipping industry. Moreover, despite being an important part of the country's economy, the shipping industry was in many ways 'independent'. There were 'few industrial carriers, no conglomerates and little capital from other industries placed in shipping' (Seland, 1973, p. 31). This, of course, has important implications, as it means that the fate of the country's shipping companies can be explained only to a very limited extent by developments outside the maritime industry.

In order to provide a structured analysis, we should consider developments at three interrelated levels. The first is the international arena, where the Norwegians (authorities and shipowners) have had to adapt to changes in transport demand as well as to the actions of authorities and owners in other countries. The second is the domestic regulatory level, where the authorities have responded to the developments that have been taking place at the international level. The players at the third level are the individual shipowners, who have had to address and react to driving forces and challenges at the international level, but at the same time have been constrained (or helped) by the Norwegian regulatory regime.[3] Table 2.4 provides a schematic presentation of the most important driving forces and challenges at the various levels.

The chapter has so far primarily dealt with the development of the international shipping market – level 1 of this table – and the challenges and opportunities that the changes at this level posed to shipping nations and companies. The subsequent analysis will first focus on

Table 2.4 The playing field – driving forces and challenges

	Participants	**Driving forces**	**Challenges**
Level 1	All shipowners and maritime nations	Demand for seaborne transport	Adapting to development in demand, given the actions of competitors (other shipowners and other maritime nations)
Level 2	National authorities	Challenges from level 1	Enabling the country's shipowners to maintain competitiveness, given a set of political values and considerations
Level 3	Domestic shipowners	Challenges from levels 1 and 2	Finding sustainable profit-making strategies, given expectations about development at level 1 and influence from the authorities at level 2

the adaptation of the Norwegian authorities to the upheavals in the shipping industry. This 'domestic framework' will then be used to explain the business side – the investments and strategies of Norwegian shipowners.

Shipping policies – a framework

Several aspects of government policy affect companies in the maritime sector. The most obvious is shipping policy itself, which covers issues of flag and registration, manning requirements, cargo reservation, safety regulations, and so on. However, economic policies in general, and tax policies in particular, as well as education, research, business and industrial policies also influence the decisions and strategies of shipping companies. Sturmey (1965, p. 15) defined shipping policy as a policy that 'formulates, or encourages, measures to interfere with or control the impact of market forces on the employment of shipping. The interference may extend from ad hoc measures to a carefully planned and continuous policy.'[4]

So what characterized the regulatory framework of Norwegian shipping, and how did the Norwegian authorities adapt their policies to the structural development of shipping demand? There is no doubt that Norwegian shipping policies were transformed over the period. Moreover, the change was characterized primarily by liberalization, in tune with global trends, but also influenced by ad hoc measures. The development of Norwegian policies was characterized by one massive transformation – the introduction of the Norwegian International Ship Register in 1987. However, a number of incremental changes, related in particular to crisis relief and taxation, also influenced the development.

The liberalization of Norway's flag policy

The challenge for the Norwegian authorities, as presented in Table 2.4, has been to enable 'the country's shipowners to maintain competitiveness', but this is conditioned by 'a set of political values and considerations'. As long as demand for shipping was rapidly increasing, there was no conflict between the question of competitiveness on the one hand and political considerations on the other. However, the shipping crisis of the 1970s and 1980s was particularly fierce in the markets in which Norwegian owners had their main engagements. Thus a schism developed between the Norwegian authorities' desire to maintain a large shipping sector and Norwegian owners' ability to fulfil this desire.

As late as 1975 the authorities emphasized that 'Norwegian shipping, as a main rule, shall be based on vessels flying the Norwegian flag and employing Norwegian crews' (Stortingsmelding no. 23 (1975–76), p. 25). This policy stance was very much rooted in the 'old' – or traditional – way of producing shipping services, that is, based on domestically sourced factors of production (labour and equity). Two concurrent trends explain the policy changes that facilitated the subsequent internationalization of Norwegian shipping supply. The shift in Norwegian policy was both a response to the crisis within shipping *and* an adaptation to the long-term changes in the structure and hegemony of the maritime industry. An investigation of the parliamentary proceedings illustrates this.[5]

By the early 1980s economically motivated flagging out of Norwegian vessels had begun in earnest, and the authorities had come to realize that 'a flexible flag policy is necessary to maintain a Norwegian shipping sector' (Stortingsmelding no. 53 (1984–85), p. 40). Erling Dekke Næss, a Norwegian-born Bermuda-based shipowner who had been among the main protagonists of the Flag of Convenience (FoC) institution, suggested in 1984 the establishment of an 'international register' that combined the use of foreign labour with Norwegian ownership.[6] The initial responses from both the shipping organizations and the authorities were lukewarm, and the reactions of the seamen's unions were downright hostile.[7]

The continuing, and escalating, flight of tonnage from the Norwegian flag made it patently clear that something had to be done. In 1986 alone the Norwegian fleet was reduced by more than six million dwt, representing more than a third of the fleet (Ot.prp. no. 45 (1986–87), p. 4). This exodus changed the attitudes of the authorities and the shipping organizations. After a bout of parliamentary indecision, an act establishing an open Norwegian ship register was passed, and the new institution came into effect from 1 July 1987. Around the same time, liberalization of the foreign exchange legislation made it easier for Norwegian shipping companies to establish subsidiaries abroad and for foreigners to invest in Norwegian companies.

Through the establishment of the Norwegian International Ship Register (NIS), the authorities sought to maintain and develop the country's maritime competence, while at the same time countering the flight of Norwegian vessels to foreign flags (Sletmo and Holste, 1993; Goulielmos, 1998). A combination of the depressed market and competition from the rapidly growing FoC fleets had paved the way for an institutional rethink. The register, which had initially been viewed with scepticism by authorities and shipowners, turned out to be an instant success, with a helping hand from a market that had finally left the doldrums and once again facilitated new investments.

Following the introduction of the NIS, the Norwegian fleet was split into three parts: foreign-flagged ships, NIS registered vessels and tonnage registered in the Norwegian Ordinary Register (NOR). Tonnage-wise, the majority of the Norwegian-owned fleet today is still flying foreign flags. Some Norwegian-owned vessels did not return to the Norwegian flag when the NIS was introduced, and the share of the Norwegian-owned fleet registered abroad has in fact grown in the first years of the twenty-first century. The second part is the NIS fleet: vessels that did not trade in Norwegian waters and could utilize low-cost foreign labour. Finally, the vessels that trade domestically, or for other reasons occasionally enter Norwegian ports, are included in the NOR registry, where the traditional nationalist manning requirements are still more or less intact.

Figure 2.1 shows the dramatic reduction of the Norwegian-registered fleet as vessels were flagged out or sold to foreign interests in the first part of the 1980s, as well as the reversal of the development in the latter part of the decade. The basis for the strong growth after the introduction of the NIS was a combination of repatriation of previously

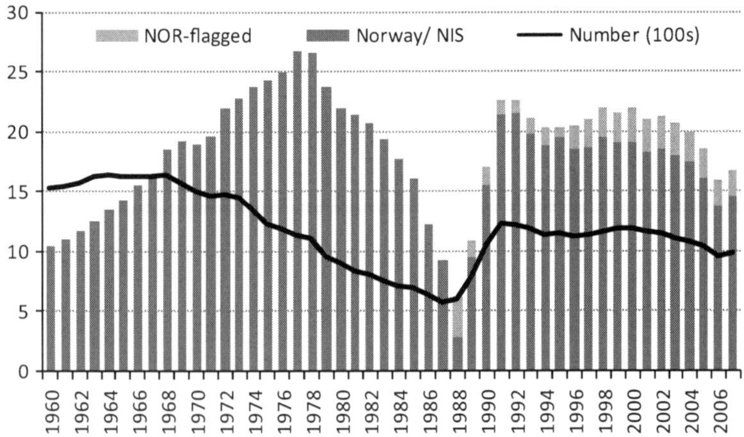

Figure 2.1 Norwegian-registered fleet, million grt and number (in 100s), 1960–2007

Note: Based on data from Lloyd's Register, as adapted by the Institute of Shipping Economics and Logistics, Bremen; includes all ships larger than 300 grt.

flagged-out ships and investments in new transport capacity encouraged by an upswing in shipping demand.

The general economic policy regime

The flag policy was instrumental in shaping the possibilities for shipping under the Norwegian flag. The relatively pragmatic enforcement and adaptation of this policy has been crucial in maintaining Norway's role as a major shipping nation. However, general economic policies – and tax policies in particular – have also had important implications for Norwegian shipowners. Again, impulses from the international stage have been decisive for the development. Just as lower manning costs in competing countries paved the way for the use of low-cost foreign crews on Norwegian ships, the fact that a lot of their competitors operated within zero-tax regimes influenced the taxation of Norwegian shipowners. For example, the 1996 introduction of a tonnage tax regime in Norway is frequently presented as a response to similar regulations in other countries (van den Noord, 2000, p. 14; Lassen and Sørensen, 2002, p. 47).

The taxation of Norwegian shipping has been – and continues to be – a controversial topic, as it has been directly influenced by two opposing motives. On the one hand, it has been seen as desirable that the tax treatment of shipping corresponds to the tax treatment of other Norwegian industries – thus creating 'tax neutrality' between the various sectors of the Norwegian economy. On the other hand, it has been regarded as important that Norwegian shipping companies should not be subject to tax-induced disadvantages relative to their competitors in other countries.

Table 2.5 gives a schematic overview of the tax systems under which Norwegian shipping companies have operated. Traditionally, formal corporate tax rates in Norway have been relatively high, when viewed from an international perspective. In reality, though, actual taxes paid by shipping companies were influenced by a number of methods of reducing tax obligations. Specifically, generous depreciation rules and the ability to defer revenues from vessel sales meant that the actual tax burden levied on Norwegian shipowners was substantially below that of other industries. However, in order to take advantage of this, a strategy of frequent renewal of tonnage was necessary.

According to van den Noord (2000, p. 14), before the 1992 tax reform 'an investment in a ship ... was profitable even with negative pre-tax returns due to very generous depreciation allowances'. Until the shipping crisis this in fact meant that shipping companies paid relatively little corporate tax – as long as earnings were reinvested

Table 2.5 An overview of Norwegian shipping taxation

Year	Main features	Effects
Pre-1992	High formal tax rates, but substantial depreciation and classification allowances, as well as tax deferral	Low taxes paid on shipping activities for companies with continuous reinvestment
1992	Reduced tax rate, broader tax base (limits on depreciation allowances)	Increased tax burden
1996	Choice of tonnage tax for companies, given some limitations	Taxation only when profits are paid out (tax deferral, not exemption)
2007	Tonnage tax – new system	Very low tax burden – in line with EU-countries

in new capacity. However, this system also affected the strategies of Norwegian shipowners. By promoting the ordering of new ships in years with high revenues – in order to take advantage of the generous depreciation allowances on new contracts – the tax system provides one explanation of the pro-cyclical contracting behaviour of Norwegian shipping companies.

The aim of the 1992 tax reform was to put shipping taxation more in line with the system within which other parts of the Norwegian economy operated. The corporate tax rates were reduced from 50 per cent to 28 per cent. At the same time, however, the generous depreciation allowances were reduced, meaning that the net effect for shipowners was negative. An international comparison from the early 1990s acknowledges the deterioration of the regime: in seven out of ten selected shipping centres, it was possible to 'operate as shipowners without being subject to ordinary taxation' (Knudsen, 1997, p. 45). The exceptions were Denmark, Norway and Sweden.

The subsequent 1996 tax reform aimed at remedying the now unfavourable tax conditions for Norwegian shipowners, and a tonnage tax regime – of the kind already introduced in the Netherlands – was established. In practice, however, the system was based on infinite deferral of tax burdens, rather than tax exemption, and subsequent changes to the system rendered the arrangement 'diluted and uncompetitive' (Nightingale, 2005, p. 8). The 2007 introduction of a tonnage tax regime more or less identical to that of the EU countries was accompanied by hefty tax and legal bills. In the end a High Court ruling found the claim for repayment of deferred taxes unconstitutional.

Norwegian economic policies affected not only the costs of shipping companies, but also their ability to attract investment capital. This was partly a result of the general limitations on capital movements before the late 1980s and partly a result of specific tax policies that favoured shipping investments. In particular, the personal tax deductions related to participation in limited partnerships (*kommandittselskap*) secured large amounts of tax-motivated investment capital for the industry. Over the period 1986 to 1991, for example, a total of 38 billion kroner of committed capital was raised for shipping investments through limited partnerships. To put this into perspective, the shipping companies listed on Oslo Børs (the Oslo stock exchange) only raised 5.5 billion kroner through equity issues over the same period (*Dagens Næringsliv*, 29 June 1992, p. 16).

In addition to the developments presented above, two other economic policy decisions have had important ramifications for Norwegian shipping in the period 1960 to 2008. The first was the 1975 establishment of 'Garantiinstituttet for skip og borefartøy' (the Guarantee Institute for Ships and Drilling Vessels), an institution officially aimed at alleviating the liquidity difficulties of the shipping companies and avoiding the sale of ships to foreigners at low prices (Tenold, 2001a). The second was the introduction of a tax reimbursement system, often imprecisely referred to as a 'net wage compensation'. The seeds of this system – which is primarily targeted towards vessels in the NOR registry – were sown in the mid-1990s, but substantially scaled up from 2002 onwards (ECON, 2010).

In general Norwegian shipping and economic policies have developed in a manner beneficial for the country's shipping companies, though not without setbacks, such as the 1992 changes in shipping taxation. Nevertheless, the piecemeal and vague character of the reforms has been a target for criticism by agents working in the maritime industry. Typically, when shipping companies have used frameworks in other countries as their point of reference, rather than the policies adopted for other Norwegian sectors, the authorities' maritime strategies look weak. There has also been much criticism of the frequency of changes and the limited long-term commitment to a permanent pro-shipping policy.

Other implications of policies

In addition to shipping and economic policies per se, the room to manoeuvre for Norwegian shipping companies was affected by general policy decisions. For example, the decision to exploit the petroleum resources of the North Sea provided shipping companies with an opportunity to use their financial resources and maritime knowledge in a new arena. At the same time, however, the oil industry quite rapidly eclipsed shipping as the main export sector.

The shipping community played a crucial role when Norway entered 'the oil age'. Norwegian shipowners were among the leading investors in a number of areas related to petroleum exploration and production, including oil companies, drilling rigs and supply vessels. For example, eleven of the twenty companies that established the oil exploration company Norwegian Oil Consortium AS in 1965 were shipping companies (Glenne, 1997, p. 12). Similarly, the list of Norwegian enterprises' investments in drilling rigs in 1971 contains nineteen shipping companies, one ship broker and only three companies from other sectors (*Norwegian Shipping News*, 1972, pp. 39–40). There were two main reasons for large investments in the oil sector by Norwegian shipping companies. First, these investments reflected the relative abundance of capital in the shipping sector as a result of the boom in the late 1960s and early 1970s. Second, the offshore oil industry provided the shipping companies with a new activity in which they could utilize their maritime competence.

The Norwegian Rigowners' Association was established in 1972. Given the overlapping membership and the corresponding interests of the members, it was merged twelve years later with the Norwegian Shipowners' Association.[8] By 2006 the value of Norwegian rigs and offshore service vessels amounted to some US $14 billion, compared with around US $20 billion for the rest of the Norwegian fleet (Norges Rederiforbund, 2006, p. 5).[9] There is little doubt that oil exploration in the North Sea presented shipping companies with new opportunities, and some of the companies ended up exiting the shipping sector altogether to concentrate on offshore activities. This transformation from shipping to offshore oil activities, or to a combination of shipping and offshore activities, also became an important means of diversification for other agents in the Norwegian maritime milieu, including shipyards, brokers and banks. Nevertheless, the return to the home waters of the North Sea was only one of many strategies followed by Norwegian shipping companies in the period after 1960.

Norwegian responses II – shipping company strategies

At the start of the period analysed in this chapter, three features made the Norwegian shipping sector stand out in an international, and also in a Nordic, perspective. The first was the sheer size of the industry and its crucial role in the economy (Norman, 1971). Norway's fleet was among the largest in the world, and the gross revenues from the export of shipping services had on average accounted for more than 50 per cent of total Norwegian export revenues during the 1950s. The second distinguishing feature was the widespread dispersal of ownership. In 1960 a total of 164 Norwegian companies owned ships larger than 5000 grt: more than twice the total of the other Nordic countries. The third feature was the manner in which shipping companies were dispersed geographically. The fleet in 1960 was registered in 26 different home ports, so shipping was an important activity all along Norway's long coastline. Oslo, the largest home port, held around half of the Norwegian tonnage.[10]

The heterogeneity of the Norwegian shipping sector makes an all-embracing analysis difficult: it is evident that changes in the international market and domestic shipping policies affected Norwegian shipping companies in very different ways. The final part of this chapter therefore concentrates on general developments – the main trends in tonnage supply and company strategies of Norwegian shipowners – seen in relation to the demand and supply developments presented in the introduction to the chapter. However, from a business point of view, the macro picture may be too crude. The presentation of the general development is therefore followed by some broad typologies of company strategies in the various periods.

The main unit of analysis is the managing owners (*rederi*): the companies that were responsible for the operation and management of the ships. Long-term strategies were usually chiselled out at this level, with the managing owners controlling vessels legally owned by one or more 'shipholding' companies. The number and incorporation of these shipholding companies were usually determined by tax, accounting, financing and legal issues, so they are not suitable units of analysis in the longer term. For example, 'one-ship' companies have been established to alleviate the knock-on effects of culpability in marine accidents, and a managing owner would typically control vessels owned by a number of such 'one-ship' companies.[11] An analysis based on the legal owners of the vessels would therefore not reflect the actual mechanisms that determine the growth and development, and create the structural changes, taking place in the Norwegian shipping sector.

The main Norwegian trades

An overview of dominant strategies in the various post-war periods was given in Table 2.1. In the boom period, up to 1973, Norwegian shipping was characterized by large investments, primarily in ships utilizing economies of scale or vessels aimed at specialized segments. During the shipping crisis there was massive disinvestment, accompanied by a strong reduction in the number of companies. As previously noted, a number of shipping companies were successful in embracing the new opportunities of the offshore oil industry, but for Norwegian shipping as a whole this was a period of unprecedented turbulence and decline. Some companies, however, continued to invest in the specialized shipping niches, where a number of Norwegian owners had managed to build up and maintain substantial market shares. Finally, with the revitalization of the shipping sector, and the decoupling of the supply side, the picture becomes more complex. After 1987, to the extent that there *was* a 'Norwegian strategy', it was two-pronged. First, the investments in specialized segments continued, but there was renewed growth in other segments as well, and the links between shipping and offshore were strengthened. Second, the changes in the organization of the shipping supply blurred the linkages between the shipping companies and the Norwegian economy. Increased flexibility with regard to manning and cross-border investments diluted the 'Norwegian' aspect of the country's shipping industry.

The tanker trades

Independent Norwegian shipowners had been pioneers in the tanker market in the interwar period and continued to play important roles in the post-war decades. The focus on the growing tanker trades in many ways revitalized Norwegian shipping in the 1920s and 1930s, enabling the country's shipowners to recapture much of the position in international shipping that they had lost during the transition from sail to steam (Tenold, 2008).

In 1960 Norwegian owners controlled 8.6 per cent of the world fleet, but more than 15 per cent of the world tanker fleet. New competition – particularly from Greek shipowners – led to a reduction in Norwegian dominance, but Norwegians were nevertheless arguably over-represented in this segment of the shipping sector. By 1973 Norway's share of the world tanker fleet had fallen to around 10 per cent, while the share of the world fleet was more or less unchanged.[12]

From an international perspective, the Norwegian tanker owners were seen to be particularly vulnerable when the shipping market collapsed; they had invested in the largest ships, which were hardest hit by the crisis, they operated them in the spot market or on relatively short time charters and also had a substantial amount of unfixed newbuildings on order – vessels that were sometimes mothballed straight from the building berths (Norman, 1999; Tenold, 2006). As a result, Norwegian lay-up rates were substantially above the world rates and the fleet was drastically reduced through distress sales.

With the renewed growth of the country's shipping activities after the introduction in 1987 of the NIS, tanker shipping increased again, though never to the same levels – in relative or absolute terms – as before the crisis. Moreover, a large proportion of the Norwegian participants were new agents rather than the traditional tanker owners. There was also, at least for a period of time, a shift to asset play strategies.

The Norwegian engagements in the tanker sector after 1987 illustrate several of the changes in the fabric of the shipping industry. First, the oil tanker industry witnessed technological innovations, including the Norwegian concept of Floating Production Storage and Offloading units (FPSOs), which have led to increased diversity among oil tanker owners. Whereas the tanker fleet in 1960 was primarily made up of ships for the transport of crude oil and oil products, there are now also FPSOs and shuttle tankers, in addition to specialized tankers for chemicals, gas, etc. This means that the market for tanker services has become much more diverse.

Second, some Norwegian ventures in the tanker sector have been taken over by foreign interests, reflecting the increased internationalization of the industry. For example, Teekay Corporation, one of the leading tanker owners internationally, has grown through the acquisition of the Norwegian-based companies Ugland Nordic and Navion. Conversely, some of the most prominent Norwegian-born tanker owners – including John Fredriksen, who controls the world's largest tanker fleet – operate from a foreign base. Although the tanker segment has lost its hegemony in the Norwegian shipping industry, Norwegian owners continue to play important roles internationally, as owners, operators and innovators.

The dry bulk trades

During the 1950s several Norwegian owners were among the first investors in ships for the rapidly growing dry bulk trade. In the following decade this activity escalated, with large investments both in the relatively new ore and dry bulk carriers and in combination carriers that could alternate between dry and wet bulk cargoes. Fon (1995, p. 195), who has looked at the dry bulk investments in more detail, refers to Norway as 'The world's leading dry bulk nation' in the period 1960 to 1973. He emphasizes two elements of the Norwegian expansion in the dry bulk market. First, the foray into that market was characterized by 'an entrepreneurial attitude, in the Schumpeterian sense of the word' (Fon, 1995, p. 288). Second, the investments seem to have been characterized by co-operation, both with regard to joint ordering of vessels – which enabled smaller owners to participate – and with regard to the operation of ships in pools.

In 1960 Oslo-based shipowners held a dominant position within the dry bulk segment, owning more than 70 per cent of the Norwegian dry bulk fleet. However, in the period up to 1973 the relative position of Oslo declined as the concept was spread geographically. By then, about a hundred Norwegian owners had invested in dry bulk vessels, and the fleet had multiplied by a factor of 12.5 relative to 1960.

Although the dry bulk market was less affected by the shipping crisis than the tanker market, the last part of the 1970s and the first part of the 1980s were difficult years for the dry bulk owners as well. The influx of combination carriers from the tanker market and heavily subsidized dry bulk newbuildings put a downward pressure on freight rates and aggravated the effects of lower demand growth. At the same time, operation under the Norwegian flag became increasingly uncompetitive. After a downscaling of the Norwegian involvement up to the mid-1980s, there were substantial investments in new capacity after the introduction of the NIS. However, the Norwegian owners never regained the dominant position that they had held in the 1960s, and today Norwegian owners appear to be somewhat under-represented in the general dry bulk market.

As in the tanker sector, however, there was some degree of specialization in the dry bulk sector. Norwegian owners were – and are – among the major owners of 'open hatch' dry bulk vessels. It is doubtful whether this niche, based on novel technological solutions that enable owners to take a premium in the freight market, should be included as part of the dry bulk market per se. In many ways, the leading Norwegian presence within this niche of the dry bulk market reflects the third, and most sustainable, strategic avenue: specialization.

The specialized trades

As the supply of shipping tonnage became more diversified during the 1960s, Norwegian owners were at the forefront in the introduction and expansion of the new ship types. Moreover, as the crisis hit the commodity segments – the tanker and dry bulk trades – in the 1970s and 1980s, specialized vessels came to be the most dynamic part of the Norwegian shipping industry. From the mid-1970s onwards, the continued investments in technologically advanced specialized tonnage were a stark contrast to the massive disinvestment in the commodity segments.

Stopford (2009, pp. 66–7) presents the five main specialized shipping sectors today: motor vehicles, forest products, refrigerated foods, liquid gases and chemicals. Within all of these segments, Norwegian shipowners have been both pioneers and dominant market players. Moreover, the earliest purpose-built specialized vessels for forest products, cars and liquid petroleum gases were not only built at Norwegian yards but owned by Norwegians.

In the commodity trades ship sizes were growing until the mid-1970s and this led to a reduction in unit transport costs, facilitating the rapid growth of international trade. This reduction of costs was probably even larger in the specialized trades, though less easy to quantify. In these markets the basis for the cost decline was a combination of economies of scale – including the introduction of the bulk cargo concept for new commodities – and significant improvements in cargo storage and handling. Moreover, the new technological solutions enabled the seaborne transport of a number of commodities for the first time.

The basis for increased technological sophistication differed from segment to segment. For the transportation of motor vehicles, for example, general cargo and liner vessels were initially replaced by bulk carriers with some car-carrying capacity in the 1950s, before the pure car carriers were developed in the subsequent decade.[13] Similarly, chemical parcel tankers also represented a refinement of known concepts, though in the end a combination of incremental and more revolutionary technological changes added up to create a whole new segment of the shipping industry.

Table 2.6 shows that by the mid-1970s, the participation of Norway in several of the new segments was much higher than its position in world shipping in general, with the role of vehicle carriers and

Table 2.6 Norwegian participation in various sub-segments (share of world fleet = 100), 1977

Type	Oil tankers	Gas carriers	Chemical tankers	Bulk and combination	General cargo	Container ships	Lighter-aboard ships	Vehicle carriers
Index	117	142	503	135	29	10	131	355

Note: Based on data from Lloyd's Register, as adapted by the Institute of Shipping Economics and Logistics, Bremen. Includes all ships larger than 300 grt.

chemical tankers being particularly impressive. However, the international distribution of specialized shipping tonnage has followed a Vernon-like cycle. This means that the role of Norwegians as pioneers has become less dominant as the markets have matured and the technology has become standardized (Thanopoulou, 1995; Tenold, 2009a).

The early Norwegian entry into the specialized shipping markets is partly explicable by a combination of maritime knowledge, innovative approaches and close relations to customers, brokers, and, in particular, classification societies, shipyards and ship equipment producers. Interestingly, in some of the niches in which Norwegians were pioneers, such as car carriers and chemical and gas tankers, Norwegian shipyards and their subcontractors held large market shares in the initial growth period (Wergeland, 1992, pp. 123–5).

Norwegian reliance on specialized tonnage was substantial in the years before the introduction of the NIS; measured by the number of ships, the proportion of specialized vessels in the Norwegian fleet increased from around 18 per cent in 1977 to almost 50 per cent ten years later. This increasing proportion reflects the fact that such vessels had proved to be relatively good investments, but it was also a result of reduced ownership of conventional tonnage. As the specialized ships were both more expensive and technologically more advanced than other tonnage, Norwegian owners could still afford to pay the wage premium associated with the Norwegian flag. The advantage of having highly skilled Norwegian personnel on board the ships outweighed the cost benefits of foreign seamen. Subsequently, the standardization of the specialized technology, combined with dedicated efforts by Norwegian owners to train seamen abroad, has enabled the use of foreign manning also for such vessels.

Several of the Norwegian specialized shipping pioneers still maintain their large market shares. Odfjell, Stolt-Nielsen and JO Tankers, a company that was spun off from Odfjell in the late 1970s, are among the most important players within the chemical tanker segment. Star Shipping and Gearbulk, as well as the Japanese-owned Saga Forest Carriers, which is headquartered in Norway, are market leaders within forest products.

The strong growth of world trade over the last 50 years has partly been a result of political liberalization. Yet there is little doubt that productivity improvements within shipping further increased the benefits of international trade. The mode of production in shipping – in technological as well as organizational terms – has changed tremendously.

Norwegian shipowners have been at the forefront of this development as handmaidens of trade. In particular, they have played a crucial role with regard to technological innovations.

Although an overview at the macro level helps to show the main trends in the development of the shipping sector, progress has not been made as a result of collaborative efforts at improvement. Rather, it is the many individual decisions made by the main actors – the shipping companies – that have determined the path of development. Thus, in order to understand the dynamics of the industry, we need to take a closer look at the different strategies of individual companies, and how these have added up to create the broader picture.

Strategies of individual companies

Although it is useful to look at specific companies in more detail, some kind of simplification has to be made in order to create a 'typology' of Norwegian shipping companies and their strategies. A categorization of shipping companies could be made based on a number of parameters, such as fleet size, age and ownership of the company, home port or region, main market segment, company organization or links to other maritime businesses. Furthermore, we have to take into account the fact that the strategic challenges were different in the three main periods: the boom to 1973, the crisis to the late 1980s and the revitalization era.

Figure 2.2 provides an overview of the structure of the Norwegian shipping sector in 1960. The chart shows that the smaller companies – those owning only one or two ships – made up almost 40 per cent of the population of shipping companies, but owned only 10 per cent of the fleet. The rest of the fleet was more or less equally divided between the other two groups: the 80 medium-sized companies, which owned from three to nine ships, and the companies with more than ten ships. There were 20 companies in the last of these groups in 1960. The giants of Norwegian shipping thus owned around 45 per cent of the fleet, despite making up only 12 per cent of the population of companies.

The diversity that is apparent from Figure 2.2 makes generalizations about company strategies difficult. However, it is evident that the size of the fleet at the start of the period is an important indicator of the challenges that were facing the companies, and also influenced the 'menu' of strategies from which they could choose.[14] The following presentation thus looks in more detail at four template types of companies – small, medium-sized, large and newly established companies.

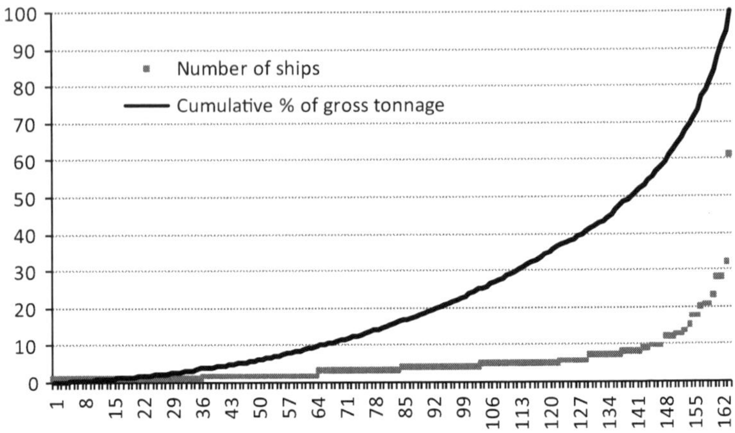

Figure 2.2 Norwegian shipping companies, ranked by number of ships, 1960

Note: The data in this part of the article originate with a set of databases, made on the basis of *Det Norske Veritas* (various issues). All Norwegian-registered ships larger than 5000 grt tons are included.

Small shipping companies

The period since 1960 has seen increasing concentration in the shipping sector, both in company and geographical terms, in Norway as well as internationally. As shipping became more capital-intensive and the vessels and shipping markets became more complicated and specialized, the demand for general cargo tramp vessels declined. Strategies based on specialization and utilization of economies of scale increased competitiveness, and for Norwegian shipping per se, the new technological opportunities served the industry well. For Norwegian shipowners that were unable to join in, however, the increased productivity of their competitors was detrimental. The smaller companies – struggling to make a profit from one or two relatively small and old vessels – were stuck with obsolete 'hardware' and an increasingly futile strategy that undoubtedly belonged to the past.

For the smaller shipping companies, the technological development during the post-war boom and the favourable demand conditions that facilitated the new technologies therefore had adverse effects. The starting point was unfortunate: the ships owned by these companies in 1960 were on average both smaller and marginally older than those owned by the medium-sized and larger companies. There was therefore one major challenge for the companies with small fleets and limited

Table 2.7 Three categories of owners in 1960 and their survival rates to 1973 and 1987

	No. of ships	No. of cos.	No. of ports	Average company size (grt)	Survival to 1973	Survival to 1987
Small companies	1–2	64	22	14,078	45%	8%
Medium-sized companies	3–9	80	15	50,790	88%	33%
Large companies	10+	20	7	217,388	100%	70%

financial muscle: how would it be possible to replace their ageing tonnage with new, larger and much more expensive ships?

Table 2.7 shows that the majority of the small companies were in fact unable to solve this conundrum. By 1973, more than half of the companies had disappeared, and were no longer registered as shipowners. This might seem puzzling, given the generally beneficial market conditions in the 1960s. However, the small companies started out with a clear handicap: as the boom favoured new and expensive vessels, companies that did not have the financial muscle to invest in such ships were quickly left by the wayside.

The smaller companies typically ended up with one of three possible strategies. First, some small shipping companies had an offensive strategy, financing investments in larger tonnage by means of external funds. Second, some companies chose, or were forced, to exit the shipping sector altogether. Finally, some companies sold off their fleets, but reinvested the sale revenues in parts of ships managed by other shipowners.

In the period from 1960 to 1973 slightly more than a third of the small companies increased their transport capacity. Four of them expanded particularly rapidly, and had growth rates of more than 500 per cent from 1960 to 1973. Nevertheless, while these investments might have been successful for a period of time, closer analysis of the data presented above shows that none of the companies managed to sustain their expansion as markets turned sour after 1973. Consequently, by 1987 more than 90 per cent of the small companies from 1960 had disappeared, and the five that remained had all been reduced to one-vessel companies.[15]

Many of the smaller shipping companies sold their assets, usually to foreign operators with lower operating costs who could squeeze a few more years out of the tonnage, and left the shipping sector altogether.

Some companies disposed of their fully owned ships, but joined forces with other, usually larger, owners, investing in more competitive tonnage. Such solutions were beneficial for both parties. The larger owners got access to equity, while the smaller companies could piggyback on transport concepts that were superior to those they could exploit on their own. A case in point is the medium-sized Bergen-based shipowner Odfjell, pioneers in the chemical tanker market. In the period 1965 to 1973 the Odfjell group entered into joint investment projects with nine small shipping companies, eight of whom had disposed of their last fully owned ships a year or two before entering into the partnership (Thowsen and Tenold, 2006, pp. 335–9). The degree to which the smaller companies were passive investors or actually maintained some in-house shipping activity – for example commercial management, technical management or the manning of the vessels – varied from partnership to partnership.

The fact that practically all the small shipping companies from 1960 had disappeared 30 years later does not imply that small companies were unimportant in the long run. Almost by definition, newly established companies will start out with limited amounts of tonnage, and some of these in fact became very successful. It is thus likely that the forces of the market – the processes of 'creative destruction' – are stronger in this part of the shipping sector than among the larger companies. However, periods of substantial market turmoil – such as the shipping crisis of the 1970s and 1980s – create a lot of turbulence even for the medium-sized and larger companies.

Medium-sized companies

In terms of numbers, the medium-sized companies that controlled from three to nine ships made up the largest part of the Norwegian shipping population in 1960. The group itself was relatively diverse, with fleet sizes ranging from slightly more than 20,000 grt to almost 140,000 grt, and with a large variety of ship types.

In the period from 1960 to 1973 the medium-sized companies had the highest rate of expansion. In 1960 they had controlled an aggregate fleet that was slightly smaller than the 20 largest companies, while by 1973 their fleet was larger than that of the top 20 companies from 1960. This expansion was, however, not evenly distributed, and a handful of high growth companies had major impact. In fact, almost half of the growth in this group – which numbered 80 companies in 1960 – can be traced back to the six companies with the highest rate of expansion. Chief among these was Sig. Bergesen d.y. & Co, an Oslo-based company established in the interwar period. In 1960 the company controlled a fleet of seven vessels, amounting to slightly less than 140,000 grt. By 1973, primarily as a result of massive investments in large tankers, Bergesen's fleet had multiplied by a factor of more than ten. The company was responsible for almost a quarter of the growth of the medium-sized companies, and had become Norway's largest shipowner, measured by tonnage, by the early 1970s.[16]

The ten medium-sized companies that disappeared in the period from 1960 to 1973 were all relatively small, controlling from three to five ships in 1960. The reasons for their demise are varied – from restructuring, through deteriorating health, to family feuds. After 1973, however, another 45 companies disappeared, so by 1987 less than one-third of the 80 medium-sized companies from 1960 still existed. The main reason for the reduction after 1973 was the adverse effects of the shipping crisis. The hazardous combination of revenue reduction, lay-ups, falling vessel values and an increasingly difficult competitive situation led to bankruptcies and disinvestment. Several of the medium-sized companies did not have the financial reserves necessary to survive as the crisis dragged on. The Guarantee Institute did alleviate the problems for some of the companies, but the length of the crisis meant that this support – aimed at overcoming temporary financial difficulties – was insufficient in the long run.

Figure 2.3 illustrates the fates of companies in the various size categories from 1970 to 1987. It shows the percentage of companies in each category that disappeared in the various years – the basis is the owners that survived from 1960 to 1970. The figure shows a striking difference between the categories. There appears to have been a wave-like pattern of company deaths, spreading from small companies in the early 1970s to medium-sized companies in the late 1970s and onwards to large companies as the crisis dragged on for a considerable period of time.

The fact that the majority of the smaller companies disappeared in the early 1970s reflects the problems of reinvestment described above. Over a period of five years, the number of small companies was more than halved. The reduction in the number of medium-sized companies was most prominent in the latter half of the 1970s, reflecting the fact that their ability to withstand a deterioration of the revenues from the freight market was limited. Interestingly, the apparent reprieve for the medium-sized companies in 1980 coincides with a temporary improvement of freight rates. All the larger companies survived into the 1980s – though some were reorganized and needed state support. From 1983 onwards, however, the crisis found its victims among the larger companies as well.

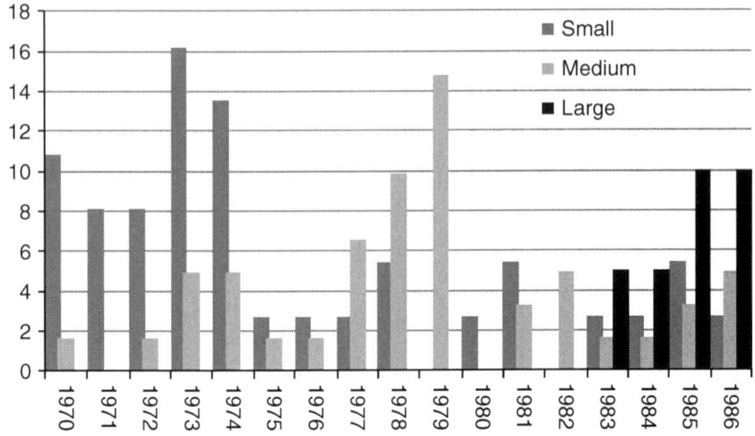

Figure 2.3 Percentage of companies disappearing by year, 1970–87

Note: The categories are based on the number of vessels owned in 1960, as presented previously in the text, but include only companies that survived until 1970. The bars show the proportion of companies that disappeared in the various years, as a percentage of the number of companies in each category in 1970.

Despite the haemorrhage as a result of the freight market breakdown, some of the medium-sized companies from 1960 – for example the Grimstad-based Ugland companies, Anders Wilhelmsen and Sig. Bergesen d.y. in Oslo and the Bergen-based Odfjell group – continue to play a crucial role in world shipping today. Again, it is therefore important to emphasize the heterogeneity of the development over the longer period. The majority of the medium-sized shipping companies disappeared as a result of the long-lasting depression in the industry. Some owners, however, had managed to carve out sustainable strategies that insulated them from some of the most violent effects of the shipping crisis. Moreover, the demise of their competitors enabled them to 'pick and choose' – for example with regard to labour on shore and at sea. Thus, while none of these companies were unaffected by the shipping crisis, and some were indeed in deep trouble, they were relatively well equipped to take on the new challenges in shipping after 1987.

Large companies

The category 'large companies' in 1960 includes the 'royalty' of Norwegian shipping – companies such as Fred. Olsen & Co.,

Westfal-Larsen & Co. and Wilh. Wilhelmsen – which were already established shipowners in the early twentieth century and have continued this activity into the twenty-first. The largest companies in 1960 all had diversified fleets, owning both tankers and general cargo or dry bulk carriers. This is in contrast to the 'streamlining' that subsequently occurred, where many shipowners would typically focus on one market segment. Moreover, throughout the period the number of activities or segments in which the large Norwegian shipping companies were involved was much lower than, for example, that of the shipping companies operating in or controlled from the UK (Casson, 1986, pp. 24–5).

Only three of the 20 largest companies in 1960 did not expand their fleets in the period up to 1973, and the five most expansive owners multiplied their tonnage by a factor of three or more. In spite of the fact that the fleets controlled by the companies more than doubled, the number of vessels was actually reduced, because average sizes were increasing. However, there is no indication that the large companies were keener to utilize economies of scale than the medium-sized owners.

Figure 2.3 revealed that there were no casualties among the largest companies during the 1970s. This does not mean that the large companies remained unaffected by the difficulties – the Guarantee Institute played a crucial role in the survival of some big companies, while several others were reorganized and refinanced, sometimes with the position of the original owners heavily diluted.[17] After 1983 even some of the larger companies were forced to give in to the troublesome market – ships were sold as the longevity of the crisis also led to casualties among the giants of Norwegian shipping.

Despite the disappearance of some of the large shipping companies, there has been an element of continuity at the top of Norwegian shipping. A list of Norway's 30 largest shipping companies in July 2003, for example, reveals that six of the companies were also among Norway's ten largest companies in 1960 (Stortingsmelding no. 31 (2003–04), p. 25).[18] Of the 30 companies, 18 were established shipowners in 1960, although two of them only owned small vessels at the time. Three of the companies had links to other companies that were operating in 1960, having been established independently by individuals from families with shipping traditions or spun off as ownership was divided among different branches of the family.[19]

Table 2.8 shows the 'top ten' of Norwegian shipping companies in the period 1960 to 2008; some of the companies that show particular resilience at the top have been noted. Although the table reveals a fair

Table 2.8 Norway's largest shipping companies (based on dwt), 1960–2008

1960		1970		1980	
Wilh. Wilhelmsen*	631	Sig. Bergesen d.y. & Co.	2,221	Sig. Bergesen d.y. & Co.	4,234
Anders Jahre†	523	Anders Jahre†	1,466	Rederiet Johan Reksten	3,144
Leif Høegh & Co. AS‡	500	Wilh. Wilhelmsen*	1,248	Anders Jahre†	2,407
Torvald Klaveness	411	Hilmar Reksten	1,215	Leif Høegh & Co.‡	1,839
Fearnley & Eger	378	Fearnley & Eger	1,000	Wilh. Wilhelmsen*	1,738
Westfal-Larsen & Co. AS§	366	Leif Høegh & Co. AS‡	9,81	Einar Rasmussen	1,653
Sigurd Herlofson & Co. AS	340	AS Thor Dahl	877	Sigurd B. Sverdrup AS	1,273
Knut Knutsen O.A.S.	338	Mosvold Shipping Co. AS	745	Halfdan Ditlev-Simonsen & Co.	1,198
A. F. Klaveness & Co. AS	236	Einar Rasmussen	617	Lars Krogh & Co. AS	1,152
Einar Rasmussen	229	Westfal-Larsen & Co. AS§	490	AS Thor Dahl	1,071
Total	**3,952**		**10,860**		**19,709**
1990		**2000**		**2008**	
Bergesen d.y.	6,785	Bergesen d.y. ASA	9,449	BW Group	4,309
Norman International	3,163	Wilh. Wilhelmsen*	1,815	Teekay Shipping Norway	2,982
Fred. Olsen	1,943	Jahre Dahl Bergesen†	1,657	Knutsen OAS Shipping AS	2,881
Bulls†	1,800	Red Band AS	1,442	Kr. G. Jebsen Skipsrederi	2,446
Wilh. Wilhelmsen*	1,337	Leif Høegh & Co.‡	1,425	Odfjell SE	1,897
Torvald Klaveness	1,284	NAVION AS	1,398	Eitzen Group	1,401
Ugland-gruppen	1,274	Odfjell ASA	1,392	Viken Shipping AS	1,127
Mosvold	1,271	Ugland Nordic	1,334	Westfal-Larsen gruppen§	1,090
Leif Høegh‡	1,253	Kr. G. Jebsen	1,269	Spar Shipping AS	1,047
Bergshav	1,259	Knutsen OAS	1,101	Leif Høegh & Co.‡	935
Total	**21,369**		**22,282**		**20,115**

Note: The table is based on data from the Veritas registry for the years 1960 to 1980, and on data acquired by the author from the Norwegian Shipowners' Association for the remaining years. Note the strong positions retained by Wilh Wilhelmsen*, Anders Jahre/Bulls/Jahre Dahl Bergesen†, Leif Høegh‡, and Westfal-Larsen§.

degree of consistency in the medium term, only one company – Leif Høegh & Co. – is represented on the list throughout the period.

One interesting element of Table 2.8 is that the criterion for inclusion in the Norwegian shipping top ten – the tonnage of the tenth-largest company – more than doubled from 1960 to 1970 and then more than doubled again in the subsequent decade. From 1980 to 1990 the growth was much more modest, whereas after 1990 both the cut-off point and the aggregate tonnage of the ten largest shipping companies have declined. This is, however, to some extent a reflection of the fact that the basis for the table is the size of the companies' fleets measured by dead-weight tonnage. With the increased sophistication of the tonnage – both as a result of investments in specialized niches and the increased technological contents of the ships operating in the commodity trades – a reduction in dead-weight tonnage does not necessarily reflect lower investments or activity. Indeed, the tonnage reduction might be regarded as a testament to the strength and capacity for innovation of Norwegian shipping, rather than as a sign of an industry that is losing its position within Norway, and where Norwegians are losing their position internationally.

Despite this positive spin, however, it is evident that the largest Norwegian shipowners no longer hold the 'aristocratic' position that they once held in Norwegian society. They do not play a prominent role in politics, as they did in the early twentieth century, and their positions as lynchpins and benefactors in local communities have disappeared. There are three main reasons for this reduced influence. First, while 'the shipowner' was previously an easily identifiable individual, the largest fleets today are owned by corporate entities, usually with dispersed ownership. Second, the companies now source their inputs from an international base, and the importance of local capital and labour has been greatly diminished. Finally, the general increase in wealth in Norway – coupled with the growing number of career paths available for entrepreneurially minded individuals – has produced a plethora of Norwegian individuals who have become rich from other industries. While there have always been wealthy persons from outside shipping in Norway, the share of Norwegian tycoons who found their fortunes at sea has fallen conspicuously. Nevertheless, even in the last part of the twentieth century, there was a large portion of successful rookie sailors in Norwegian shipping. The members of this group, the newcomers, are a testament to the fact that there are still opportunities within the Norwegian shipping industry.

Newcomers

The newcomers – companies that were either non-existent in 1960 or owned ships below the 5000 grt threshold – are perhaps the most interesting category from an entrepreneurial and business development point of view. To some extent it is the establishment of such companies that has enabled Norway to sustain its maritime hegemony, in spite of all the problems and 'disappearances' witnessed in the other categories.

The 'newcomers' category is even more heterogeneous than the other groups, as it includes everything from companies that lasted only a year or two to those that were established after 1960 but today rank among the country's largest shipowners. Moreover, several of the newcomers developed and conducted their business in a way that makes the traditional definitions of 'shipowner' inadequate.

Perhaps the best example of the new structures within shipping is the empire of John Fredriksen, which is noteworthy for two reasons. First, Norwegian-born Fredriksen today controls one of the world's largest tanker fleets. Second, the growth of this fleet provides a very good example of how the fabric of Norwegian and international shipping has changed since 1960. Although the degree of his success clearly makes John Fredriksen an atypical example, the development of his enterprise sheds important light on the increased complexity of the shipping industry. As such, it shows that the old, locally based owner-manager system has become increasingly refined. There have been transformations with regard to ownership, the business and operational dimensions, as well as nationality.

John Fredriksen has been doing business through foreign-owned companies since the early 1970s.[20] His main vehicle in the shipping industry – the company Frontline Ltd – was originally Swedish, but in 1997 changed its domicile to Bermuda. The main shareholder of Frontline, with more than a third of the shares, has been Hemen Holding Ltd, 'a Cyprus holding company, the shares of which are held in trusts established by Mr. John Fredriksen for the benefit of his immediate family' (Frontline, 2010, p. 72). John Fredriksen emigrated to Great Britain in 1978 (Thowsen, 2004). In 2006 he became a Cypriot citizen, but due to his Norwegian roots he undoubtedly warrants an inclusion here.

The companies in the newcomer category generally fall into one of three subgroups. Two of these subgroups were relatively short-lived and are directly related to the shipping crisis and its consequences. The first is the 'involuntary' shipowners – banks and other financial institutions that were registered as managing owners when they had to take over ships from debtors in distress.[21] The second subgroup is made up of interim companies established in connection with the reorganization and closing down of companies with economic difficulties.[22]

The third subgroup among the newcomers consists of entrepreneurs who have entered the shipping industry and been able to build up sustainable companies. Some of these have had links to other shipping companies, and have used their 'inheritance' or family ties as the basis for their enterprise. Others have started from scratch, gradually building up fleets from retained earnings or investment capital.

There were nine newcomers on the list of Norway's 30 largest shipping companies in 2003. This includes five companies involved in the offshore service sector, one of which was in fact owned by foreign interests. Some of the newcomers have been particularly successful. Three of the companies in the 2008 top ten in Table 2.8 were established after 1960. The three newcomers, Kristian Gerhard Jebsen Skipsrederi AS (KGJS), Viken Shipping AS and Spar Shipping AS, are all based in Bergen. KGJS was established in the late 1960s, when Kristian Gerhard Jebsen left the family shipping company to start out on his own. The company was the driving force behind the open hatch operations of the Gearbulk partnership, but has subsequently expanded strongly within other segments. Spar Shipping and Viken Shipping both date from the early 1990s, although the owners' involvement in the shipping industry – through, for example, minority ownership of vessels – goes further back.

The Norwegian maritime network

The main focus in this chapter has been Norwegian shipping companies and their actions and adaptations. While the international dimension and links to domestic economy and policies have been emphasized, the shipping companies' relationships with the other agents in what is often referred to as 'the Norwegian maritime cluster' have only been mentioned briefly.

The shipping companies are typically presented as the 'core' of the model in theories about maritime clusters (Wergeland, 1992; Benito et al., 2003; Sornn-Friese, 2003; Wijnolst et al., 2003). However, this pattern has been disputed in the Norwegian case. Econometric analysis of the industry suggests that the co-existence of two subclusters – one within transports and related services and one within manufacturing – appears to give a better representation of the actual relationships within 'the maritime cluster' (Knarvik and Steen, 1999).

The expansion of Norwegian shipping companies in the 1960s was accompanied by a parallel growth of related services and industries:

domestic brokers, classification societies, financing institutions, insurance companies, shipyards and ship equipment producers all saw their activities increase substantially. The Norwegian owners were particularly important for the country's yards. While Norwegian yards supplied only around a quarter of the newbuildings delivered to Norwegian owners in the period 1960 to 1975, Norwegian shipowners were responsible for more than 75 per cent of the vessels ordered at the country's yards.

Several Norwegian shipyards – including the leading Aker group – ended up in financial difficulties as a result of the dearth of new orders during the shipping crisis. However, there is still a vibrant shipbuilding industry in the country, though the really large vessels of the type built during the 1970s are no longer constructed in Norway. The yards have also, like shipowners, utilized the opportunities arising from the slicing up of the value chain. Hulls constructed abroad are fitted out at Norwegian yards, and the ship equipment industry is also still substantial.

Endangered endurance – 40 years of Norwegian shipping

In the beginning of the 1980s the Norwegian shipping industry was in a more precarious state than it had been at any point over the previous 150 years. The international shipping market was in the middle of its most severe crisis ever. Owing to the difficult circumstances, the size of the Norwegian fleet was in rapid decline as a large number of shipping companies had gone bankrupt, had been forced to sell their tonnage or had transferred their vessels to FoCs. The Norwegian ability to compete had deteriorated in what was becoming an increasingly cut-throat freight market, where more and more competitors were keeping costs down through low-cost labour. Previously, Norwegian owners had been able to neutralize their labour cost disadvantage by investing in large and technologically advanced vessels. The dearth of new investment, caused by the persistent overcapacity of tonnage, made the continuation of this strategy almost impossible.

By the end of the 1980s the outlook for Norwegian shipping was far more positive. Two factors are particularly important in explaining the shift. First, the demand for seaborne trade had started to recover, and the freight markets were rapidly improving. This positively affected shipowners in all nations. Second, the introduction in 1987 of the Norwegian International Ship Register gave Norwegian shipping a 'kiss of life'. By enabling owners to utilize less expensive foreign labour, this new institutional arrangement revitalized the Norwegian shipping industry and created optimism among the country's owners. Since the introduction of the NIS, Norway's share of the world fleet has fluctuated, though around a persistently higher level than what would have been the case if the Norwegian authorities had not reformulated their policies.

This snapshot of the Norwegian shipping experience during the 1980s provides three important insights into the shipping industry.

First, shipping is a global industry, very closely linked to the patterns and volumes of world trade, where the domestic demand for transport services is of very little importance. Indeed, the international demand dimension has been a necessary condition for the expansion of Norwegian shipping ever since the nineteenth century. As the tanker market collapsed during the shipping crisis of the 1970s and 1980s, and most other markets were also characterized by overcapacity, there was practically nothing that the Norwegian authorities or owners could do to change the development of demand. The fate of Norwegian shipping was at the mercy of an international market – as it has been throughout the twentieth century, and as it continues to be.

Second, the supply of shipping services has also become increasingly international in the post-war period. This aggravated the effects of the limited international demand. Challenges from foreign owners who could undercut the rates and offer shipping services at a lower price, as well as the drain on the financial resources resulting from unfortunate investments in the period before the freight market collapsed, are also important in explaining the predicaments that Norwegian owners faced in the first part of the 1980s.

The third insight is related to the remarkable turnaround witnessed in the Norwegian shipping sector; while shipping truly is an international industry, the domestic political regime is undoubtedly of great importance for the economic well-being of owners in a given country. As shipping is a footloose industry, most shipowners have more freedom in choosing where to base their operations than companies in other industries.

The history of Norwegian shipping over the last 50 years shows how the inherent cyclicality of the freight market both poses threats and creates opportunities for shipping companies. The strategies followed by Norwegian companies varied between the successful and the outright foolhardy. However, when some of the old stalwarts succumbed to the merciless forces of the market, new agents with fresh perspectives and sustainable strategies were ready to take over.

Despite the large number of failures among Norwegian shipping companies, the Norwegian shipping industry per se has shown a remarkable resilience. Over the last 150 years the international economy in general, and the Norwegian economy in particular, has undergone a series of fundamental changes. Still, the manner in which shipping has remained one of Norway's leading sectors, despite this transformation, is nothing short of remarkable.

Notes

The author would like to thank participants at the Nordic shipping workshops, as well as Professors Bjørn Basberg and Siri Pettersen Strandenes, NHH, for fruitful comments. Financial support from the Norwegian Research Council and Norges Rederiforbunds Fond for NHH, through the NORTRASHIP (Norwegian Transformations in Shipping) programme, is gratefully acknowledged.

1. For an overview of the long-term development of the shipping industry, see Kaukiainen (2006, 2008).
2. Liner ships and pseudo-liner ships constituted only around 8 per cent of the Norwegian fleet in the mid-1960s, and this share had dwindled to 4 per cent by the mid-1970s. Small companies that utilized economies of scale at the ship level, for example in the tanker sector, rather than at the fleet level, as would be necessary in the liner sector, is one factor that can explain this. See Poulsen (2007) and Slack and Frémont (2009).
3. The division between these levels is of course not clear-cut; Norwegian authorities may to some extent influence developments at the international level, through institutions such as the GATT/WTO and IMCO/IMO. Correspondingly, shipping companies may try to influence the direction and magnitude of the domestic regulatory regime. Indeed, these interactions between the participants at the different levels provide an interesting research agenda in themselves, but one that will not be pursued within the context of this chapter.
4. See also Sturmey (1975) and Sletmo (2001). In his discussion of Norwegian shipping policy, Willoch (1971) emphasizes the recruitment of skilled personnel, but also singles out tax policies, research policies and the access to registering ships abroad (flag policies). For the development of shipping policies in other countries see, for example, Gibson and Donovan (2000), Harlaftis (1993, 1996), Harlaftis and Theotokas (2009), Jamieson (2003) or Kaukiainen (1993).
5. The extended Committee on Finance and Economic Affairs used 'the current state of the shipping industry' – the shipping crisis – to justify the first stage of the flag policy liberalization (Innst. S. no. 167 (1978–79), p. 9). Shortly afterwards the Ministry of Trade and Shipping emphasized that '[i]n the evaluation of the flag policy, allowances must be made for the fact that an increasing share of the world fleet is registered in countries with free registers' (Stortingsmelding no. 52 (1980–81), pp. 30–1).
6. The lecture in which he suggested this was later printed as Næss (1985).

7. See Halvorsen (2007) Chapters 7 and 8 for a thorough account of the process, as seen from the view of the seamen's organizations.
8. At the same time the Norwegian Shipowners' Association changed its name in Norwegian from *Norges Rederforbund* [*Reder* describes a person owning ships] to *Norges Rederiforbund* [*Rederi* refers to a company owning ships]. This linguistic change reflected a belated adaptation to the transformation of the organization of the shipping industry in the country.
9. Given the cyclical nature of the shipping and oil markets, such comparisons are of course very sensitive to the point in time at which the comparison is made.
10. Slightly fewer than 50 Swedish companies owned vessels larger than 5000 grt in 1960. Thirteen Danish companies, all based in Copenhagen, owned vessels of this size. The number was the same for Finland, but here the geographic spread was more even, with five different ports (including the Åland Islands) registered. Oslo's share of the Norwegian fleet in 1960 was 53 per cent, if the fleets of Sig. Bergesen d.y. & Co. and Wilh. Wilhelmsen, which were nominally registered in Stavanger and Tønsberg respectively, are included. If these are included in their ports of registry, Oslo's share falls to 47 per cent.
11. This is one of the present reasons for the establishment of one-ship companies. Previously, this kind of incorporation was the most common form of ownership in Norway, through the *partsrederi* – companies that were set up for the purpose of owning a specific ship, and whose operations were usually wound up when the vessel was sold or lost.
12. Based on grt data from Lloyd's Register, as adapted by the Institute of Shipping Economics and Logistics, Bremen; it includes all ships larger than 300 grt. As the Norwegian vessels were relatively large, in international terms, a comparison based on dwt would give a higher Norwegian share.
13. See Ekberg (forthcoming) for a good introduction to the historical development of the car carrier industry and Norwegian participation in it.
14. For an introduction to shipping strategies, see Lorange (2005, 2009) and Wijnolst and Wergeland (1996, 2009).
15. This refers to companies that owned vessels larger than 5000 grt in 1960. Some companies that fell below this threshold in 1960 were more successful in the longer term – see, for example, Bakka (2004). Given that they were below the 1960 'radar', such companies are characterized as newcomers in our analysis.
16. There is no switching between groups, so despite its leading position by 1973, Bergesen is still considered to be 'medium-sized' in this context, which is faithful to the 1960 categories.
17. The data on which the analysis is based are 'loyal' to the ships, rather than corporate entities. Bankrupt holding companies, have, for example, not been counted as 'deaths' in the cases where the fleet remained intact but was transferred to a new corporate entity.
18. A seventh company, Color Line, was established in 1990, originally based on the passenger services owned by Anders Jahre, who was Norway's second largest shipowner in 1960.

19. In two of these instances, JO Tankers, spun off from Odfjell, and Bergshav Shipping, which had its roots in the Ugland group, both the original company and the offshoot were among Norway's 30 largest shipowners.
20. Fredriksen's colourful career has been the topic of two unauthorized biographies Odd Harald Hauge and Gunnar Stavrum (1991, 2005); see also Lennerfors (2009).
21. It could be argued that these owners should be seen as 'holding companies', rather than managing owners – see the section on *rederi* above. However, Veritas puts them in the latter group, and as the number and lifespan of such companies were low, this poses no problem for our general conclusions.
22. A certain degree of discretion has been necessary to determine whether the reorganization was of a type that warranted categorization as a new company, or whether it was merely a restructuring without substantial implications. As a rule, demergers have been treated as new companies, while a change of incorporation or name is viewed as the continuation of the original business.

3

'Knowing the Ropes': Capability Reconfiguration and Restructuring of the Danish Shipping Industry

Henrik Sornn-Friese, René Taudal Poulsen and Martin Jes Iversen

Introduction

The development of Danish shipping over the 50 years from 1960 to 2010 has been characterized by an overall fleet growth. However, there have been important dips disrupting the general development, some of which have been long-lasting and had distressing results for individual entrepreneurs. Half a century ago, around 1960, Denmark owned about 1.75 per cent of the world fleet and Danish shipping companies engaged successfully in all the main shipping segments. A decade later, Danish shipping proved more resilient to the downturn in world shipping markets than its Nordic competitors. The survival rate for Danish companies was higher than that in Sweden and Norway. In the mid-1980s shipowners cut costs and started reflagging their ships into open registries. Throughout the 1990s Danish shipping was in the doldrums, as it were, with some companies prospering and others failing spectacularly. In the initial decade of the twenty-first century Danish shipping companies proved able to exploit the global growth opportunities created by the demand-driven upswing in North America and South East Asia. By the end of the period covered in our analysis Danish shipping proved more successful than ever, controlling almost 5 per cent of the world fleet in 2008 and, according to the Danish Shipowners' Association (Danmarks Rederiforening, 2010), carrying 10 per cent of world trade as measured in terms of the value of the goods carried.

In this chapter we study the transformation of Danish shipping in the light of the fundamental changes in the shipping industry since 1960 in terms of markets served, the means of production, the organization and administration of tasks, and the supporting local institutional environment. The development of the Danish shipping industry over the last 50 years has been remarkable in at least three important ways. First, during its restructuring the industry managed to sustain and even develop its competitive advantage in an increasingly global market, while at the same time other Traditional Maritime Nations (TMNs) generally lost out to the new – notably South East Asian – maritime nations.

Second, the Danish developments have occurred within an industry structure dominated by a few large players. The period after the Second World War and up to 1960 saw a rebuilding and expansion of the Danish merchant fleet, and there were important changes in the organization of the industry, with an overall concentration into fewer and larger companies. By 1960 the top ten largest shipping companies owned about 80 per cent of the Danish fleet (Rasmussen et al., 2000). That this development happened within such a concentrated structure makes it different from those in most other TMNs, where shipping has historically been a more fragmented industry.[1] It is also somewhat at odds with the main economic explanations of industry evolution, such as the Vernon–Posner product cycle, technology life cycles, or punctuated equilibrium.[2]

Third, the Danish development has been remarkable in that the corporate pioneers were a small group of incumbent firms that had been the leaders of the industry since its inception in the latter part of the nineteenth century. Six of the top ten largest Danish shipping companies today, as measured in terms of owned fleet – including A. P. Møller-Maersk (Maersk), DFDS, J. Lauritzen (JL), Torm, Norden, and Dannebrog – were also in the top ten in 1960. Table 3.1 gives an overview of the ten largest Danish shipping companies at the beginning of each decade, as measured in terms of operated (not necessarily owned) tonnage. Some companies have left the list and others entered it. Nevertheless, the table demonstrates a remarkable stability in industry structure, in particular with regard to the largest companies. In comparison to the Swedish and Norwegian shipping industries, the changes in Danish shipping industry structure were generally smaller and less significant (see Chapters 2 and 4 on Norway and Sweden respectively). While the shipping industries in other TMNs seem to have historically accommodated structural changes in world shipping markets by

Table 3.1 Top ten largest Danish shipping companies (operated tonnage based on 1000 dwt), 1960–2008

1960		**1970**		**1980**	
Maersk	1,099	Maersk	2,904	Maersk	6,228
EAC	484	EAC	358	EAC	779
DFDS	222	JL	254	Torm	272
JL	215	Ove Skou	237	Ove Skou	224
Dansk-Fransk	141	Torm	181	Norden	169
Torm	101	Dansk-Fransk	151	JL	157
Dansk Esso	93	DFDS	129	Dansk Esso	126
C. K. Hansen (Dannebrog)	93	Dansk Esso	103	DFDS	122
Ove Skou	75	Monthor	74	Weco Shipping (Dannebrog)	111
Norden	60	Weco Shipping (Dannebrog)	72	Knud I. Larsen	84
Total	**2,583**	**Total**	**4,462**	**Total**	**8,273**
1990		**2000**		**2008**	
Maersk	4,669	Maersk	8,974	Maersk	15,828
JL	1,289	Torm	2,408	Norden	14,652
EAC	931	Norden	2,196	Torm	3,927
Torm	495	JL	1,813	JL	3,628
Norden	478	Tschudi & Eitzen	1,649	Clipper	2,339
Mercandia	182	Elite Rederi	237	Eitzen	2,027
Knud I. Larsen	86	United Shipping	145	Bidsted & Co	972
Terkol	70	Herning Shipping	80	ID Shipping	577
DFDS	56	Armada Shipping	79	Svendborg Ship Mgmnt	415
Dannebrog	54	T&C	68	T.K.B. Shipping	381
Total	**8,309**	**Total**	**17,650**	**Total**	**44,746**

Source: SeaDirectory.com (*Scandinavian Shipowners & Ship Management Companies*) 1961–2009.

the continual entry of new shipping companies, replacing the old and established ones, such accommodation by the Danish shipping industry has thus essentially taken place through the reconfiguration of organizational capabilities in century-old companies.[3]

Our analysis is founded on the premise that conditions at company, sector and national levels interact to shape the development of capabilities and economic organization in the shipping industry, and we will include all three levels in our analysis. Our explanation is not complete, since we do not go into detail about the competitive strategy and internal dynamics of individual shipping companies, but instead generalize from the corporate-level strategies of the most important companies. To the extent that these companies are multiproduct firms, we see them as tightly-knit groupings of related business units. While we may thus devote some space to depicting the recent overall growth strategies of successful Danish tramp shipping companies such as Torm and Norden, both of which are engaged in dry cargo bulk as well as product tanker shipping, we do not delve into the different risks of dry cargo and product tanker shipping and the different responses of the companies to those market and other relevant risks.

The past 50 years of evolution in the shipping industry of Denmark can be divided into four clearly identifiable and distinct phases. In each phase, technological, organizational and institutional innovations have transformed the structure and basis of Danish shipping. This rugged development of Danish shipping over the period since 1960 serves as the inspiration for the chronological structuring of our analysis.[4]

The first phase, covering the period between 1960 and 1973, represents a period of rapidly growing demand and technological innovation. A stable growth in Danish tonnage could not conceal the fact that Danish shipowners lost global market share. The relation between liner, tramp and tanker shipping was relatively stable, as was the population of Danish shipping companies.

The second distinct phase runs from 1974 to 1987. Under the heading 'Between stagnation and crisis' we consider the rise and fall of various shipping segments during this phase. The number of Danish-registered ships fell dramatically during the period, a decline which was caused by Danish shipowners flagging out their vessels to open registers at the end of the period. The structure of the industry in terms of the main companies was intact, however: a fact that set the Danish case apart from the other Nordic countries. Most importantly, this period saw a fundamental resegmentation of Danish shipping as the dominant liner shipping companies entered container shipping in the late 1960s and the 1970s, which created possibilities for smaller shipping companies and new entrants to develop strong container feeder services.

The advent of the Danish International Ship Register (DIS) in 1988 marked the beginning of a third distinct phase of development, lasting for about a decade and a half, in which an implicit coalition between the shipowners and the shifting governments shaped a national industrial policy for Danish shipping. This was also the period in which long-established Danish tramp shipping operators took significant shares in the world dry bulk and product tanker sectors. Important in this latter development was the idea that a shipping company could prosper, not by owning vessels, but by operating vessels owned by other companies.

The recent development of Danish shipping, after 2002 but ahead of the world economic recession of 2008 to 2009, has been characterized by tremendous company growth and unparalleled economic success. Old players were rejuvenated and the Danish government maintained a supportive attitude towards the industry. In 2007 Danish shipbuilding orders moreover peaked at a record high level. In contrast to the earlier phases most of these orders were placed outside Denmark. This development mirrored a general globalization of Danish maritime industries in the decades in question.

1960–1973: A conservative approach

Fluctuating freight markets are a fact that shipowners will always face, and predicting such fluctuations is the basis of their business. The 1960s saw periods of boom and bust in shipping, and political tensions in the Middle East had an important bearing on the freight markets. Rapid growth in the Western hemisphere and Japan cascaded over into shipping, and the demand for shipping – in particular for the carriage of crude oil – grew very rapidly, as did the world fleet (Tenold, 2006; Stopford, 2009; Wijnolst and Wergeland, 2009).

Shipowners also faced rapid technological change. Economies of scale were achieved through the application of more rational cargo-handling equipment and larger vessels. The pursuit of economies of scale was most evident in the oil tankers, for which average sizes grew many times over (Gardiner, 1992; Tenold, 2006). Numerous foreign shipowners decided to build supertankers, and the first Very Large Crude Carriers (VLCCs) entered into service in 1966 followed by the first Ultra Large Crude Carriers (ULCCs) in 1968. Similarly, transportation of dry bulk cargoes went through rapid technological change with the breakthrough of bulk carriers, which had wide hatches and large holds, tailored for large-scale break bulk carrying. The new technology increased both the size of vessels and average cargo loads, but the entry barriers to this segment of the industry remained low.

Liner shipping companies struggled with increasing cargo-handling costs in the early 1960s. Conventional liner ships spent long periods in ports and required large gangs of longshoremen to load and offload cargo. Containerization, however, revolutionized liner shipping from the mid-1960s, not only increasing efficiency and achieving economies of scale but paving the way for integrated transport chains. Originally a North American speciality, containers gained global significance from the late 1960s when containerization was initiated on all the main east–west trade routes. It involved massive investments and scale became a key success factor. Frequent services, large liner networks and high capacity were crucial and the new technology proved disrupting to many traditional liner shipping companies (Broeze, 2002; Levinson, 2006; Donovan and Bonney, 2006). The North Atlantic liner service of the oldest Danish shipping company, DFDS, presents an illustrative case of failure. In 1966, when its competitors introduced container vessels, DFDS built conventional liner vessels, which quickly proved uncompetitive and the service was closed down approximately two years later (Poulsen, 2010).

In the generally expansive climate of the 1960s, shipowners in many TMNs remained optimistic, but Danish shipowners were more cautious, being less expansionist and more hesitant with regard to adopting the new technologies. Danish tonnage investments were smaller than the global average and Danish shipping companies were generally technological late movers.

Liner trades, on which several Danish shipowners had been engaged for decades, were generating the main income, but Danish owners also turned out to be late movers with regard to containerization. Some first attempts at containerization in the 1960s were made in the short-sea trades in Northern Europe when DFDS introduced ro-ro (roll-on roll-off) container carriers on its Esbjerg–Grimsby line in 1967. In its domestic services DFDS had also experimented with unitized cargo systems as early as the early 1950s – however, they were using the company's own system (small, wooden containers), and not the future winning standard twenty-foot equivalent unit (TEU) system. In general however, Danish shipowners, like everybody else, continued to build conventional liner ships for the overseas lines until the mid-1960s (Graae, 1966; Thorsøe et al., 1991).[5] When foreign competitors decided to go for full-scale containerization and demonstrated the viability of the new technology, the main Danish companies – the EAC and the Maersk subsidiary Maersk Line – planned to do the same. By waiting, Maersk Line avoided some of the disruptive problems experienced by the pioneers (Poulsen, 2007, 2010; Lauring, 2008, see also below).

The dry bulk trades grew rapidly in the 1960s, but Danish shipowners were generally reluctant to invest in bulk carriers. This is evident from newbuilding lists published in the Danish maritime newspaper *Søfart*. According to annual reports from the Danish Shipowners' Association, this was due to particularly high Danish manning requirements, which made such vessels uncompetitive under the Danish flag until the late 1960s. Under the Danish flag such vessels had to operate with larger crews than elsewhere in Western Europe, thus raising Danish crewing costs and building costs for vessels with large crew accommodation (Danmarks Rederiforening, 1961, 1962, 1964, 1965, 1967, 1968). Nevertheless, a significant investment in this segment was made by Norden, which sold the main share of its fleet of technologically obsolete, conventional general cargo ships during the 1960s. This company was looking for new investments at the time, the alternative being to abandon the shipping industry altogether. Norden entered the bulk business on a large scale between 1973 and 1978 when it took delivery of five new bulk carriers, three of which were paid for in cash (Falkensteen, 1996). Two of the bulkers were fixed on ten-year time charters (t/c) to the Seaboard Shipping Company of British Columbia in Canada, at highly profitable rates. An additional two bulkers were later fixed on shorter t/c to Seaboard. The latter had expected to pay a charter rate above the freight market during the first years of the charter period, and then earn money in the latter part of the period. For most of the ten years, however, the freight market remained below the charter rate, so the t/c agreement was a profitable one for Norden and allowed the company to stay unaffected by the depressed period from 1975 to 1978 and set for the subsequent goods years in dry bulk, 1979 to 1980.

The tonnage strategies of Danish shipowners differed in other ways from those of their foreign competitors, a fact which was clearly evident from their newbuilding programmes. Shipping is generally a capital-intensive industry, so shipowners' choice of vessels is a key strategic component. Owners can generally choose between newbuildings (efficient vessels with high capital costs) and second-hand vessels (older vessels with lower capital costs), or a mix of the two. Since the 1950s Danish shipowners had focused on young and efficient high-quality tonnage, thus accepting high capital costs (see Figure 3.1). The prevailing

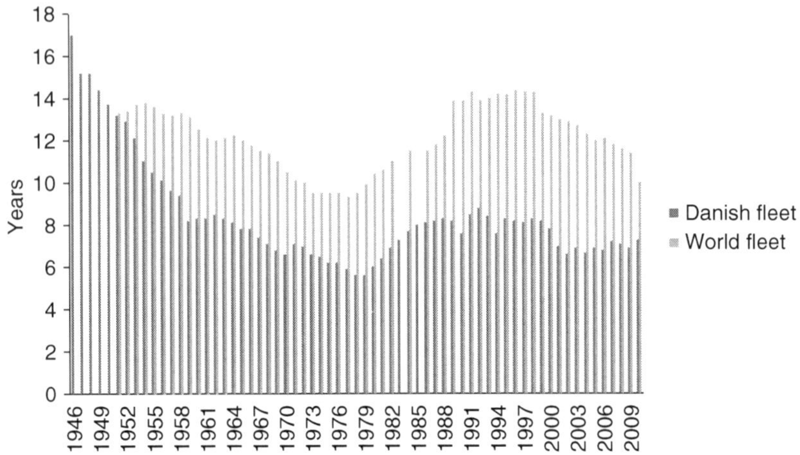

Figure 3.1 Average age of tonnage in the Danish and world fleet, 1946–2010
Source: Danmarks Rederiforening (various years), annual report.

tonnage strategy in Denmark differed markedly from the low-cost alternative applied by numerous owners in the large Greek shipping community. Greek shipowners were famous for their operation of second-hand vessels at low costs (Harlaftis, 1996). In comparison with other fleets internationally, it can be seen that a significant reduction in the average age of the Danish fleet took place up to the mid-1970s. While Danish companies were not pioneers technologically, they certainly based their competitive position on a young fleet.

Ordering new vessels also demonstrated a belief in future freight and asset markets and a willingness to take commercial risks (Stopford, 2009). Generally it appeared that the bigger the newbuilding programme, the greater the owners' optimism or willingness to take on risk. Moreover, a large newbuilding programme over time would increase the capital costs of a company. Hence, a large increase in the newbuilding programme changed the competitive position of companies and revealed important aspects of shipping company strategy.

From Figure 3.2 we can see that the Danish newbuilding programme was relatively stable until the late 1960s, as the number of vessels on order fluctuated between 7 and 17 per cent of the existing fleet. Ships typically had a commercial life length of approximately 25 years, and it took between one and three years to build a ship (from ordering to delivery), depending on the availability of shipyard berths. Hence, a shipping company with a fleet of 25 vessels needed an average order

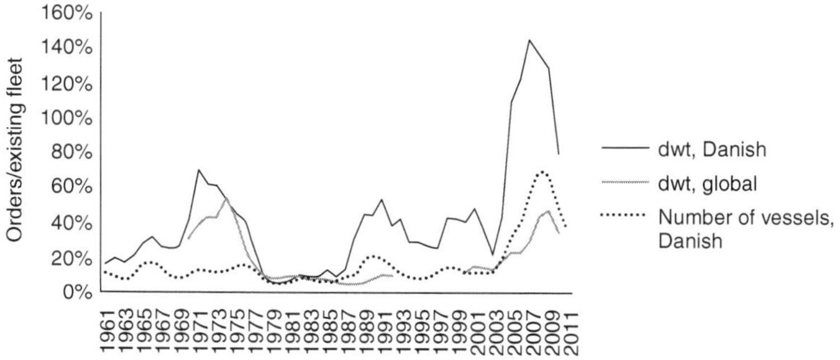

Figure 3.2 Danish newbuilding programme compared to existing Danish fleet, 1960–2011

Source: Calculated from Danmarks Rederiforening (various years), annual report.

programme of approximately two vessels (8 per cent of the existing fleet) to maintain its fleet at the same level. Figure 3.2 also clearly demonstrates the cyclical nature of shipping. In terms of deadweight, the Danish newbuilding programme started to grow noticeably in 1969. It peaked at 70 per cent of the existing fleet in 1970, even though the number of vessels on order did not rise accordingly. The Danish programme was large by international standards. According to annual reports from the Danish Shipowners' Association (1969–75) the global newbuilding programme, the tonnage (dwt) of which peaked at 54 per cent of the existing fleet in 1974, was dominated by supertankers. The Danish peak, however, was solely attributable to Maersk's orders of such vessels. This company's quest for economies of scale in the oil tanker business resembled the general trend in the industry at the time, but it differed from the strategy of the other Danish companies, which refrained from such investments. If we ignore Maersk's supertanker orders it is obvious that the Danish programme was of a modest size in global terms. Moreover, in the case of Maersk, the investments in supertankers only represented a small part of the total investments of the business (D/S Svendborg and D/S af 1912, annual reports, 1968 to 1978).

The fact that Danish shipowners did not venture into the supertanker business reflected a conservative approach, which contrasted with that of Norwegian and Swedish companies. Political factors (high manning requirements for tankers) clearly also played a role. Several medium-sized and large Danish shipping companies, including the EAC, JL and Dannebrog, were experienced in the tanker business, and entry barriers were generally low, so they could have invested in supertankers. From 1967 to 1973, the global market for supertankers was the most expansive and profitable shipping market, and several foreign shipowners made fortunes in a short period of time. However, the market for supertankers was also highly volatile and thus risky (Tenold, 2006). The conservative approach of Danish shipping companies precluded Danish companies from reaping the benefits of the boom in oil shipping from 1967 to 1973, but it also proved a blessing after the oil price shock of 1973.

In contrast to other Danish shipping companies, Maersk increased its risk exposure in the oil-related industries. Not only did it invest in supertankers, it also entered the business of oil exploration in 1962, when it gained a concession from the Danish government to operate in the North Sea. Partnering with foreign oil majors, the company discovered oil and gas in the North Sea a few years later, and offshore oil production commenced in 1972. The investments in oil exploration were highly risky due to the low probability of discoveries. Moreover, field development programmes were costly after discoveries were made (Hahn-Pedersen, 1997).

The 1960s were also a significant period because shipping capital was raised in new ways. A small group of entrepreneurs managed to build up large fleets of coasters in less than a decade. The most important of these were Per Henriksen, who founded the Mercandia shipping companies, Asger Lindinger (the Shipping Company Lindinger), Bent Waagesen (Bewa Line), and Helmer Lønborg (Lønborg-Line), none of whom had a maritime background (they were merchants and stockbrokers). Lacking the necessary financial resources themselves, these entrepreneurs raised capital through the K/S system (*kommanditselskab*). Shares in the K/S system were often small; investors were entitled to a postponement of income tax, and the system attracted numerous passive investors with no maritime background and little insight into shipping. Some of the K/S financed ventures proved short-lived, but Mercandia expanded into a large Danish shipping company during the 1970s and 1980s and it remained an important company until its shipping activities were gradually closed down after the retirement of Mr Henriksen (Henriksen, 2004). In the 1980s the reputation of the K/S system was damaged by heavy losses in several ventures (Jensen, 1993; Erhvervsministeriet, 1996). Following a heated public debate, the K/S system was changed by law in 1994 to 1995. The maximum legal number of investors per vessel was radically reduced, raising entry barriers for investors. The system remained, however, and has played a significant part in the continued restructuring of the Danish shipping industry, especially as a vehicle for fleet expansion. The more recent investment companies that have entered into Danish shipping – especially DIFKO 47, CS & Partners, and Investment Group Denmark (ID Shipping) – profited greatly from the limited partnership system during the boom in shipping from 2002 to 2008.

With the exception of manning issues, the regulation of shipping did not cause any major political battles in Denmark during the 1960s. However, international developments were a main concern for Danish shipowners, who depended almost completely upon cross-trades, and they remained a concern into the 1970s and even later. Hence access to foreign markets was crucial, and from the annual reports of the Danish Shipowners' Association over the period it is obvious that Danish shipowners feared that various government subsidies and the protectionist policies of the United States would inspire many countries to restrict cross-traders. In South America, in particular, various measures were taken to build up large national fleets, and within the liner trades – the most regulated shipping segment – there was intense conflict between developing countries and countries with large cross-trading fleets (De la Pedraja, 1999). Developing countries wanted to build up their own merchant fleets and used the United Nations Conference on Trade and Development (UNCTAD) in this process. From the establishment of UNCTAD in 1964 the so-called 'Group of 77' required that the industrialized countries recognize the legitimacy of the developing countries' efforts to secure a larger share of their seaborne trade on their own vessels. Also, they saw liner conferences as an unjust remnant of colonialism and therefore demanded that international liner shipping should be controlled by the United Nations (UN).

From 1964 onwards, a 40–40-20 code was discussed within UNCTAD, according to which only 20 per cent of liner cargoes would be allocated to cross-trading shipping lines.[6] The remaining 80 per cent of the cargoes would be split equally between shipping companies from the exporting and importing countries. Denmark, Finland, Great Britain, Norway, Sweden, Switzerland and the United States voted against this compromise, and Denmark and Great Britain began lobbying within the European Community (EC) for a new shipping policy. The potential damage threatened by the UNCTAD Code brought previously competing lines together in a fight for free market access, and Scandinavian liner shipping companies took part in this process. Fear of cargo restrictions had a direct bearing on the cross-trading shipping companies in the 1960s, which worked determinedly to keep markets open (Poulsen, 2010). Later, however, those fears proved to have been exaggerated. In 1979 the European countries agreed that UNCTAD rules should apply within the Organisation for Economic Cooperation and Development (OECD) and that the developing countries would have preference over 40 per cent of their trade, while 60 per cent would be subject to open competition. With this provision ('the Brussels Compromise'), the code was ratified in 1983. As it turned out, the damage to Danish shipping that the shipowners had feared did not materialize. Containerization had changed the nature of liner shipping and liner networks, and the code never gained the significance that had been anticipated.

1974 to 1987: between stagnation and crisis

The long and deep international shipping crisis that lasted from the mid-1970s to the mid-1980s, was caused by what some economists have called a 'perfect storm'. The two oil crises in 1973 and 1979 to 1980 caused, first, stagnation and then decline in the hitherto booming oil tanker segment, which was combined with the breakthrough of a new maritime transport paradigm – containerization – and with difficult macroeconomic circumstances, in particular in the late 1970s and early 1980s. Finally, the rise of open registers, or what the International Transport Workers' Federation (ITF) termed 'Flags of Convenience' (FoCs), made the circumstances even more difficult for the TMNs.

Danish shipping was obviously damaged by these transformations, but not to the same extent as other traditional northern European maritime nations (e.g. Norway, Sweden and Great Britain). The Danish fleet continued to grow until the late 1970s and did not decline to the same extent as the Norwegian and Swedish fleets. Moreover, Danish shipping suffered remarkably few casualties during the crisis years. The only notable company failures were the liner and bulk shipping company Dansk-Fransk Dampskibsselskab, which went bankrupt in 1979, and the bulk shipping company Ove Skou, which after several difficult years that had wiped out its capital by 1985, was finally dissolved in 1988 (Lund, 1995; Sornn-Friese and Iversen, 2011). Hence, in contrast to the Norwegian and Swedish cases, the structure of the Danish shipping industry remained practically unchanged (see Table 3.1).

There were three important reasons for this. First, the generally cautious strategic approach of the Danish shipping companies during the 1960s, as described above, gave them a relatively strong position in the early 1970s. In the Norwegian and Swedish cases, large newbuilding programmes quickly turned into dangerous liabilities. This was not the case in Denmark. Second, as already mentioned in the introduction to this chapter, the Danish shipping industry was dominated by old, relatively large, shipping companies. As shown in Chapter 2, large shipping companies in Norway had the financial strength necessary to survive during the difficult years in international shipping, and they were thus able to endure longer than their smaller competitors. Structural concentration may also, from this perspective, have been an important contributor to the relatively stable development in the Danish case during this period. Third, Danish shipping to a large extent depended on the relatively stable liner segment. Maersk alone was exposed to the drop in the supertanker markets, and that only to a limited extent, according to annual company reports (1974–87). For that reason, Danish lay-up rates never reached Swedish and Norwegian levels. When the Norwegian and Swedish rates peaked in 1976 at 24 and 27 per cent of the tonnage, respectively, Danish rates were only 11 per cent (Tenold, 2006). The tanker segment lost its relative importance during the period as some supertankers were sold for scrap. Bulk shipping – and most notably the coaster fleet employed in short-sea shipping – also declined. These small vessels were hit by lower demand due to the economic crisis combined with enhanced competition from alternative transport means, such as trucks and trains, but also – perhaps most significantly – from container shipping (Industriministeriet, 1980).

Liner shipping proved to be the most prosperous segment, and the Danish market share rose from 2.9 per cent in 1975 to 4.4 per cent in 1980. In 1980 liner vessels constituted 20 per cent of the merchant fleet but contributed approximately 45 per cent of the national net currency income (Industriministeriet, 1980). The defining years for Denmark as an important liner shipping nation were the period from 1975 to the early 1980s, and this was closely related to the strategic development of the two corporate giants in Danish shipping, Maersk and EAC. Both were conglomerates with interests in several shipping segments as well as various other types of industry. But then the similarities end: at the dawn of this period the subsidiary Maersk Line was one of the world's strongest liner companies, while EAC struggled with the necessary transition and finally sold its container fleet in 1993 – to Maersk Line.

In the period between 1974 and 1986 Maersk took over EAC's historical role as the largest and most important corporation in Denmark. As illustrated in Figure 3.3 the annual turnover of EAC was almost 15 billion DKK in 1974, when EAC was a diversified group with various activities in manufacturing, trade and shipping.

Figure 3.3 Total annual revenues of Maersk and EAC, 1974–86 (billion DKK)
Source: Mapping Corporate Denmark (http://ilex.cbs.dk/corporatedk/CorporateDK/Welcome.asp).

Containerization

EAC had been engaged in liner shipping between Europe and South East Asia since its establishment in 1897, and had gradually expanded its network to include Africa, Australia and the US West Coast. EAC was a diversified trading company engaged in shipping, trading and manufacturing. By the mid-1970s it had become the largest corporation in Scandinavia (in terms of turnover). It had a long tradition and was keenly aware of its history as a technological pioneer.[7] The company's liner traditions, its access to internal financial resources, which emanated from its large assets in activities outside shipping, and its ambitions to continue as a pioneer in technology were all important factors for EAC's early investments in container shipping. After experiments with various semi-container vessel designs in the late 1960s, EAC received its first fully cellular container ship in 1971.

To enter full scale into container shipping EAC joined forces with several foreign lines in various international consortia. On the Europe–Asia run EAC entered into an extended co-operation with its close and long-standing shipping partners Wilh. Wilhelmsen in Oslo and Svenska Ostasiatiska Kompaniet (Ostasiat) in Göteborg. This enabled the company to provide a customer-friendly liner schedule and share the heavy demands for capital investment. Soon a Dutch and a French partner joined, and the venture was renamed ScanDutch, with operating headquarters in Copenhagen (Poulsen, 2007). EAC also joined forces with other liner shipping companies on its other major routes, further extending its co-operative strategy.

EAC early on established its own business college to provide the company's employees with thorough practical and theoretical training in finance, trade, shipping and logistics, based on the special EAC 'way of doing things'. In its glory days as a shipping company EAC would graduate 60 to 70 young company managers yearly (Westphall, 1978). As we shall argue below, EAC's co-operative capabilities would, in the development phase of Danish shipping (1988–2001), spread into the whole Danish shipping industry and form an important basis for the development of Copenhagen as an international centre for the commercial management of, in particular, pools of product tankers.

While EAC was quite successful with its initial co-operative container strategy its next strategic move from 1976 was an expensive failure, which eventually contributed to its final exit from shipping in the mid-1990s. In 1976 and 1977 the company received seven Liner Replacement Vessels (LRVs). These were rather small and highly energy-efficient ships with a capacity of 600 TEU combined with flexible capacity for various cargo types. On delivery they were put into service on the transpacific line. This decision was, as it would turn out, decisive for the economic troubles that would follow for the company. The ships were too slow and the freight rates too low and, because of the 'jack-of-all-trades' nature of these vessels, EAC could not achieve the necessary economies of scale (Bjerrum, 1993; Lauring, 2008). In many ways, the liner replacement vessels reflected EAC's nature as a general trading company rather than as a specialized shipping company (unlike Maersk, which understood that success with containerization would require focused large-scale investments). EAC had invested in ships that neither contributed to large-scale containerized logistics, nor formed a sustainable high-value shipping niche.

Taking delivery of its first fully cellular container ship in 1973, Maersk was a late mover in containerization compared to EAC. Its background in liner shipping also differed markedly from that of EAC. While EAC had worked as a conference member, operating its main liner network from of the Nordic home market, Maersk had always worked as a cross-trader, mainly with its historical transpacific service that had been set up as early as 1928 (in fact named the 'Maersk Line'), and its Europe–Far East service, set up in 1968, and as an outsider to the established liner conferences. Hence, Maersk had a stand-alone experience that set it apart from EAC's more traditional position in liner shipping (Rasmussen et al., 2000; Lauring, 2008). Despite the relatively late investment, the owner of the company and chairman of the board, Mærsk Mc-Kinney Møller, had predicted the importance and requirements of container shipping as early as the annual report of 1970 and argued that the company should expect to be engaged with container vessels. Maersk also noted the huge requirements to capital investments that would follow from such a change in strategy.

In 1975 and 1976 the company bought nine fast container vessels for its transpacific line, the largest investment in the company's history, and ships of a radically different design from EAC's contemporary LRVs. In contrast to EAC's co-operative approach, Maersk Line adopted a standalone strategy, running the service single-handedly according to the company's annual report for 1975 (see also Broeze, 2002). As predicted by Mr Mc-Kinney Møller, large investments in land-based transport facilities followed the container operations. It also provided new opportunities for related diversification, such as the establishment of Maersk Logistics in 1977, Maersk Container Industry in 1992 and APM Terminals in 2001. During the shipping crisis in the mid-1980s, Maersk adopted a strategy of strong growth in container shipping, complementing its services between Europe and Asia and the transpacific, which had been fully containerized by 1975, with a US West Coast–Middle East service, based on transhipments in Hong Kong, a major hub in Algeciras in southern Spain, which provided the foundation for the company's own feeder lines in the West Mediterranean as well as access to the West African coast, and a hub in Dubai, which provided the basis for services to the East African coast (Fremont, 2007). Moreover, it extended its services with major investments in land-based infrastructure in several countries. During the 1980s Maersk thus spanned the globe with an extensive container hub-and-spoke network. The company expanded fast and by the early 1980s Maersk Line was among the world's ten largest container shipping companies (Donovan and Bonney, 2006).

The cases of EAC and Maersk Line stand out in the history of Danish containerization, but a number of specialized container feeder companies, such as Knud I. Larsen (1942–98), Elite Shipping (1977–99), Hansen & Lange (1976–), Unifeeder (1977–), and Fabricius Marine (1984–), also appeared on the scene during this period and remained successful for many years. Unifeeder, which built its liner services on chartered-in tonnage, is the leading container feeder company in Northern Europe today and among the top five largest container feeder companies in the world.[8]

The difficult 1980s

While the large Danish shipping companies were well positioned during the crisis of the 1970s, an erosion of their competitive position started in the early 1980s. In the first half of 1985, on average one vessel was sold abroad every five days and one-sixth of the total fleet was officially on sale. These figures alarmed the shipowners' association, which in its annual report for 1985 warned that the demise of shipping under the Danish flag was imminent. From 1979 to 1985 the fleet was reduced by more than two million dwt, according to their annual report for 1987. The pessimism of Danish shipowners' was also evident in the historically low level of the Danish newbuilding programme (Figure 3.2) and the rapid rise in the average age of the Danish merchant fleet (Figure 3.1). Finally, the flagging out of the Danish merchant fleet accelerated rapidly. In the 1970s Danish shipowners had been relatively cautious in their use of open registers. Only 50 Danish-owned ships – up to around 300,000 grt, or 5 to 6 per cent of the total fleet – were registered abroad in 1978 (Industriministeriet, 1980). In 1980 the Ministry of Industry concluded that the problem of flagging out was not a major cause for concern. However, the situation changed dramatically in the mid-1980s. During the first half of 1987 the use of foreign flags by Danish shipowners had increased from 20 to 30 per cent (both in number of ships and in tonnage) and over the following months an alarming number of Danish-owned ships were transferred to open registries. By October 1987 40 per cent of Danish-owned ships sailed under foreign flags and there were severe losses of jobs and foreign currency income from shipping.[9]

Both market conditions and unfortunate strategic choices played a role in the problems of Danish shipping in the 1980s. In the main shipping markets, freight rates remained at a low level until late in the decade and, within the group of large Danish shipping companies, there were several cases of overstretching in depressed markets. EAC's ill-fated trans-pacific venture represents one such example, but J. Lauritzen (including the partly-owned DFDS) showed this even more clearly. For decades JL had stayed at the very top of Danish shipping together with EAC and Maersk, but in the late 1980s it represented an almost classical case of overinvestment in difficult markets. Like its peers, EAC and Maersk, JL was engaged in several shipping segments as well as shipbuilding and manufacturing. As a major player in specialized reefer shipping, and strongly consolidated in 1979, JL embarked on a diversification strategy in cruise, drilling and heavy lift vessels in the early 1980s. The company's plans failed, however, as market conditions deteriorated and its resources were consequently heavily strained. Divestment from several shipping segments followed (Lange, 1995). However, poor strategies and difficult market conditions were not alone in explaining the problems of Danish shipping.

1988 to 2001: The break with established frames

The depressing drift of Danish shipping in the mid-1980s had turned into a crisis for Denmark as a maritime nation-state. The shipowners and the Conservative–Liberal Danish government agreed that the survival of Danish shipping was at stake, and for the first time there were serious attempts to cultivate a national strategy for Danish shipping, focusing on the competitiveness of the national merchant fleet.[10] The following decade and a half saw a number of important institutional changes that were essential for building up a vigorous shipping environment, particularly in Copenhagen – much in the spirit prescribed by Michael E. Porter (1990). These included the creation of the Danish International Ship Register (DIS); the establishment of the Danish Maritime Authority; the adoption of the tonnage tax scheme; and the rising professionalization of maritime education, the rationale for which was a growing concern about shipping as the engine driving developments and competitiveness in the broader Danish maritime sector. The latter concern was chiefly expressed by the notion of a Danish maritime cluster, also known as 'Blue Denmark' (Sornn-Friese, 2003). These changes were all important building blocks in what would later be presented as a comprehensive and coherent Danish maritime growth strategy (ibid.; Økonomi- og Erhvervsministeriet, 2006).

From the mid-1990s Danish shipping developed in two directions: first, with further expansion and specialization in container shipping with a focus on building up comprehensive logistics systems and, second, with an increasing focus on operating rather than owning ships – the latter entailing the flexible chartering-in and pooling of ships generally operated for particular large customers. Danish shipowners have increasingly entered into co-operative relationships with foreign shipowners, thus complementing classical shipowning with capabilities in commercial management. The total tonnage controlled from

Copenhagen has more than doubled since 1998 and more than half the income of Danish shipowners today derives from operating foreign-owned tonnage.

Creating national competitiveness

In the 1980s the shipowners were heavily engaged in strategic agenda-setting and, through their association, published analyses of markets and competitors, drafted proposals, and communicated their ideas to policy-makers and the wider public. In their centenary jubilee publication in 1984 they addressed the situation regarding competition in Danish shipping, tackling such issues as open registers (now known as 'flags of necessity') and competitiveness. They concluded that developments in international shipping since the late 1970s had eaten into their capital and that this would force them to seek out solutions, such as reflagging their ships under open registries. In a later brief they claimed that, with the low freight market at the time, it was impossible for Danish shipowners to cover capital and operating costs, and that the real issue was not about making money but about how to minimize losses (Danmarks Rederiforening, 1987). Again they argued that manning costs constituted the main problem for the competitiveness of Danish international shipping, since these were the only costs that varied under different flags and were thus the only real factor in competitiveness. This cost argument was central to the general discussion about the competitiveness of nations at the time, which focused on the clearly detrimental effects of increasing relative unit labour costs on market shares and economic growth.[11]

The shipowners proposed a 35-point plan with suggestions for improvements in national shipping capabilities (Danmarks Rederiforening, 1986). In a letter to the Minister of Industry that accompanied the plan, they pointed to five major issues that distorted the competitiveness of Danish shipping, including manning requirements, requirements to vessel fittings and equipment, unfortunate tax provisions, burdensome administration, and deficiencies in the Danish maritime educational system. The letter concluded by stating that a rapid and positive reaction from the authorities would be essential for the survival of many Danish shipowners if they were to continue registering their vessels under the Danish flag. The plan prompted an independent analysis by the Ministry of Industry. It was released in a comprehensive White Book only a few months later (Industriministeriet, 1987a) and became an essential document in the subsequent Danish shipping policy process.

The shipowners, however, soon realized the need for more radical steps than those introduced in the 35-point plan. With ever more vessels registering under open registries, the Danish merchant fleet was being reduced rapidly and at an accelerating rate. At the same time, Norway was about to establish the Norwegian International Ship Register (NIS), which inspired the shipowners in Denmark to suggest a similar special Danish register. They were backed by the Ministry of Industry, which in an important memorandum on Danish shipping policy suggested the establishment of a Danish International Ship Register (DIS) applying to large vessels engaged in foreign trade (Industriministeriet, 1987b). The Conservative-Liberal government supported the suggestion, but the trade unions and the Social Democrats opposed it, as they feared it would lead to the loss of Danish jobs and jeopardize safety on board Danish ships. The shipowners and the government ensured that every ship would continue to employ Danish seamen and follow all the standards agreed upon by the International Maritime Organization (IMO). But more persuasion was needed to get the proposal through parliament. The shipowners did two things in this regard. First, they promised to bring back home a significant share of their vessels registered abroad. JL, EAC, Norden, Torm, Knud I. Larsen and Mortensen & Lange – together controlling more than a quarter of the Danish-owned fleet under foreign flags – promised they would reflag a number of their ships back into DIS. Second, they emphasized more strongly the positive externalities generated by shipping for the rest of the Danish economy. It had often been claimed that sustaining a Danish-flagged merchant fleet manned primarily by Danish nationals would be essential in order to retain Danish maritime know-how. The shipowners now went a few steps further, arguing that a passive maritime policy would hurt not only the shipping industry but the entire Danish maritime value chain, which also included the shipyards, specialized maritime suppliers and maritime research units (Pontoppidan, 1987). This 'maritime cluster' argument centred on the claim that, in the long term, the retention of Danish seafarers and officers in the national fleet would be essential to the further development of Danish maritime know-how and the adaptive ability of Danish shipping and other maritime companies. DIS was thus enacted as the universal remedy to the problems faced by Denmark as a maritime nation.

The shipowners presented their arguments at a time of change in Danish economic and industrial policy. According to Christensen and Ydesen (2009) there was an apparent neo-liberal turn in Danish policy around 1980, where not only the Conservative–Liberal parties but also the Social Democrats adopted elements of neo-liberal thinking: classical liberal concepts such as competition, markets and efficiency were coupled with the view that, in an increasingly global economy, markets can only function under certain institutional conditions that must be actively constructed by government. The neo-liberal problem of 'national competitiveness' also became a central concern to government around this time (see, for example, Pedersen, 2008). In this regard, the general focus was initially on cost-competitiveness but from around 1986 it was being recast in terms of 'structural competitiveness', directing policy towards flexible labour markets and taxation structures, as well as privatization, outsourcing and the like (Campbell and Pedersen, 2001).[12] In line with the neo-liberal ideal, the Danish government moved actively towards creating favourable regulation and institutions to attract and retain mobile factors such as labour and capital. Industrial and business targeting initiatives soon came to include the shipping industry, which was not only the most truly global, indeed footloose, Danish industry but also considered as critical to the Danish economy.[13]

In December 1987 the government proposed a Bill on the Danish International Ship Register. The maritime cluster argument presented by the shipowners was adopted by several of those politicians in favour of DIS and used many times during the first reading of the Bill (Sornn-Friese and Iversen, 2010). The bill for the DIS was passed by the Danish parliament in June 1988. Although there were important differences between the Norwegian and Danish policies, the latter was clearly inspired by NIS, in this respect, DIS should be regarded as an adaptive rather than a creative institutional response to the globalization of shipping (Schumpeter, 1947).

A number of other events in the late 1980s and early 1990s marked a new and more active Danish policy towards shipping, essentially concerned with creating national competitiveness. For more than 300 years the public governance of shipping in Denmark had been institutionally fragmented, but with a major structural reform of the Ministry of Industry in 1987 to 1988 the many public maritime agencies that existed at the time (the Ship Register, the maritime training and education institutions, the Ship Inspection Agency, the Seamen's Welfare Agency, the Danish Ice Service, the Seamen's Directorate and the Department for Maritime Affairs) were merged, creating the Danish Maritime Authority.[14] The ministry also established a shipping policy secretariat, which was later relocated with the Danish Maritime Authority in 1996. This institutional reorganization was part of a wider series of public management reforms in Denmark in the 1980s, all of which combined a broad liberal foundation with a corporate managerial approach to public-sector management.[15]

The concern for national competitiveness was clearly demonstrated with the increasing popularity among public officials of the concept of 'industry clusters' in the early 1990s. A group of researchers undertook case studies on 15 Danish industries, which, together with similar case studies in other countries, were summarized in Porter's (1990) influential book. Among these was a case study of the Danish shipping industry (Petersen, 1991). The cases were later used as a foundation for one of the earliest cluster studies reported for the Danish economy, which identified five Danish clusters: the food cluster, the technical cluster, the pharmaceutical-biotech-medico cluster, the mink cluster and the maritime complex (Pade, 1991).[16] The Ministry of Industry, at the same time, published a survey analysis, with approximately 100 Danish maritime companies, with the purpose of defining and analysing 'Blue Denmark' (Industriministeriet, 1991). Throughout the 1990s the shipping community in Denmark made still more frequent reference to Blue Denmark. The maritime authorities added more detail and rigour to the notion and gradually moved the policy focus away from a narrow concern for the shipping industry towards a broader concern for the entire maritime cluster. At the close of the 1990s they published a second report on Blue Denmark, which tightened the definition of the cluster with attention to historical traits and in accordance with official national statistics (Søfartsstyrelsen, 1999). More importantly, it was influential in the introduction of tonnage taxation in Denmark, for which the shipowners had been arguing for years. Within a few months of entering office in November 2001, the new Conservative–Liberal coalition government under Mr Fogh Rasmussen proposed the tonnage tax scheme as part of the targets for the 2002 budget, and in May 2002 a majority decision in parliament made tonnage tax law in Denmark.

A renewed optimism emerged in Danish shipping following the establishment of DIS and Danish shipowners embarked on a more expansive course, increasing the newbuilding programme (see Figure 3.2). During the period 1986 to 1991 the number of vessels on order more than doubled relative to the existing Danish merchant fleet, corresponding to an increase in the order programme from 9 to 54 per cent of the existing fleet. This is largely explained by large VLCC orders made by Maersk, but it also reflected a general expansion in Danish shipping and particularly in the container segment, where Maersk Line and some of the smaller feeder companies dramatically expanded their fleet. From 1985 to 2000, Denmark's share of the world merchant fleet more than doubled.

Emerging business models and the revival of dry bulk and product tanker shipping

From the mid-1980s, the largest Danish shipping companies started gradually abandoning old axioms of vertical integration; since 2000 this has meant that shipping companies are more focused. Since the 1910s EAC, DFDS, JL and Maersk had had their own shipyards and maritime equipment manufacturing companies in Denmark, and while vertical integration between shipping and shipbuilding was not a solely Danish phenomenon, it was more extreme and persisted longer in Denmark (Poulsen and Sornn-Friese, 2011). JL and EAC divested themselves of shipbuilding in the 1980s, closing down loss-making yards, and in 2000 JL finally exited shipbuilding completely and sold its industrial assets, refocusing entirely on owning and operating ships – particularly within dry bulk. While the development of Maersk in the previous decades had been characterized by related and unrelated diversification, this shipping conglomerate also became a more focused company from the late 1980s and onwards, reinforcing sectors where it was already strong and especially developing its activities in tanker and container shipping (Sornn-Friese and Iversen, 2011). Its offshore oil and gas business also began an international expansion programme from the 1990s, making it a major cash-generator for the group (Maersk annual reports, 1990–2010).

Between 1986 and 1991, as mentioned above, the growth of Maersk was mainly organic as it took delivery of a series of new supertankers and 12 new container vessels (the M-series), built at Maersk's own shipyard in Lindø. By 1988 all of its liner activities had been reorganized as container shipping (Jeppesen et al., 2001). In 1990 it entered into an operating agreement with P&O Container Lines on the Europe–Far East service, but when P&O merged with the Dutch company Nedlloyd in 1996, Maersk terminated the agreement. The great leap forward happened in 1993 when Maersk took over EAC's remaining container fleet (the 'EAC-Ben Line') and thus became the world's largest container shipping company. The massive growth of the company in the 1990s culminated in 1999 with its purchase of Sea-Land, which strengthened Maersk's position on the east–west trade route, and its purchase of Safmarine, which made Maersk a major shipping line in the expanding north–south trades.

The focused growth of Maersk, especially during the 1990s, made it a truly global company, managing a highly sophisticated and diversified global network of shipping lines and shore-side facilities. In 1993 the company established its own management trainee programme MISE (Maersk International Shipping Education). While Maersk had always taken on young apprentices and trained them for a management career in the company, MISE was an attempt to systematically build up a more broadly composed staff that would reflect the increasingly global scope of the company. MISE was a major step up for the company's internal organization, enhancing the loyalty of its staff and instigating a great corporate spirit, and it gained a world-class reputation for its leadership education, annually attracting more than 85,000 applicants from more than 80 different countries and admitting less than 500 trainees a year (that is, approximately one trainee for every 200 applicants).

Other century-old Danish tramp shipping companies, as well as some newcomers, greatly expanded their fleets during the 1990s, either by forming and managing bulk shipping pools in collaboration with foreign shipowners, or by leasing vessels from foreign shipowners on long-term bareboat or time charter agreements. Alongside the liner shipping conferences, pooling had been used in shipping since the transition from sail to steam (Sickel, 1914). However, ship operation – more broadly conceived – emerged as a distinct maritime profession in bulk shipping during the 1970s. As a new type of specialist companies, ship operators would contract for cargo to be shipped and exploit their profound shipping market knowledge, hence taking over risk from both ship and cargo owners. Profits were then determined by the degree to which freight rates would develop as forecasted by the operator. There has since been a tendency for old-established shipping companies to turn to running ships belonging to others as their single most important shipping activity (Farthing, 1987). In Denmark the phenomenon emerged specifically in the network of people in and around the shipbroking company H. Bang & Co. (1958–83), which became the Danish ship operator par excellence. Ship operation diffused from Bang and its sister company Carib Shipping Co. into the wider Danish shipping community through spin-offs and other movements of people, as well as through takeovers.[17] An important part of JL's refocusing, as mentioned above, has to be seen in the light of this increasing focus on commercial management by Danish shipping companies.

Torm provides the prototype case of an established shipping company greatly expanding through the development of bulk shipping pools. This company expanded its product tanker fleet markedly during the

1990s. Central to this expansion was the introduction of the bulk shipping pool concept into the product tanker segment. A shipping pool is a grouping of ships of similar size and characteristics with different owners that are commercially operated by a pool manager – either one of the pool partners or a joint venture organization – set up by the partners. The main reason for creating a shipping pool is the increased opportunity to undertake large Contracts of Affreightment (CoA), thus allowing pool participants to undertake the transportation of large volumes of cargo for particular shippers at regular intervals over longer periods of time without necessarily taking on excessive market risk (Torm, 1990–2010).

Via three pools established in the 1990s – each of which centres on a particular class of ships – Torm has proven able simultaneously to achieve a critical mass of vessels necessary to operate in the product tanker market, to increase unit income for participating shipowners and to provide better services for customers. In 1991 Torm and BurWain Tankers International, an offshoot of the B&W shipyard in Copenhagen, established a joint chartering office to co-ordinate the employment of their own and chartered-in product tankers and strengthen their capacity to cultivate new markets. The partnership was subsequently renamed the LR1 Pool. It is currently the world's largest operator of Long Range vessels and a considerable market player, controlling an estimated 30 per cent of the world's total LR1 tonnage. In 1998 Torm established two additional tanker pools, the LR2 Pool and the MR Pool. The three pools were conceived and established by Klaus Kjærulff who had been trained in EAC. In 1976 he had come to Torm and in 1981 became the manager of its tanker department, which at that time operated two tankers. During his years in EAC he had gained significant experience with shipping markets, but most importantly he had been transferred to a position in ScanDutch, where he gained key knowledge on how to build and manage a shipping pool.

The number of foreign-owned vessels being controlled from Copenhagen has expanded markedly since the introduction of bulk shipping pools, and nowadays Danish shipowners and operators dominate as commercial managers of shipping pools, especially in the product tanker markets. Indeed, Danish shipowners and operators participate in ten of the more than 40 active international shipping pools, eight of which are commercially managed from Copenhagen (see Table 3.2). As commercial managers of these pools, Danish companies arrange employment for the fleets operated through the pools, collect freight and pay voyage costs, manage the fleets' commercial operations, and distribute the net earnings of the pools to the participating shipowners under a pre-arranged weighing system, which is most often an equitable distribution. Most of these tasks require profound knowledge of shipping markets and excellence in conducting business.

Norden is the strongest example of an established shipping company expanding its fleet through chartered-in vessels. While Norden was still a relatively small international operator in the 1980s, it expanded its dry bulk fleet considerably and at a rapidly accelerating rate in the latter part of the 1990s, mostly through the chartering-in of vessels. The year 1998 marked a paradigm shift in which the company gained advantageous access to a number of Japanese-owned Handymax bulkers on long-term time charters with purchase options (t/c-pops). In that year, the company almost doubled its operated fleet of bulkers and product tankers from 18 vessels in 1998 to 31 vessels in 1999. This happened at a time when the outlook for the dry bulk sector was bleak, affected particularly by the commotion in the South East Asian dry cargo market that was caused by the Asian financial crisis and which created a devastating recession lasting into the new millennium. However, the significant increase in the company's tonnage exposure from the late 1990s took place alongside continued expansion in CoAs and favourable employment of ships on time charter. Indeed, active portfolio management has proved to be one of Norden's major competitive strengths and an

Table 3.2 Shipping pools with Danish management

Pool name	No. of vessels	History	Pool Manager
Handytankers K/S	125	1999	Handytankers (DK)
Swift Tankers	24	2006	Maersk Tankers (DK)
Maersk Tankers VLGC Pool	12	2008	Maersk Tankers (DK)
Norient Product Pool	68	2004	Norden (DK)
LR1 Pool	31	1991	Torm (DK)
LR2 Pool	30	1998	Maersk (DK) / Torm (DK)
MR Pool	41	1998	Torm (DK)
SkandiGas	20	Dissolved 2009	Maersk (DK)
Island View Shipping & Lauritzen Bulkers	53	2001	Lauritzen Bulkers (DK)

Source: Fearnley Consultants (2006), company web pages and other industry sources.

important reason why the company could expand its fleet in a time of generally depressed markets.

The timing of fleet expansion proved exceptional for the further growth of Norden since its control over Japanese-owned tonnage prepared the company for the Chinese-led boom in dry bulk shipping in 2002. In the late 1990s the company had been able to charter-in tonnage at much lower than expected rates and it had thus acquired an extraordinarily inexpensive fleet. This has to be seen in the light of the financial crisis in Japan that had occurred a decade earlier. The Japanese shipping industry was hit hard by the rapid appreciation of the yen and the concurrent weakening of the US dollar between 1985 and 1987, and it continued to face hardship until the latter part of the 1990s. Norden had been in a particularly privileged situation for engaging with the relevant Japanese companies, a privilege that arose from its ability to employ long-standing maritime traditions, trust-based personal relationships and empathic leadership.[18]

2002 to 2008: Massive growth

The development of a maritime cluster strategy continued in the new millennium. In the early 2000s the authorities initiated five major studies that would lead to a new national maritime growth policy, focusing on the maritime educational system and again embracing an overall industry cluster perspective (Søfartsstyrelsen, 2003). The specific aim of the growth strategy was to assess the size of the Danish maritime cluster, determine the forces keeping it together, examine in a Danish as well as an international perspective the education and employment pattern of people with a maritime education, and resolve the question of how government-funded education in Denmark could add to growth in Blue Denmark. DIS and its associated tax exemption for seamen together with the tonnage tax scheme were the cornerstones of the strategy.

Over the short period from 2002 until 2008 the Danish merchant fleet grew by 38 per cent, from 6.7 million dwt in 2002 to 9.2 million in 2008, and the growth in turnover was even more significant. This remarkable growth of Danish shipping happened in all the major segments, where Danish companies already had strong positions, and it was expansion both through the growth of individual companies – organically as well as through mergers and acquisitions – and through the entry of new companies, some of which expanded very fast. As an example of the latter, CS & Partners was founded in 2004 as an investment company providing tonnage to ship operators, and within a couple of years it was one of the top ten largest shipping companies in Denmark.[19]

The operation of foreign-owned tonnage was an important aspect of the expansion of Danish shipping after 2002, but a large Danish newbuilding programme also fuelled growth. Figure 3.2 shows that the programme peaked around 2007 to 2008 at 68 per cent and 145 per cent of the existing fleet in terms of numbers and tonnage respectively. The average size of the newbuildings was thus clearly greater than that of the existing vessels. When comparing the peaks of the Danish newbuilding programme in 1970 and 2007 to 2008 we see significant differences, and the unique characteristics of the latter peak are obvious. First, the peak in 2007 to 2008 was considerably higher than the peak in 1970. In fact the newbuilding programme of the 2000s was unprecedented in the history of modern Danish shipping. Second, the recent peak was attributable to numerous players' investments in a diverse fleet of container ships, bulk carriers and product and crude oil tankers. Maersk topped the list in terms of the number of vessels on order, but Norden, Torm, JL and the two more recent entrants, Clipper Group and Eitzen Bulk, also expanded greatly within bulk and tanker shipping. In relative terms, the expansion of the bulk and tanker shipping companies was even faster and greater than that of Maersk. Finally, according to unpublished data for 2004 and 2007 provided by Søfart, several small product and chemical tanker companies (e.g. Erria and Herning Shipping) grew rapidly through ambitious newbuilding programmes in the segments for small vessels below 10,000 dwt. In contrast the 1970 peak had been due to only one company's investments in one type of vessel, namely those of Maersk's in supertankers. The world fleet also grew rapidly between 2002 and 2008 but the Danish newbuilding programme proved even more expansive. For example, at the peak of demand for shipping at the end of 2007, global orders for Panamax bulk carriers, product tankers and VLCCs amounted to 35–40 per cent of the existing fleet (Wijnolst and Wergeland, 2009).

The result of the Danish expansion after 2002 was one of the youngest and most modern merchant fleets. This was in line with the strategy pursued by the majority of Danish shipowners since the 1950s. After 1960 the average age of the Danish fleet never exceeded nine years, even though the commercial lifespan of a vessel was considerably longer. The competitive position of Danish shipping was built on new vessels, delivered directly from shipyards to Danish shipowners. Often such vessels were more expensive and capital-intensive than older, second-hand vessels, a fact which underlined the general Danish commitment to high-quality tonnage.

Maersk continued expanding in a more focused manner, strengthening its activities in tanker and container shipping as well as in offshore oil and gas extraction, and selling off and closing down other activities. In the container segment, the company continued a highly expansive course in the period 2002 to 2008, continuing its acquisition strategy from the 1990s. In 2002 it acquired Torm's liner division (Torm Lines) and thus strengthened its coverage of the Atlantic. When acquiring the British-Dutch competitor P&O Nedlloyd at a cost of 2.4 billion US $ in 2005, Maersk's global market share peaked in 2005 at approximately 18 per cent. However, severe integration and IT problems following the acquisition of P&O Nedlloyd caused a drop both in market share and profitability. In December 2007 CEO Eivind Kolding introduced the 'StreamLINE' recovery plan for Maersk Line, which contained a series of dramatic cost-cutting and productivity-focused initiatives. When the container line was struggling, Maersk Oil and Gas made up for the losses. In fact, the oil business has generated the major part of Maersk's earnings after 2000, even though it only represented a minor share of the total turnover of the company. In 2009 and 2010, during the global financial crisis, return-on-investment after tax in the oil business was of 23.4 and 34 per cent, respectively (Møller-Maersk Annual Reports, 1999–2011). In the production tanker segment, Maersk also applied an acquisition strategy, in 2008 acquiring the Swedish competitor, Broström Tankers. This happened shortly before the financial crisis set in. While keeping the Broström brand and operational headquarters in Sweden for the smallest tanker segments, in September 2010 Broström decided to transfer all its vessels from the Swedish flag to DIS, where policy conditions were considered more attractive.

In the bulk segment China's rapid growth after 2000 produced an expansive business climate. Bulk freight rates rose rapidly as Chinese imports of raw materials accelerated, creating what has been termed the 'bulk supercycle' (Tenold, 2009b). Danish shipowners – and in particular Norden, JL and Torm – were well positioned to profit from this development, and the Danish-operated fleet grew quickly. The period from 2002 to 2008 proved the strengths of the Danish position, developed in the 1990s, and players expanded faster than the global average. Clipper moved its headquarters from the Bahamas to Copenhagen from where it expanded greatly in the bulk and product tanker business, but also diversified into ferry, ro-ro and cruise shipping. Eitzen had entered Danish shipping during the 1990s by acquiring the remains of the failed Skou Shipping and Knud I. Larsen as well as the remaining bulk fleet of EAC, and also expanded from its Danish headquarters. Danish ship investment companies – especially DIFKO47 and the two newcomers CS & Partners and ID Shipping – also expanded greatly after 2002. Especially noteworthy in this latter regard is that the tonnage tax system had once again made the limited partnership system an attractive model for investors that were peripheral to the shipping industry. A major difference from the earlier experience with this model in Denmark was that, this time around, it attracted large-scale investors with a professional approach to asset management.

It is worth noting that DIFKO47, originally a tonnage provider for other shipping companies, developed into a full-scale shipping company, Nordic Tankers, with commercial and technical operations in chemical and product tankers. In 2007 the company was listed on the Copenhagen stock exchange and two years later, Clipper became a large shareholder. Clipper transferred its chemical tanker fleet to Nordic Tankers, which currently operates a fleet of 70 vessels.

Recent challenges

As the financial crisis unfolded and demand and freight rates dropped rapidly, another turning point in global shipping was reached in the autumn of 2008. As if reiterating the demanding situation of the great shipping crisis of the 1970s and 1980s, the latest depression happened at a time when global newbuilding programmes were at a historically high level. The combination of falling freight rates and record-high shipbuilding order books has forced shipowners, including the Danish companies, to reconsider their business models and cut costs. The development depicted in Figure 3.2 shows clearly that the Danish newbuilding programme started a rapid contraction as some orders were cancelled. Some Danish owners turned instead to the second-hand market, which they had previously avoided. In particular, they acquired second-hand, but young, product tankers. While these investments did not represent a departure from the long-held Danish focus on quality tonnage, it demonstrated some owners' belief in future trading opportunities and possibly also future rises in asset values (Norden, 2010a, 2010b).

The container segment was badly hit by the financial crisis. On many trades, cargo volumes dropped by 20–30 per cent. In contrast to its major competitors, Maersk Line had already initiated the streamline project before the financial crisis set in, and this earlier cost-cutting move prepared the company for the crisis, which may partly explain why Maersk was able to make profits again after 2008, much faster than its rivals. In continuation of the streamline project, Maersk quietly shut down its educational MISE programme, which had proved to be extremely expensive and organizationally demanding. Instead of recruiting talented young people straight out of high school and providing them with an all-round, high-quality shipping management education, the company announced that it would instead focus on bringing in university graduates and providing them with two years' intensive management training in business-specific entry-level programmes. The Maersk Line Graduate Programme (MLGP) was launched later that same year as the first business-specific programme to replace MISE. In 2010 Maersk Line returned to high profitability and it embarked on an expansive newbuilding programme, ordering up to 30 ultra-large container carriers named Triple-E's. According to Maersk, this series of vessels can increase economies of scale while, at the same time, significantly reducing emissions (Maersk, 2011). In the twenty-first century, fuel emission and climate issues have entered the agenda of shipping and Maersk has decided to improve the environmental performance of its fleet, reducing fuel costs and emissions at the same time. The company published its first environmental or sustainability report in 2007, and as stated in the 2010 report it continues to aim at gaining competitive advantages from a proactive environmental policy.

In the dry cargo and product tanker markets, rates also dropped rapidly in the autumn of 2008, and shipowners had to respond accordingly. For example, Torm's programme 'Greater Earning Power', established during the boom before 2008, was replaced by cost-cutting exercises. Torm and Norden both reduced their operated fleet, increasingly focusing on owned tonnage. Torm, for example, announced that it would reduce its pool operations and focus more on its owned fleet instead (Lloyd's List, 2011). The actions of the Danish dry cargo and product tanker operators demonstrated the flexibility of their business models and the importance of their profound knowledge of shipping markets. During times of rapid growth, they had proved able to quickly build up large fleets, and in times of decline, they could scale down easily. Norden, to give an example, had shown itself able to expand its fleet through short-term t/c, and thus increase its earnings, in periods when freight rates were on the rise and, conversely, to reduce the number of vessels fixed on short-term t/c (and refrain from exercising their extension or buying options) in periods of decline. In the spring of 2008, when the dry cargo market was growing, Norden had thus fixed a number of vessels on short-term t/c. In the second half of 2008, it returned 116 units, thereby adjusting its capacity and costs to the vastly changed market conditions. Norden and JL produced handsome profits in 2010, despite the difficult market conditions, whereas Torm and Eitzen Bulk (the latter now under new ownership and renamed U-Sea Bulk) made net losses (annual reports, 2010). The structure of Danish shipping has so far remained largely unaltered.

The institutional set-up – including DIS, tax exemptions and tonnage tax – has remained unaltered despite the changes in market conditions. A modification in the DIS legislation, however, will allow Danish owners to use foreign captains on their vessels, which had previously been prohibited by law. The international financial crisis and subsequent economic recession tested the strength of Danish shipping. What has been built up in Danish shipping over the past three decades appears to be robust.

Conclusion

In contrast to the three other Nordic countries dealt with in this book, Denmark was by 2010 a more important nation in global shipping than it had been in 1960. The growth of the Danish fleet was particularly intensive after 2000, as may be seen in the country statistics presented in Chapter 6, with an average annualized growth rate between 2005 and 2008 of 16.76 per cent. In the same period, the average world growth rate was 7.30 per cent. Around 2010 Danish shipping included the world's largest container shipping company, several world-leading dry bulk carriers, and one of the largest product tanker companies in the world. The historical background for this successful development, as outlined in this chapter, was marked by complexity, which leaves little room for simple explanations. There would probably not have been such growth in Danish shipping without the breakthrough of South East Asian economic growth after 2002 and continuously strong North American demand for goods until 2008. In short, one could say that Danish shipping after 2000 was based on a capability to exploit the opportunities caused by increasing integration of the global economy. The critical question is of course how Danish shipowners exploited these opportunities, and why they apparently did so more successfully than their Nordic peers. This chapter has pointed at two important sets of explanations essential to the Danish development: the accommodating changes in the national institutional set-up, and the ability of the large, century-old Danish shipping companies to reconfigure their organizational capabilities successfully in response to structural changes in international shipping.

There were three important pillars in Denmark's new institutional environment. First, the development of a shipping-friendly tax and ship registration regime, which built upon a 'level playing field approach', meaning essentially that Danish framework conditions should, as a minimum, match those in other leading TMNs such as Norway, Great Britain and the Netherlands. The second pillar was an active strategic maritime growth policy based on close public–private co-operation. This Michael Porter-inspired cluster policy was introduced in the late 1980s and enhanced in the 2000s, when several maritime policy initiatives were developed in intensive interaction between the maritime authorities and the private actors in the maritime community, the latter often represented by the Danish Shipowners' Association. The third important public-institutional pillar was Denmark's legal and political stability. Shipping is an industry marked by a combination of long-term investments, capital-requiring assets and unpredictable markets. This combination imposes a need for institutional stability, which has been present in Denmark since the mid-1990s. Shipowners have made huge long-term investments since that time, trusting that tax and legal conditions were stable and would not be unexpectedly changed overnight by a new political regime.

The corporate–strategic factor was marked by a combination of a concentrated structure in Danish shipping, with a few dominant, old and large corporations on the one hand and on the other, a strategic heterogeneity, including shipping companies in very different shipping segments.

Table 3.3 provides an overview of the development of the most important Danish shipping companies that still exist, which are also in large measure the companies that have been at the forefront of developments in Danish shipping over the past 50 years. They are all headquartered in the Greater Copenhagen area and it is worth noting that the bulk of them are between 107 and 178 years old.

The table shows what is the perhaps the most important feature of Danish shipping, namely its heterogeneity. In the growth period after 2000 the largest Danish shipping companies operated in very different segments of global shipping, each with its own dynamic: the container industry (Maersk), product tankers (Torm), dry cargo bulk (Norden and JL), offshore support (Maersk and JL) and short-sea (DFDS). These segments were very varied, and it is critical to our understanding of the transformation of Danish shipping that there was not a 'single Danish way' – neither in terms of corporate strategies, nor in terms of the mechanisms through which the leading companies were able to

Table 3.3 Strategic change and capability reconfiguration by the leading Danish shipping companies

Firm (year founded, HQ location)	Original product lines	Current product lines	Decisive strategic moves
Maersk (1904, Copenhagen)	General cargo tramp shipping	Container shipping; tankers (VLCCs, product, LPG); niche shipping (supply and tugs)	Construction of own shipyard in 1917; establishment of liner service in 1927; acquisition of crude oil tankers in 1928; post-war expansion in liner and tanker shipping; concession for Danish oil and gas exploration gained in 1962, marking the build-up of an oil company; containerization of liner services from 1975; large-scale mergers and acquisitions from early 1990s to mid 2000s
Torm (1889, Hellerup)	Short sea general cargo tramp shipping in the North and Baltic Seas	Product tankers; Dry bulk (Panama)	Transition from short-sea to deep-sea shipping in 1909; refocusing from tramp to bulk and liner shipping in late 1950s; refocusing into product tanker shipping in 1976; establishment of product tanker pools in the 1990s and subsequent major expansion in this area; divestment from liner shipping in 2002.
Norden (1871, Hellerup)	Deep-sea general cargo tramp shipping	Dry cargo bulk in all major segments, product tanker shipping in handy-size, MR and LR1 segments	Refocusing from tramp to bulk shipping in early 1970s; related diversification into product tanker shipping in the 1990s; enormous expansion as operator of dry bulk vessels on long-term charter with purchase options (t/c-pops) from 1997–98 and onwards; entering into product tanker pool in 2004.
JL (1895, Copenhagen)	Northern European tramp shipping	Bulk carriers; LPG; product tankers; offshore support vessels	Refocus on niche shipping from 1930s (reefers, LPG tankers, ice strengthened tonnage, offshore and passenger shipping); conglomerate strategy with diversification in manufacturing and shipbuilding from 1930s to 1990s; divestment from shipbuilding and manufacturing in 1990s (return to basics, focusing on shipping only).

DFDS (1866, Copenhagen)	Liner shipping in the North and Baltic Seas	Short-sea shipping; Northern European Logistics	Build-up of overseas liner services in late nineteenth century to complement North Sea and Baltic liner network; divestment from overseas liner services (1970s) and failed cruise venture in 1980s; focused growth in northern European short-sea shipping through acquisitions (from 1980s to the present).
Dannebrog (1883, Rungsted)	Tramp shipping	Liner shipping and product tankers	Abandoning tramp shipping in 1960s upon acquisition by new owners; entry into small tanker market in 1960s; acquisition of liner services from DFDS and Dansk-Fransk in 1980s; expansion in product tankers and niche liner services in 2000s.
Svitzer (1833, Copenhagen)	Local surveys, salvage and rescue around Copenhagen and in the Sound	Worldwide port, terminal and ocean salvage, rescue and towage, some offshore services	Internationalization in 1853; related diversification into towage in 1870s; related diversification into offshore services in late 1970s; Maersk becomes majority shareholder in 1970s; refocusing on port towage in early 1980s; regional expansion in 1999 trough company acquisitions; global expansion through company acquisition in 2001; focus on core business from 2003 onwards (including divestment of survey activities, coal barges and crew boats).
DIFKO47/Nordic Tankers (1984, Copenhagen)	Tonnage provider	Tonnage provider	Supplier of K/S financed product tankers built at Danish shipyards and managed commercially and technically by Danish and foreign shipping companies in 1980s and 1990s; launching of new strategy in 2009, to build up a full-scale shipping company; take-over of Clipper Tankers' fleet in 2009.

Sources: Bramsen (1983), Eriksen (2005), Falkensteen (1996), Frandsen (2008), Graae (1966), Hornby (1987), Lange (1995), Søfartsstyrelsen (2010) and company web pages.

reconfigure their capabilities. Each of the major firms developed and executed specific strategies, which reflected the dynamics of its own segment. Maersk combined an acquisition strategy with the vertical integration of a complex global logistical system. It is also worth mentioning that EAC, although eventually unsuccessful, managed to reconfigure its organizational capabilities to compete, early on, in global container shipping. Norden's growth within dry cargo bulk shipping was based on expertise in flexible fleet operation combined with long-term charter agreements and CoAs, while Torm's growth in the product tanker segment, to a large extent, was based on their expertise in managing pool agreements with other shipping companies, as well as CoAs and close relationships to their customers. These corporate strategies were all very different and required different types of organizational capabilities.

The mechanisms through which the major Danish shipping companies managed to reconfigure their organizational capabilities were also varied. According to Lavie (2006), three distinct mechanisms of capability reconfiguration can be discerned from the diverse literature on organizational capabilities, namely what he refers to as substitution, transformation and evolution. As a general framework, these mechanisms may be used to highlight some of the differences in the ways Danish companies were able to respond to structural changes in international shipping. Capability substitution, which is a process of drastic immediate response to aspects of technological change, characterized EAC's venture into container shipping around 1970, while Maersk's entry into container shipping in the mid 1970s may be better described as capability transformation, which is a synchronized, directed response based on the integration of new routines with the carryover of existing routines. Finally, the bulk shipping revival in the late 1990s, which happened through the flexible use of mainly foreign-owned ships, and which was experienced by Norden, Torm, JL and the newcomer Clipper, resulted from continuous experimentation and the gradual modification of existing routines. As such, it is best understood as capability evolution, which is a process strongly influenced by path dependence on prior configurations.

The one thing the various strategies did have in common, and which was perhaps the common trait of Danish success, was the deep historical roots of their organizational capabilities in commercial shipping: Danish shipping companies 'know the ropes', so to speak. Competencies had been carried over from decade to decade in Danish shipping. After 2000 these competencies would flourish in conjunction with increasingly global economic integration.

Notes

1. Greek-owned shipping may serve as an illustrative example, as it has remained highly fragmented throughout the course of its history. Only in recent years has there been a tendency towards concentration, with the number of companies after 2000 decreasing steadily and with a parallel reduction in the market shares of the smaller companies (Thanopoulou and Theotokas, 2007).
2. Important references to the product cycle include Posner (1961) and Vernon (1966). The theory of technology life cycles has been put forward by especially Abernathy and Utterback (1978) and Klepper (1996), and major contributors to punctuated equilibrium theory include Tushman and Anderson (1986) and Henderson and Clark (1990). The last-mentioned, in particular, predict that when markets or technologies change, incumbents have great difficulty in adapting to the new circumstances and often fail.
3. In Greek-owned shipping, although also notable for the extraordinary robustness of existing companies, industrial rejuvenation has occasionally been characterized by the replacement of incumbents by new firms. There were two major transitions in the twentieth century during which several of the top ten Greek shipping companies were replaced by other companies (Harlaftis and Theotokas 2002, 2004). In the interwar period, the family-owned shipping companies of the Ionian Islands, which had dominated Greek-owned shipping throughout the latter part of the nineteenth century, were replaced by the family groups of the Aegean Islands, which would then, during the aftermath of OPEC I and II, gradually give way to a new breed of shipping companies originating in mainland Greece.
4. We believe this approach to be a natural choice for describing the development of an industry which is as concentrated and as dominated by incumbent firms as the Danish shipping industry.
5. See also newbuilding lists published by the Danish shipping newspaper *Søfart* over the years 1960 to 1970. For the Danish shipping industry there are consistent statistical data sets on newbuilding programmes covering the period 1960 to 2010. Data on the aggregate, national level were compiled by the Danish Shipowners' Association and published annually (see Figure 3.2). Data on individual companies' orders are available in *Søfart*, which has collected and published detailed lists from 1960 to 2002. In the 2000s the newspaper continued to compile the information and has kindly granted us access to the unpublished material for the years 2004 and 2007. Whenever we refer to individual company orders, unless otherwise stated, we rely on the newbuilding lists published in *Søfart*.
6. Sturmey (1986) and Cafruny (1987) provide excellent historical accounts of the UNCTAD committee on shipping and the development of the Liner Code.
7. Most importantly, EAC introduced the marine diesel engine in 1912 onboard the famous ship *Selandia*. On its first journey *Selandia* broke a world record by sailing around the globe in less than 40 days.
8. Knud I. Larsen entered into container shipping in the late 1970s as a subcontractor to Maersk Line. It was an expanding shipping group until the end of the 1990s and remained among top ten Danish shipping companies

for two decades. Elite Shipping became one of the fastest-growing Danish shipping companies ever. During the 1980s it built up a great fleet of small feeder ships to service the container shipping industry. The founders of Hansen & Lange are still active today within container, feeder and multi-purpose shipping. Through collaboration with Hansen & Lange, Fabricius Marine became engaged in container feeder services, and – now operating under the name Erria – only recently divested itself of container shipping.

9. The increase in flagging out by Danish shipowners during 1987 was described in the notes to the Bill on the Danish International Ship Register proposed to parliament by the conservative Minister of Industry, Nils Wilhjelm (proposal No. L 110 'Proposal for a law on a Danish International Ship Register' brought in on 2 December 1987).
10. The conservative government (or 'four-leaf clover government') headed by Poul Schlüter included the Conservatives, the Liberals, the Centre Democrats and the Christian People's Party.
11. Unit labour costs (ULC) are defined as the wages and social costs of workers at current prices divided by gross product at constant prices. Relative unit labour costs (RULC) are ULC converted to an international currency and divided by the average ULC for the country's trading partners (Fagerberg, 1988).
12. See Fougner (2006) for a more elaborate discussion of international competitiveness, neo-liberalism and state governance.
13. In the words of Selkou and Roe (2004), the shipowners' reference to cost-competitiveness, as well as their increasing use of open registers, was a reflection of a neo-Fordist regime, while the activism of the Danish government in the latter half of the 1980s would be more accurately characterized as a post-Fordist regime.
14. Recent years have also seen attempts to improve co-ordination between the many different private Danish maritime associations. Particularly interesting is the observation that over the past 10 to 15 years a number of maritime associations – including Danish Maritime (the former Danish Shipbuilding Association), the Shipbrokers Association and the Maritime Development Centre of Europe – have moved their headquarters into the premises of the Danish Shipowners' Association, thus providing a sort of one-stop-shopping agency. There were also some mergers between associations in the same period.
15. The liberal foundation of this development was evident in the general public-sector management emphasis on privatization, outsourcing, user charges, profit centres, decentralized wage negotiations, and so on. The managerial logic was visible in new philosophies (quality control, management accounting, management-by-objectives, purchaser–provider models, performance assessments, and so on) and new job titles (e.g. director) in public-sector organizations (Klausen, 2010).
16. It should be mentioned that prior work on related phenomena (industrial complexes, industrial districts and cluster-like dynamics of individual sectors) had already been carried out in the early 1980s. It is also worth noting that the first Michael Porter-inspired competitiveness studies in Denmark – published three years earlier (Møller and Pade 1988) – did not mention shipping or related maritime industries.

17. Numerous small ship operating companies were established by former Bang employees, but the most important spin-offs would be Armada Shipping, Clipper Group and T. K. B. Shipping. Armada was founded in 1971 by two former Bang employees, Jørgen Poulsen Dannesboe and Torben Gülnar Jensen, and was forerunner of both Clipper Group, which was created by a demerger from Armada in 1991 by Torben Gülnar Jensen, and the smaller Interbulk, which was demerged from Armada by a third former Bang employee. The founder of T. K. B. Shipping had been employed in Bang in the late 1970s. Other former Bang/Carib Shipping employees have advanced into managing positions in leading Danish shipping companies (e.g. Knud I. Larsen, JL, Norden, Dannebrog and Eitzen) and honorary offices in maritime interest organizations (e.g. the Institute of Chartered Shipbrokers, Intertanko, BIMCO, the Maritime Development Centre of Europe and the Danish Shipowners' Association). When Bang went bankrupt in the early 1980s a number of the company's charter parties were transferred to JL and this became a key element in JL's return to tramping in the global dry bulk markets.
18. SS *Norden*, the company's very first steamer, had called at Nagasaki as early as 1876.
19. It did not survive the subsequent crisis, however: only five years after it had been established, CS & Partners went bankrupt. Within these five years the company managed to build more than 20 vessels, all of them financed by capital raised through the K/S system.

4
The Two Declines of Swedish Shipping

René Taudal Poulsen, Hans Sjögren and Thomas Taro Lennerfors

Introduction

Over the last five decades the structure of the shipping industry has changed dramatically, and in this process numerous players and countries have declined, while others have prospered. Sweden, once home to vibrant shipping and shipbuilding industries, is a prime example of a maritime centre in decline. In 1960 Swedish shipping companies controlled approximately 2.9 per cent of the world fleet, but after 1973 the Swedish position was heavily eroded. By 2010 the figure was well below 1 per cent, and the Swedish industry itself currently anticipates a further decline (Sveriges Redareförening, 2010). A comparison of the structure of the industry in the late 1950s with the 2010 situation clearly demonstrates the magnitude of the decline.

In the late 1950s Swedish shipping companies were global players, generating more than 70 per cent of their income from worldwide trade, that is, outside the North European short-sea trades.[1] The companies were active in all the main shipping segments: liner and general cargo shipping, tanker and dry bulk shipping, passenger shipping and short-sea shipping. Swedish liner services spanned the globe and Swedish tankers, dry bulk and general cargo ships were equally common worldwide. In many cases Swedish shipowners were at the forefront of technological development, operating a very young deep-sea fleet by international standards. In the mid-1950s, 35 per cent of the vessels were less than five years old, compared to 21 per cent for the world fleet as a whole. At the same time several owners were experimenting with new cargo-handling systems in liner shipping and car carrying (Björklund et al., 1984; Poulsen, 2007, 2010). Furthermore, Swedish shipping companies participated actively in the shipping industry's quest for economies of scale, building ever-larger tankers and dry cargo ships.

Shipping was centered in Stockholm and Göteborg, which housed several renowned maritime conglomerates that dated back to the nineteenth century. In addition, more than 26,000 Swedish mariners were employed at sea. In terms of tonnage per capita, Sweden was only surpassed by one country, Norway, and it was on a par with Denmark. Even mighty Great Britain had a lower tonnage per capita than the Scandinavians. The shipping industry was even more significant to Sweden at the time, because six of the world's largest and most efficient shipyards were located on the Swedish west coast. In Göteborg alone approximately 10,000 people were directly employed in the yards. In the late 1950s Swedish shipbuilders held approximately 10 per cent of the global shipbuilding market, and during the 1960s they managed to strengthen their global position further through ambitious expansion programmes (Stråth, 1987; Bohlin, 1989; Olsson, 1996).

By 2010 Swedish shipping had clearly declined. The old structures had broken down and the global position of Swedish shipping, as well as that of most of the related maritime activities, had been substantially reduced or disappeared altogether. The old maritime conglomerates of Stockholm and Göteborg were gone and few new companies had replaced them. The Swedish shipping market in 2010 was characterized by fragmentation, with only two large companies remaining, the Stena group and Wallenius. Swedish companies are currently active only in passenger and roll-on roll-off (ro-ro) shipping and in product and chemical tankers. The shipyards are long gone, and the last large commercial ship built in Sweden was delivered in 1989. The number of Swedish seafarers had declined to 13,500, mainly engaged in short-sea and passenger shipping in Northern Europe (Sjöfartsverket, 2010, p. 2). The average age of the Swedish-flagged fleet was very high relative to other European counterparts. In 2005 only 10 per cent of the vessels were less than five years old (Palmberg et al., 2006, p. 95). Shipping's relative contribution to Sweden's exports and the Swedish economy had dwindled, and accordingly, shipping had a much reduced role in the public mind (Palmberg et al., 2006, pp. 83–4).

The decline in Swedish shipping happened in two phases, the first from the mid-1970s to the mid-1980s and the second from the late 1990s to the present. The period from the mid-1980s to the mid-1990s represents a short period of recovery. During the global boom in the shipping market from 2002 to 2008, Sweden's share of world shipping tonnage was substantially reduced. In this chapter we examine the causes of these two declines, asking what caused Swedish shipping to decline when the shipping industries in some of the other Nordic countries was thriving.

We have applied an analytical scheme to structure our discussion of the causes of the remarkable decline of Swedish shipping over the last five decades (see Figure 4.1). The scheme makes two important distinctions. First, the vertical axis identifies structural and organizational conditions. Structural conditions are common to several if not all players in the field of shipping, while organizational conditions are individual and are likely to differ between players. In other words, structural conditions are found at the macro level, while organizational conditions belong to the micro level, where they are attached to the various companies. Secondly, the horizontal axis identifies economic and policy conditions. Economic conditions refer to the demand for shipping services, as well as to the properties of the agents supplying such services, while policy conditions refer to decisions made by regulators and corporate managers.

At the intersections of the various conditions there are four explanatory factors: markets, regulations, strategies and know-how/resources. Markets are economic and global by nature and hence common to all players. Know-how and resources are also economic by nature, but differ greatly between players. Thus they also form part of the organizational conditions. Regulation concerns policy conditions and is common for players in the same country when imposed by national governments, or

Figure 4.1 Relationship between economic, structural, policy and organizational conditions

Note: See also Sjögren (1999a, p. 35).

common to the shipping industry at large when imposed internationally. Strategies vary greatly between players, depending on individual choices of, for example, markets and technology. We analyse the influence of each of the four explanatory factors on the players – the Swedish shipping companies. At the end of the chapter, we evaluate the interaction between the four factors with regard to the two periods of decline of Swedish shipping.

The term 'markets' encompasses changes in demand for, and supply of, shipping at the international level. Demand is determined by the development and composition of world trade and shifts in seaborne trade routes, whereas technological innovation, such as new vessel types or new cargo-handling equipment, and changes in shipbuilding, labour and fuel prices determine the supply side of the equation. By 'regulation' we mean international and national policies governing and directing the shipping industry. International maritime labour conventions and codes on the safety of life at sea are examples of international maritime regulation, common to all players. National regulation of shipping, for example through taxation and national manning requirements, are usually common for players in the same country, but differ on a global scale. 'Strategies' are decisions made by corporate management with the intention of substantially changing the direction of shipping companies. Strategies include such issues as the scale and timing of investments, as well as the choice of shipping markets and vessel types. Finally, 'know-how and resources' refer to two related elements. 'Know-how' denotes human capital, embedded in human competencies and sustained by training, whereas 'resources' applies to asset capital and financial capital.

Market conditions and regulations change over time, and so do strategies, resources and know-how. This suggests a dynamic analysis where these four factors may be treated as four variables. The scheme thus allows us to follow certain long-term processes. It also considers the interaction between the variables, which enables us to analyse mechanisms in a mix of conditions. This in turn permits discussion of which variables have been the most decisive for the transformation of the Swedish industry. The analysis of these four variables therefore forms the framework for this chapter.

Markets

The world economy set the pace of the shipping industry and shipowners always depended heavily on the balance between the supply of and demand for seaborne transportation. Growth rates in the global economy determined the demand for shipping, but changes in average haul (the distance between producers and consumers) also substantially influenced demand. The supply of shipping was determined by a multitude of factors, including the size, speed and efficiency of the existing fleet and global shipbuilding capacity (Stopford, 2009). This section examines how changing shipping markets influenced the opportunities for Swedish shipping companies between 1960 and 2010.

During the 50 years from 1960 to 2010, international shipping went through several periods of boom and bust, generally caused by political changes, notably conflicts in the Middle East, and shipping markets proved inherently unstable and unpredictable. Nevertheless, in the first post-war decades, shipping experienced one of its longest periods of continuous growth, as the economies of the West and Japan expanded rapidly. Demand rose substantially from 1950 to 1973. In particular, the demand for crude oil expanded heavily, and demand for oil shipments rose accordingly. Freight rates were at a very high level between 1967 and 1973. In response, the world fleet grew rapidly, in particular the fleet of oil tankers (Stopford, 2009).

On the supply side, technological changes transformed the nature of the industry prior to 1973. In tanker shipping, average vessel sizes grew rapidly throughout the 1960s. Very Large Crude Carriers (VLCCs) and Ultra Large Crude Carriers (ULCCs) changed the transport economics of oil shipping. Bulk carriers, tailored for shipping large bulk cargoes, started to replace traditional and small general cargo vessels (Fon, 1995; Tenold, 2006). Finally, container vessels gradually superseded conventional liner ships and paved the way for integrated transport chains (Broeze 2002; Levinson, 2006; Donovan and Bonney, 2006). Changes did, of course, not take place overnight, but the period from 1960 to 1973 saw many of the technological changes becoming more widespread. Consequently, shipowners faced new opportunities and new challenges.

In 1973 market conditions changed rapidly following the oil price increases initiated by OPEC. Referred to as OPEC I, the oil crisis after 1973 contributed to the structural problems of Western economies, where stagnation and inflation slowed down the growth in demand for shipping. Gradually, changing energy consumption patterns in the OECD countries reduced the average haul of oil transportation and the oil shipping markets contracted significantly. Problems started in the oil tanker market but gradually cascaded into other segments. Combination carriers, capable of carrying both oil and dry bulk cargoes, shifted from the oil trades to dry bulk markets. In a similar way, oil tankers on order were converted to other ship types. Thus the problems in the shipping industry generally accelerated throughout the 1970s (Tenold, 2006).

With regard to the supply of new ships, problems gradually became evident in the 1970s. Globally, shipbuilders held large order books in the 1970s, and overcapacity in the shipbuilding sector exacerbated and prolonged the problems in the shipping sector. Governments, including that of Sweden, subsidized yards in order to keep up shipyard employment. In the long run, however, the structural change in shipbuilding could not be avoided. The shipbuilding policies of Sweden and other European countries contributed to a long-term overcapacity in shipping (Stråth, 1987; Todd, 1991; Sjögren, 1999a; Poulsen and Sornn-Friese, 2011). The substantial increase in the world fleet between 1972 and 1976 significantly reduced the prospects in shipping for many years. When shipping company managers finally realized that there was a surplus in supply, global shipbuilding capacity proved difficult to reduce. Further problems in the shipping markets followed OPEC II, the second massive oil price increase, which was partly caused by the fall of the Shah of Iran in 1979. Demand for shipping generally remained low, and global shipping overcapacity continued into the late 1980s.

Demand for shipping started to rise again in the late 1980s. Scrapping of ships and shipyard closures had reduced the overcapacity in most shipping markets, thus creating a balance between supply and demand, which had not existed for more than 15 years (Stopford, 2009). Most notably, the market for container ships increased, as the process of containerization accelerated. Simultaneously, global container carriers emerged with liner networks that spanned the globe (Broeze, 2002). The tanker and dry bulk segments also recovered, whereas certain niche segments, such as car carrying, proved even more expansive.

A general rise in shipping freight markets took place from 2002, mainly driven by China's booming economy. Freight markets skyrocketed, and freight rates increased massively from that date. On the supply side, shipowners were induced to large-scale ordering and new yards were set up in Asia in order to satisfy an almost insatiable demand for new ships. However, the growth of the world merchant fleet could not outpace the growth in demand, and freight rates rose to high levels (Stopford, 2009, pp. 118–30). In the Nordic case, Denmark's rapid rise in shipping was particularly remarkable (see Chapter 3 on Denmark).

Shipping markets collapsed en masse in 2008, when the financial crisis caused demand for shipping in all segments to stagnate or decline. Numerous ships were sent into lay-up, but shipbuilders still held historically large order books. The supply side could not react as quickly as demand, even though some orders were cancelled.

Despite the difficult market conditions, the capacity of the global fleet is set to rise rapidly in the years to come. Observers therefore currently believe there are new challenges ahead for global shipping (Stopford, 2009; Wijnost and Wergeland, 2009). This also influences the potential of Swedish shipping.

It is clear that changing international markets set the pace of shipping and are a major influence on Swedish shipping companies' business opportunities. Clearly, the massive recession from 1973 to 1987 explains why old structures in Swedish shipping came under very heavy strain. However, changing market conditions in themselves cannot explain why most Swedish shipping companies continued to underperform relative to their foreign competitors after 1973. By their very nature, shipping markets are global and opportunities in the markets are in principle the same for all nations. Moreover, the second decline in Swedish shipping happened during a period of boom in world shipping markets. Swedish peculiarities contributed to this development.

Regulation

Swedish shipowners have repeatedly argued that Swedish shipping policies have hampered, and continue to hamper, the development of Swedish shipping. In particular, the shipowners have pointed out the detrimental role of labour unions in relation to the development of the shipping industry.[2] This section addresses the shipowners' arguments, by assessing the impact of regulations on the performance of Swedish shipping companies. Or, to address the problem differently, did Swedish policies put Swedish shipowners at a disadvantage vis-à-vis foreign competitors?

International shipping regulation requires shipowners to register their vessels in a flag state. The flag of a vessel has a symbolic significance, but, more importantly, also has a direct bearing on the costs of running the vessel. Flag-state policies vary, and the operational costs vary accordingly. Since at least the sixteenth century, shipowners have registered ships under low-cost flags, and the practice accelerated after 1945. In 1950 an estimated 5 per cent of the world fleet was registered under so-called 'Flags of Convenience' (FoCs), with low-cost regulation, and the figure had grown to 32 per cent by 1987 (Tenold, 2000, p. 7). By 2005 an estimated 48 per cent of the world fleet flew FoCs (Stopford, 2009, p. 670). Panama and Liberia were the two most popular low-cost flags, but there were many others, and new low-cost flags continue to come into existence. The development of low-cost flags was an important regulatory factor for all international shipping firms after 1945 and contributed to the changes in the competitive structure of the industry (Carlisle, 1981; Stopford, 2009, pp. 666–75). European shipowners and politicians also had to consider the issue carefully.

The costs of flying the Swedish flag exceeded the costs in, for example, Liberia or Panama, but during the prosperous years of the 1960s the issue of costs did not cause major debates in Sweden. Indeed, compared with later periods, regulation issues did not lead to major contests. The issue of low-cost flags, however, was discussed extensively in the Swedish parliament in the 1970s, when Swedish shipowners became increasingly interested in achieving cost reductions through the flagging-out of tonnage to low-cost countries. Shipowners' and labour's interests clashed in a time of economic recession, as they did elsewhere in Scandinavia, but in the Swedish case the anti-flagging-out view prevailed. In 1977 Sweden enacted a law to restrict Swedish shipowners' use of low-cost flags. This law hindered the transfer of a Swedish ship, or a share in a ship, to a low-cost flag, without prior permission from the government. It contributed to the strong decline in Swedish shipping after 1977 (Sjögren, 1999a, pp. 160–87). Shipowners accused the government of making it impossible to compete internationally, since foreign competitors could more easily use low-cost alternatives. Approximately 160 Swedish ships were sold abroad between 1975 and 1979 (Lennerfors, 2009).

During the 1980s FoCs continued to grow as European shipowners tried to reduce crewing costs. Western European seamen's salaries were high relative to the salaries of seafarers from low-cost countries such as the Philippines and India, and this put European shipowners and European policy-makers in a difficult situation (Poulsen, 2011). In Sweden an internationalization agreement (*Internationaliseringsavtalet*) was made in 1983, which allowed Swedish seamen living in Sweden to work on Swedish-owned ships flying foreign flags and receiving substantial tax relief if they worked for more than 183 days a year. It reduced certain crewing costs for Swedish owners compared to flying the Swedish flag, but it was still unfavourable compared with the foreign shipping registers with foreign crew (Lennerfors, 2009, p. 164). Many European countries took more drastic measures, however, by setting up second registers: International Registers of Shipping. These registers were established to counteract the flagging out from Europe to FoCs. The European Union attempted to set up a common European register (EUROS).[3] However, when Norway established the Norwegian International Ship Register (NIS) in 1987, followed by the Danish International Ship Register (DIS) and the German International Ship Register (GIS), the concept of second registers became an important way of organizing shipping in Europe. Denmark and Norway successfully boosted their national flags in this way (see Chapter 2 on Norway and Chapter 3 on Denmark, as well as Tenold, 2006). In the international registers of shipping, shipowners were allowed to employ non-EU citizens, mainly Asians and East Europeans, at local salaries. Hence, the second registries were also competitive relative to the traditional FoCs. Safety standards in the second registries were generally high, but salaries were more competitive than under the traditional national flags (DeSombre, 2006; Poulsen, 2011).

Sweden did not establish an international register of shipping, and Swedish shipping companies clearly preferred to register new ships under foreign flags in the 1990s. The fleet under the Swedish flag had declined since the 1970s, and stabilized at a low level in the late 1980s and 1990s. In contrast, the foreign-flagged fleet, controlled by Swedish owners, started a new expansion after 1987, tripling in ten years (see Figure 4.3 below). This was mainly due to a new expansion in the fleet of foreign-flagged crude oil tankers, controlled by newly established shipping companies in Stockholm and Göteborg.[4] Attempts by the Swedish shipping industry, the seafarers' associations, and the state to unite around a shipping policy generally failed. Nevertheless a gradual change in the Swedish government's policies started in the 1990s, and the Flag Act from the 1970s was abolished in 1992. Crewing costs under the Swedish flag were still high, however. In the 1990s, at least two studies analysed the competitive conditions for Swedish shipping, and identified clear Swedish disadvantages relative to foreign competitors. Sjöfartsverket's report of 1998 concluded that labour costs for Swedish shipowners, using the Swedish flag, were often 45 per cent higher than under NIS or DIS (SOU, 1998, p. 129; Sjöfartsverket, 1998).

Sweden joined the European Union in 1995 and from then on there was a gradual change in Swedish shipping policies. Most importantly, the so-called 'TAP system' was established in 1998, after the Swedish government reached agreements with the employers' associations and the unions. The TAP system (Swedish: *Tillfälligt anställd personal*, temporarily employed personnel) legalized Swedish shipowners' employment of non-EU citizens in half of the positions on board Swedish-flagged ships. Significantly, the non-EU citizens received local salaries, which were lower than the Swedish ones. The TAP system required the captain and the chief engineer to have a Swedish nautical education and was restricted to merchant ships, excluding ferries in Northern Europe. While improving overall Swedish competitiveness, the system did not fully remove the Swedish cost disadvantage. In 1999 Swedish-flagged vessels had an average cost disadvantage of 24, 25 and 30 per cent compared to DIS, NIS and the Dutch flag, respectively. Cost disadvantages differed between ship types, however, with the greatest cost disadvantages for product tankers and bulk carriers and smaller disadvantages for ro-ro ships.[5]

In 2001 the Swedish government introduced a new type of shipping industry aid, the net wage system. The government granted Swedish owners a tax rebate, which equalled the mariners' income taxes and social costs. Henceforth, shipowners would only pay net wages to the mariners, thus saving considerable manning costs. This resembled the conditions offered to Danish and Norwegian owners under the DIS and NIS, respectively. Obviously, for the Swedish shipowners, this was good news.[6] However, their rhetoric soon changed again.

Around 2000 most European countries implemented tonnage tax regimes. Greece was the first, followed by Norway and the Netherlands in 1996, Germany in 1999, Great Britain in 2000 and Denmark in 2002. Under this regime, ordinary corporate taxes were abolished for the shipping industry. Instead, shipping companies paid taxes based on the tonnage controlled, regardless of profits and losses made. The principle was simple: the higher the tonnage, the higher the tax. Shipowners argued that tonnage taxes ensured that sound, commercial decisions were made within the shipping companies. Under a tonnage tax regime, shipowners have no incentive to invest in ships in order to avoid taxation, which would have been the case under an ordinary corporate tax regime. A committee comprising tax experts, government officials and the director of the Swedish Shipowners' Association was established in 2004 with the goal of looking into the tonnage tax issue. The committee concluded with a report in 2006, recommending the introduction of a tonnage tax regime to ensure competitive conditions for Swedish-based companies and retain both a fleet and maritime know-how in Sweden (SOU, 2006). For Swedish taxpayers, the committee predicted no negative consequences. A tonnage tax would generate a tax income for the Swedish government equal to the income from the existing taxation system (ibid., p. 25).

Despite the advice of the committee and the change of government from the Social Democrats to the Conservatives (Moderaterna) in 2006, Sweden did not implement the suggested tax legislation. Ever since, shipowners have continuously criticized the government for insufficient industry support.[7] The Swedish shipowners' arguments for the tonnage tax indicate that this issue is very high on their agenda. Indeed, the owners found themselves disadvantaged vis-à-vis their foreign competitors, even though it is difficult to measure precisely the negative impact of the Swedish tax regime on Swedish shipping. Interestingly, if tonnage taxes were introduced in Sweden, there would be no significant differences between engaging in the shipping business from Sweden and from other EU countries. In 2009 the Swedish Shipowners' Association announced their support to individual shipowners, should they wish to reflag vessels to more competitive, foreign flags.[8]

To sum up, Swedish shipping institutions were less favourable to the shipping industry than their counterparts in Norway and Denmark. Throughout the period the Swedish government reacted slowly in terms of shipping aid. We have assessed three important institutions, all of which had a clear negative impact on the industry. The Flag Act of 1977, the government's refusal to introduce an international register of shipping in the late 1980s, and its continued rejection of a tonnage tax regime in the mid-2000s all hampered the growth of Swedish shipping. Indeed, these negative policy conditions were a major contributing factor in the poor Swedish performance from the mid-1970s and in the decline of Swedish shipping.

The reasons for the negative Swedish policy conditions have never been properly researched. It is reasonable, however, to assume that the policies were influenced by the Swedish state's traumatic involvement in shipbuilding in the 1970s and 1980s. During the crisis of those decades, all the major shipyards came under government ownership. To save employment in the sector, the government implemented large reconstruction programmes, all of which ultimately failed (Olsson, 1996; Kuuse and Olsson, 1997). Shipping, which employed fewer people than the yards, got less attention from the government. It is also noteworthy that shipping issues are handled by the Ministry of Communications and Infrastructure. This clearly indicates that government officials currently perceive shipping as a provider of transport for Sweden, rather than just another free-standing industry. In contrast, in Denmark shipping issues have been handled by the Danish Ministry of Economics and Business, which has a more positive approach to shipping. In the 1990s and 2000s, the Danish administration worked determinedly to support Danish shipping companies, for example by launching a plan in 2006 to develop Denmark into 'Europe's leading shipping nation' Økonomi- ogErhvervsministeriet, 2006).

Strategies

In the world of shipping, fluctuating markets and changing policy conditions powerfully influence the performance of individual shipping companies. For that reason, shipping companies need effective corporate strategies to cope with the challenges they encounter (Porter, 1980; Lorange, 2009; Wijnolst and Wergeland, 2009; Stopford, 2009). This section identifies various corporate strategies in Swedish shipping and discusses how they influenced the competitiveness of Swedish shipping.

In the late 1950s, Swedish shipping companies were global players, engaging in all the main shipping segments. In liner shipping, Broström, Transatlantic, Nordstjernan and Sveabolaget were the main actors, controlling large liner networks. Liner shipping, however, was going through a period of radical change, both in terms of technology and organization, caused by containerization and an emerging protectionist movement in the Third World. Container vessels and new cargo-handling systems replaced the conventional liner ships and the older general cargo-handling systems. At the same time, strong interest groups in the Third World demanded a larger share of the liner shipping market and protectionism was a means to achieve that. This threatened the position of Swedish companies, which relied on access to foreign markets. The Swedish companies applied a co-operative strategy, forming liner consortia with foreign lines. The aims of this co-operation were to achieve economies of scale, to ensure political bargaining power and to maintain access to foreign markets. Combined with investments in new container and ro-ro ships, the co-operative strategy ensured the survival of the Swedish liner companies into the 1980s. Many foreign lines left the liner sector at the same time, but the Swedish companies managed this process better as a result of their strategic and technological changes (Poulsen 2007, 2010).

In the 1960s Swedish shipowners also had considerable investments in the tanker and dry bulk segments. Several companies responded to the growth of oil shipping by ordering more and larger ships, and Sweden was able to maintain its share of the world fleet. In the 1960s and early 1970s, VLCCs and ULCCs were delivered, and large ore and bulk carriers and combination carriers (oil-bulk-ore, OBO) also entered the Swedish merchant fleet. To a large extent, the growth in the Swedish fleet was attributable to the large-scale investments in VLCCs and ULCCs, as seen in Figure 4.2 (Kuuse and Olsson, 1997; Sjögren, 1999a, 1999b; Dahl, 2003, pp. 102–8). In this regard the Swedish companies

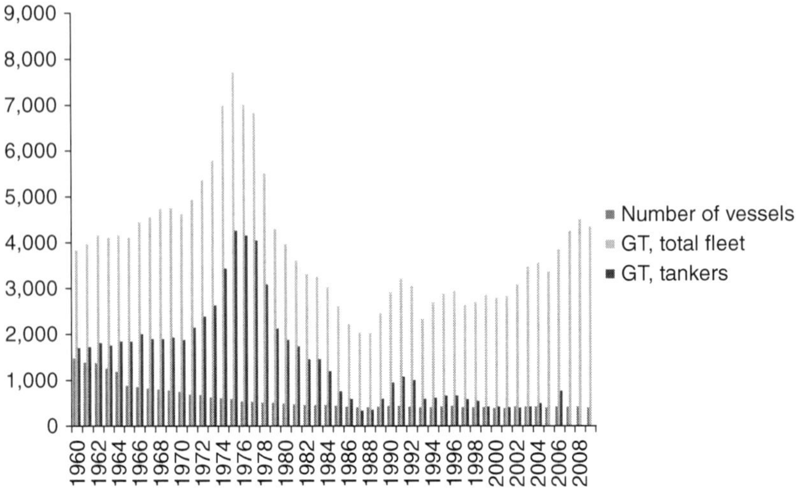

Figure 4.2 Swedish-registered fleet, GT in '000s and number of vessels, 1960–2009

Note: Based on data from SCB, SOS, Sjöfart 1960–2009. The category 'GT, tankers' includes combination carriers (oil/ore carriers) for the period 1960–77. From a peak of 30 vessels in 1964, the fleet of combination carriers had declined to six vessels in 1977 and never regained its former significance. From 1978 onwards, combination carriers are included in the total category. No specific data on 'GT, tankers' available for 2005 and 2007–9.

followed a general trend in the shipping industry at the time. Fuelled by the optimism of the 1960s, the Swedish fleet, and in particular the tanker fleet, grew rapidly. Swedish shipping companies also engaged in shipping niches, most notably reefers (for refrigeration of fish, meat and vegetables), ro-ro vessels (for cars) and ferry services. Since the 1930s, Saléninvest had been a market leader in reefers, but ro-ro shipping emerged as a new Swedish speciality during the 1960s (Björklund et al., 1984; Tor Line, 1985; Sjögren et al., submitted).

Since the early twentieth century, diversification had been a common strategy in Swedish shipping and three major Swedish players, Saléninvest, Nordstjernan and Broström, engaged in several shipping segments and also invested in other sectors, including shipbuilding and industry (Fritz and Olsson, 1994 ; Sjögren, 1999a, 1999b). Clearly diversification was a means of reducing risk. Profits from one investment would make up losses made elsewhere in the group. Moreover, Swedish yards could develop new, competitive vessels for the owners and supply tonnage even in times of boom, when yard berths were in short supply globally (Olsson, 1983). Strategies of vertical integration and diversification were not a Swedish speciality. Foreign shipping companies, most notably in Denmark, employed similar strategies (Poulsen and Sornn-Friese, 2011). However, in the Swedish case the strategy proved particularly problematic. Diversification per se did not produce fatal results, but the particular combination of investments in shipping and shipbuilding, chosen by major Swedish shipping companies, proved dangerous in the 1970s. To a large extent Swedish shipyards relied on the construction of series of large, standardized tonnage, in particular crude oil carriers and large bulk carriers, for which demand plummeted during this period. The shipping crisis of the 1970s eroded the basis of the Swedish shipbuilding industry, and problems cascaded onto the owners in the shipping companies (Olsson, 1996). In the 1970s and 1980s, when shipping and shipbuilding went through a period of radical transformation, the diversification strategies that had been chosen caused severe problems for several large players in Swedish shipping.

After 1973 the oil and shipping crises posed serious challenges to all shipping companies, and in many cases strategic misjudgements caused companies to collapse (Tenold, 2006). This also happened in Sweden, even though the main exits from the industry only took place after 1980. Most of the Swedish shipping companies waited for the next boom, but this did not come as soon as they hoped. In hindsight, Swedish owners were clearly mistaken and by the latter half of the 1970s, many of the Swedish shipping companies were forced to restructure their businesses (Sjögren, 1999a; Sjögren et al., submitted). One company, however, managed to quit oil shipping before the crisis: Wallenius sold its last oil tanker in 1973 to focus on ro-ro shipping, which turned out to be a very fortunate decision. This strategic sale saved the company from the misfortunes suffered by other Swedish companies.

After 1975 a radical reduction of the Swedish fleet began. The development in Sweden reflected the European trend, but the Swedish contraction was particularly strong. The overseas sales of Swedish ships culminated in 1978 and 1979 (Sjögren, 1999a, pp. 56–8). Not only did the Swedish merchant fleet contract, but all the prominent players who had built up successful maritime conglomerates in shipping and shipbuilding since the nineteenth century, experienced deep problems. All of these conglomerates exited shipping, including the old core of the industry – Broström, Saléninvest, Nordstjernan and Rederi AB Transatlantic – during the 1980s. The basis for the exits was either outright bankruptcy or shipping disinvestment. By the late 1980s, the main structures of the industry, as well as the maritime conglomerates, had gone bankrupt (see Table 4.1).

Table 4.1 Sweden's ten largest shipping companies, 1960–2010, based on operated dwt (calculated from Svensk Sjöfarts Tidning 1960–2010)

1960	Broströms-rederierna	668,675
	Trafik AB Grängesberg-Oxelösund	477,470
	Trans-rederierna	360,970
	Red. AB Nordstjernan	308,085
	Salén-rederierna	268,990
	Svea-rederierna	249,064
	Wallenius-rederierna	214,933
	Onstads-rederierna	197,090
	Kihlströms rederier	161,731
	Trelleborgs Ångf. AB	144,278
1970	Salén-rederierna	1,189,712
	Broström-koncernen	1,110,705
	Grängesbergsbolaget	855,985
	Red. AB Nordstjernan	436,766
	Malmros Red. AB	365,662
	Trans-koncernen	339,325
	Wallenius-rederierna	294,742
	Kungsbacka-rederierna	205,190
	Oljekonsumenterna-OK	177,925
	A.K. Fernströms Rederier	174,875
1980	Salén-koncernen (inc. Tor Line)	1,964,350
	Munkedals AB	616,800
	Rederi AB Malmoil	606,820
	Broström-koncernen	475,480
	Johnson-koncernen (inc. Rederi-Svea)	335,017
	Dalen & Fraternitas	316,550
	Wallenius-rederierna	307,459
	Transgruppen	295,929
	OK	293,979
	Johansson Gruppen	268,761
1990	Stena Rederi AB	4,128,591
	Argonaut AB	2,364,562
	UV Shipping AB	1,847,256
	Nordström & Thulin AB	795,785
	ScanShip AB	575,764

Continued

Table 4.1 Continued

	ICB Shipping AB	571,793
	United Tankers AB	475,894
	Wallenius-rederierna	454,775
	Johnson Line AB	151,501
	B&N Bylock & Nordsjöfrakt AB	137,600
2000	Stena	5,977,418
	Broström Van Ommeren Shipping AB	1,595,810
	Wallenius Wilhelmsen Lines	1,514,835
	Atlantic Container Line (ACL) AB	258,240
	Rederi AB Sunship	233,163
	Marinvest	207,509
	B & N Nordsjöfrakt AB	193,160
	Gorthon Lines AB	155,697
	Svenska Orient Linien AB	66,400
	Ahlmark Lines AB	43,550
2010	Stena Rederi AB	7,261,172
	Marinvest	826,953
	Laurin Maritime AB	451,058
	Rederi AB Transatlantic	370,396
	Broström Tankers/Maersk Product Tankers AB	360,033
	Rederi AB Gotland	355,941
	Atlantic Container Line (ACL) Sweden AB	258,240
	Thunrederierna	198,842
	Svenska Orient Linien AB	159,862
	Österströms Rederi AB	132,408

In the liner sector, the Swedish decline was particularly severe. For international container shipping, the late 1970s and 1980s were difficult times and most liner services suffered heavy losses (Broeze, 2002, pp. 79–113). The international consortia, which had ensured the survival of Swedish liner shipping in the 1960s and 1970s, also proved unstable. The consortia were often plagued by internal rivalry between the partners and inefficient decision-making processes. The successful co-operative strategies of the 1960s did not work in the depressed markets of the 1980s, where scale mattered. During the 1980s, consortium members would typically buy other members' shares. This happened in several consortia in which the Swedes participated and this process ultimately contributed to a Swedish exit from deep-sea liner shipping. Following losses made in tanker, dry bulk and reefer shipping, as well as in shipbuilding, the Swedish players did not have the resources necessary to compete with the foreign container lines, which built up global liner networks at the time. Moreover, entrepreneurs within Sweden could not set up new business in the liner sector. In contrast to the tanker sectors, high investments were required in the liner sector and this became a barrier to entry. These factors brought Swedish involvement in liner shipping to an end by the early 1990s.[9]

In the tanker and dry bulk sectors, the situation in the 1980s was more favourable for new players. Barriers to entry were reduced following the fall in freight rates and a parallel drop in the second-hand price of vessels. This opened new opportunities for entrepreneurs, and a number of new Swedish shipowners responded positively to the growth prospects. From the late 1980s, several new Swedish players, including Argonaut, ICB, Frontline, Nordström & Thulin, and Concordia Maritime AB, emerged and expanded their fleets under foreign flags, investing in second-hand oil tankers and dry bulk carriers. Throughout the 1990s, the fleet under Swedish flag stagnated at a low level, while the Swedish-controlled fleet under foreign flags grew rapidly (*Svensk Sjöfarts Tidning* 25 (2001), p. 117). Thus the general decline in Swedish shipping came to a halt in the late 1980s, and due to the increase in new players, Sweden regained global market share in the 1990s (see the data in Chapter 6). The timing of the market entry for the new companies was fortunate, because vessel prices were generally low at the time. Many of the companies followed a strategy of asset play in the tanker market, purchasing and selling ships at the right time, but some companies also developed long-term relations with the oil majors. The *Exxon Valdez* catastrophe in 1990, when the grounding of an Exxon tanker in Alaska caused an environmental disaster, delegitimized the asset play strategy in favour of long-term, high-quality industrial shipping. All the Swedish tanker players started to emphasize quality and long-term orientation from around 1990 (Lennerfors, 2009). They also to some extent built relationships with oil companies, such as Neste oil, BP and with state-owned companies such as Vela and Sonangol. Stena and Concordia Maritime AB started propagating the idea that 'oil should travel first class' in the late 1980s (Sjögren et al., submitted).

In the niche markets, Sweden continued to house active players. The bankrupted Saléninvest's reefer division emerged as an independent

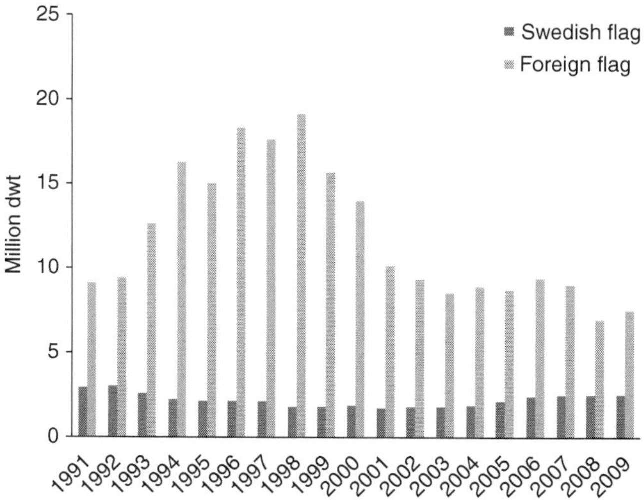

Figure 4.3 Swedish fleet under Swedish and foreign flags, million dwt, 1991–2010

Note: The chart is based on data from Sveriges Redareförening and Lighthouse (2010). The data in this figure are not directly comparable with Figure 4.2, because the data for Figure 4.2 do not include the foreign flagged fleet and data series for Figure 4.3 are only available from 1991 onwards.

company, Cool Carriers, and Wallenius continued its involvement in the deep-sea ro-ro business. While the ro-ro business proved a profitable and expansive niche for Wallenius, reefer shipping ultimately became a sunset industry (Lennerfors, 2009; Sjögren et al., submitted).

The growth in the Swedish-controlled fleet under foreign flags came to an abrupt halt around the year 2000 (see Figure 4.3), when a second decline in Swedish shipping set in. This decline reflected the fact that several prominent Swedish tanker shipping companies, including ICB, Frontline and N&T Argonaut, were acquired by foreign owners. The foreign-flagged fleet dropped significantly and headquarters were moved abroad by the new owners (Lennerfors, 2009).

Swedish shipping has never returned to its previous level. The Swedish sales were made only a few years before the boom in global shipping from 2003 to 2008. During the first decade of the new millennium, the Swedish-owned fleet stagnated, indicating that the remaining Swedish shipowners did not manage to exploit the boom to the same extent as their foreign competitors. This caused an erosion of Swedish market share, from approximately 2 per cent of the world fleet in 1995 down to approximately 0.9 per cent in 2010. The second period of decline took place just as global shipping markets boomed and competitors in Denmark experienced a period of unprecedented growth (see Chapter 3). Swedish shipping was disadvantaged at that time, because the Stockholm tanker fleet had gone a few years earlier. Among the remaining Swedish shipping companies, Wallenius and the Stena group successfully used the growing markets to expand in deep-sea ro-ro shipping and tanker shipping, offshore/drilling and short-sea ro-ro shipping, respectively. A new player with an old name, Broström, built up a large fleet of product tankers in the 2000s, but the company was acquired by the Danish giant A. P. Møller-Maersk in 2008.[10] Otherwise, there was expansion in the product tanker market by a few small companies on the Swedish West coast. Some of these have recently decided to switch to the Danish flag and move their headquarters to Denmark in response to the Swedish government's shipping policies.[11] On the Stockholm stock exchange, only two shipping companies, Rederi AB Transatlantic and SRAB Shipping, are currently listed.[12]

Strategic failures thus propelled Swedish maritime conglomerates into crisis in the 1970s and 1980s. Diversification and overinvestment in the problematic shipping segments of tankers and dry bulk vessels eroded the foundations of the old companies. In the 1980s new players were partly able to build on old strategies in the tanker and dry bulk segments and managed to build up new shipping companies. In the tanker and dry bulk sector entry barriers were low because vessel prices had dropped. This became the basis for a new expansion of Swedish shipping under foreign flags in the 1990s. However, the sale of Swedish shipping companies to foreign owners in the late 1990s started a second phase of decline in Swedish shipping and hampered its opportunities during the global shipping boom from 2002 to 2008. Currently, the niche strategies of Wallenius and the diversified strategy of the Stena group have proven to be the most successful in Swedish shipping.

To sum up: bad timing of acquisitions, overinvestment in the depressed tanker segment and diversification into shipbuilding were the major strategic mistakes made by Swedish shipowners, and all contributed to the first decline of Swedish shipping. The second phase of decline was initiated by the sale of several Stockholm companies to foreign owners. In retrospect, the timing of the sales, a few years before a global boom, was unfortunate. Clearly, strategy was an important factor in the two declines of Swedish shipping. Ultimately, the changes contributed to an erosion of know-how.

Know-how and resources

Know-how and resources are key success factors in shipping. 'Know-how' refers to human capital, while 'resources' are defined as financial capital. In this section we ask how Swedish shipping companies' performance was influenced by changes in the pool of maritime know-how in Sweden and changes in the availability of financial capital.

Technical and commercial know-how

Shipping is a capital-intensive business with high risks, and an in-depth understanding of the nature of shipping markets, both the freight markets and the sale-and-purchase markets, is crucial to shipping entrepreneurs. The tanker and dry bulk markets are inherently unstable and closely resemble the neoclassical ideal of perfect competition. Timing is crucial for freight contracting and vessel sales and purchases, and low entry barriers enable shipping companies to choose an opportunistic approach if they prefer. Liner shipping and niche markets such as reefers and car carriers work differently, but commercial know-how is equally important here. Entry barriers are generally higher and long-term relationships with customers are much more important. Moreover, large bureaucracies and agent networks are required to run the business. Liner companies have generally worked to restrict competition, using various degrees of collusion, and shipping managers have needed knowledge of and access to these networks to succeed in liner shipping.[13]

Shipping companies can rarely dictate market conditions, but they can manipulate operational costs for their fleets. Fleet management, including crewing and maintenance, is important in this regard and costs depend heavily on the flag of the vessel, which determines labour costs. Furthermore, the design of new ships also influences the competitive position of shipping companies; innovative ship designs can be a source of competitive advantage. Technical insight into fleet operations and newbuilding projects is therefore an important constituent of maritime know-how, and competence in ship insurance and shipping law is a *sine qua non* (Lorange, 2009; Wijnolst and Wergeland, 2009; Stopford, 2009).

In the early 1960s, several Swedish maritime conglomerates had both commercial and technical knowledge in-house: they retained large commercial departments with global networks, which maintained and updated market know-how. For example, the maritime conglomerate of Broström employed a large workforce in its Göteborg headquarters, which stayed in close contact with a global network of agents in approximately 100 ports in the mid-1960s (Mattson, 1965, p. 170). Considerable technical know-how was also available in-house in Broström, which owned the Eriksberg shipyard. The ownership of yards gave shipping companies easy access to technical know-how when ordering new ships. In the 1960s several large Swedish shipping companies had considerable technical organizations, many of which worked assiduously to develop innovative vessels, in particular for liner and car shipping and for the ore bulk trades. At that time, several Swedish companies were engaged in the liner sector and Swedish lines spanned the world. In a battle for survival, the companies successfully invested in innovative vessel types and managed to maintain Sweden's position in the liner segment. In the 1960s and early 1970s, container ships replaced conventional liner ships and revolutionized liner shipping. Broström successfully participated in this process, building several advanced container and combined ro-ro/container ships.[14]

The closure of the Swedish shipyards in the 1980s reduced Swedish shipping companies' access to technical know-how (Rehnström and Olsson, 2003, p. 50; Palmberg et al., 2006, p. 148). Moreover, the radical contraction of Swedish companies' newbuilding programmes after 1980, triggered by the failure of all the big old shipping companies, reduced career opportunities for naval engineers, seafarers and other technical experts in Sweden. Nautical engineering education was maintained in Göteborg, but the nautical schools in Härnösand, Stockholm and Malmö closed in the 1980s. Today, nautical education is concentrated in Göteborg and Kalmar. The decline of Swedish shipping in the 1970s and 1980s thus reduced the pool of know-how available for the remaining participants in the industry.

One notable company, the Stena group, has managed to acquire know-how from shipyards that have closed down. Stena employed personnel from the Uddevalla shipyard who became central actors in the group's new technical organization, Stena Teknik, which developed several innovative vessel designs for the group's ferry services, tanker business and offshore/drilling activities in the 1990s and 2000s. In the 2000s, according to Stena itself, no other Swedish shipping companies had comparable technical know-how in-house (Stena AB, 2009, p. 18).

In the 2000s Swedish newbuilding programmes remained at a low level, and contributed to the ageing of the Swedish-flagged fleet, which had become one of the oldest in Europe.[15] The fact that Swedish companies refrained from large newbuilding programmes during the boom years from 2002 to 2008 was clearly a strategic, commercially-based decision, but may also have been a result of the contraction of the pool of technical know-how during the 1980s and 1990s. Such know-how was no longer easily available in Sweden.

It is clear that the pool of commercial know-how also influenced the development of Swedish shipping companies. In the 1960s this knowledge enabled Swedish shipping companies to take advantage of rising shipping markets, but it did not save the industry from the structural crisis of the 1970s and 1980s. Many shipowners were too late in realizing that the shipping market had undergone a structural transformation. During this period, Sweden lost all the prominent companies in the industry. In many cases, employees in the failed companies stayed in the shipping business and set up new shipping ventures such as Argonaut, ICB and Stockholm Chartering or found employment in the government-owned shipping company Zenit Shipping (Sjögren, 1999a; Lennerfors, 2009). A generation of maritime managers carried on in Swedish shipping until their retirement in the 1990s and 2000s.

For young people, however, career opportunities in shipping and shipbuilding were reduced in the 1980s, and although many employees in the failed companies found new opportunities in shipping in the 1990s, there are few examples of Swedish shipping companies allocating large resources to the nurturing of new maritime talents. In the late 1990s the sale of several large Stockholm shipping companies to foreign owners and the relocation of headquarters abroad also reduced maritime career opportunities in Sweden and indirectly eroded the pool of commercial know-how. The recruitment of a new generation of maritime managers did not materialize in the 1990s and the 2000s.

Today there is still considerable expertise in the technical management of product tankers, mainly on the island of Donsö in the Göteborg archipelago (Friberg, 2007). However, on the commercial side, the situation does not look so bright. Many Swedish owners of product tankers work merely as tonnage providers for foreign shipping companies and in some cases turn to Denmark when they need commercial know-how (Rederi AB Gotland, 2009).

In 2008 a committee of experts was appointed under the Swedish Maritime Administration to address the recruitment problems of Swedish shipping at the time, and a report and plan for action was published two years later. The committee noted that the industry was suffering from a generational gap, caused by the high average age of employees in the industry and the low recruitment of new talent. The industry had a bad reputation and a poor image among the public, which contributed to this problem. The report made a number of recommendations to strengthen recruitment to the industry, referring to successful recruitment campaigns carried out in Denmark as a potential source of inspiration. On a broader level, the report confirmed the importance of recruitment and development of maritime know-how for the future of the industry in Sweden (Sjöfartsverket, 2010).

The pool of talent is now restricted within Sweden because numerous employees, in all functions of maritime industry, have withdrawn, and few successors have replaced them. Clearly, in an international business such as shipping there were always opportunities for recruitment of foreign experts, and some companies, including Wallenius, recently recruited top management from abroad for the first time. Irrespective of the opportunities within international maritime human resource management, a contraction of the pool of know-how, both commercial and technical, had clearly taken place. With no new players and negative national policies, career opportunities in Swedish shipping were reduced, and the recruitment of a new generation of maritime managers did not materialize in the 1990s and the 2000s. This may have contributed to the poor performance of Swedish shipping after 2000. It is not, ultimately, a requirement to have both commercial and technical know-how in-house, but easy access was clearly crucial for successful shipping companies. Lack of technical and commercial know-how may ultimately have become a barrier to Swedish shipping.

Resources

In the capital-intensive business of shipping, entrepreneurs with know-how needed easy access to financial capital (Stokes, 1997). Prior to 1970, Swedish shipping conglomerates were generally controlled by families such as Broström, Salén, Johnson, Malmros and Högberg, and for decades this was a recipe for a stable ownership. Ownership and management passed from generation to generation, ensuring a high degree of financial continuity. These conglomerates often had a main bank where they were considered preferred customers.[16]

During the structural crisis of the 1970s and the 1980s family capital was reduced or divested from shipping, when the old maritime conglomerates failed (Sjögren, 1999a; Lennerfors, 2009). The departure of family capital forced shipping entrepreneurs to go elsewhere. Many entrepreneurs gained access to financial capital through the Swedish stock market and a network of rich private individuals, related to the collapsed company Saléninvest. In these investors' eyes, shipping had a speculative character, and many of the investors ultimately proved to have an opportunistic approach to shipping (Lennerfors, 2009).

In the early 1990s the value of many shipping stocks fell dramatically, and this caused resentment among both the general public and shareholders (Lennerfors, 2009, p. 157–62). Squeezed investors lost their faith in shipping and wanted to abandon their investments. Disadvantageous policy conditions and disappointing share price developments eroded the basis for large shipping investments on the Stockholm stock exchange. At the same time, the Norwegian-born shipowner John Fredriksen, the London-based Greek shipowner John Angelicoussis and the Hong-Kong-based Sohmen family were building up large fleets of tankers in a quest for economies of scale. The Swedish tanker and dry bulk fleets were attractive targets for them and the fragile ownership structure of the Swedish companies made them ideal targets for foreign takeovers. Tankers were simply more interesting investments for large foreign owners than they were for Swedish investors, who had lost faith in shipping. Hence, the three foreign shipowners were able to acquire all the large Stockholm-based tanker and dry bulk shipping companies in the latter half of the 1990s. The ownership structure of the Swedish shipping companies proved too weak to sustain a large shipping community in Stockholm. Instead, many Swedish investors moved into other sectors. Clearly the Swedish stock market could not raise sufficient capital for Swedish shipping, and today the two largest remaining shipping companies, Wallenius and the Stena group, are family-controlled and thus not dependent on the stock market. The migration of the Stockholm shipping companies also drained the Swedish banking sector of customers, and Swedish banks scaled down their involvement in ship finance accordingly (Lennerfors, 2009, pp. 129–32).

The decline of Swedish shipping clearly demonstrates the close relationship between maritime know-how and financial capital. In shipping, commercial and technical know-how and financial capital are prerequisites for success, and both these resources gradually became more scarce in Sweden. Indeed, the problems encountered by shipping entrepreneurs, who carried technical and commercial know-how, ultimately contributed to a reduction in the industry's access to financial resources. Entrepreneurs with know-how are still present in Sweden, but their opportunities are more restricted than they were only a generation ago.

Conclusion

Few maritime centres have experienced a more rapid decline than Sweden in the years following 1973. Within a decade the whole structure of the industry changed; all the yards closed, as did most of the major shipping companies. Some businesses were reconstructed by entrepreneurs in the late 1980s, and Swedish shipping entered a period of recovery, which lasted approximately ten years. Ultimately, however, most shipping businesses were lost or sold abroad around 2000 and this started a second period of decline. Swedish shipping did not benefit from the global boom in shipping from 2002 to 2008 and this sets the Swedish case clearly apart from its Danish and Norwegian neighbours. We have analysed the causes for the two remarkable declines of Swedish shipping.

Shipping markets set the pace of the shipping industry and strongly influenced the development of Swedish shipping companies. The boom conditions from 1967 to 1973 propelled global shipping and Swedish companies into a situation of overcapacity and structural crisis. That crisis lasted for one and a half decades and knocked out many companies, including all prominent Swedish players. Recovery returned around 1987 and despite some volatility around 1990, markets recovered during the 1990s. Some Swedish entrepreneurs were able to use this positive trend for a reconstruction of tanker and bulk businesses in Göteborg and Stockholm, registering vessels under foreign flags. However, the basis of Swedish liner shipping, where high entry barriers prevented entrepreneurs from setting up new businesses, had already been lost by 1990. From 2002 to 2008, boom conditions returned to global shipping, but only a few remaining Swedish companies could profit from this golden opportunity for growth. Currently, global shipping is struggling with overcapacity, and the Swedish merchant fleet is witnessing further reductions. The fluctuations of shipping markets clearly influenced the development of Swedish shipping, and the first period of decline in Sweden coincided with the global shipping crisis. However, shipping markets have always fluctuated and changing markets cannot alone explain the decline of Swedish shipping relative to foreign competitors, who were also exposed to similar market conditions.

Peculiar Swedish regulations contributed significantly to the long-term erosion of Swedish shipping's competitiveness. During both periods of decline, Swedish regulations were more restrictive than they were in Denmark, Norway, and other comparable countries. In a global industry like shipping, competitive policy conditions are important to companies and Sweden's policies often raised the costs of doing business above international levels. In 1977 the Swedish government implemented a flag law, which hampered Swedish shipping companies' use of inexpensive foreign flags. Moreover, in the late 1980s the government refrained from establishing an international register of shipping, something other foreign competitors had done. Swedish policy conditions improved during the latter half of the 1990s and early 2000s, when the TAP and the net wage system were implemented. However, conditions soon deteriorated again, because the Swedish government did not implement a competitive tonnage tax regime, similar to the system commonly used elsewhere in Europe. It is clear that the Swedish government reacted more slowly in terms of shipping aid than most European governments. We have noted that shipowners have pointed out that the labour unions played a significant role in the formulation of Swedish regulations, but we will leave it to future research to assess their importance.

We have identified a range of corporate strategies within Swedish shipping. The old maritime conglomerates misunderstood the structural transformation of shipping after 1973, overinvesting in the problematic tanker segment and suffering from failed diversification strategies. New shipping companies proved the value of perfect timing in the rising tanker and dry bulk markets in the latter half of the 1980s. These companies entered at the bottom of the shipping market and brought the decline in Swedish shipping to a halt for more than ten years. During the 1980s and 1990s, opportunistic asset play strategies were successfully used by some of these companies, while others chose to build long-term relationships with customers. The companies built up their fleets under foreign flags in order to avoid problems caused by commercially harmful Swedish regulations. However, with the sale of most of the companies in the late 1990s, a new phase of decline started. A general shift away from the main shipping segments of oil tankers and dry bulk carriers took place, and the remaining Swedish companies mainly focussed on niches within product tankers and ro-ro shipping. Today, the winners are Stena (based on inter-industry diversification) and Wallenius (based on a niche strategy), but these provide only a partial answer to the eternal riddle of finding good shipping strategies. However, both Stena and Wallenius met changing and challenging conditions with a *creative response,* since they were (it turns out with hindsight) quite innovative in terms of market strategy and technology, while keeping a strong focus on long-term relationships with customers.

In the 1960s Swedish shipping companies and shipyards possessed considerable maritime know-how, both of the technical and of the commercial kind: Swedish companies were often at the forefront of the industry. The structural crisis that affected Swedish shipping after 1973, however, caused the pool of maritime know-how to contract considerably. Technical know-how was lost when the yards closed down in the 1970s and 1980s, and commercial know-how was reduced as shipping operations were sold or transferred abroad. In the liner sector this happened in the 1980s, and in the case of tanker and dry bulk shipping, sales took place in the late 1990s. When the old generation of former employees from the maritime conglomerates retired, the pool of know-how in Sweden dried up. With no new players and detrimental national policies, career opportunities in Swedish shipping were reduced, and the recruitment of a new generation of maritime managers did not materialize in the 1990s and the 2000s. This propelled Swedish shipping into its second period of decline after 2000.

Our analytical scheme has included four explanatory factors: markets, regulation, strategies and know-how/resources (see Figure 4.4). All these factors played important roles in the development of Swedish shipping from 1960 to 2010, but they also interacted to produce the two declines of the industry. Changes started with structural conditions, when global shipping markets fell after 1973. From here, changes cascaded into

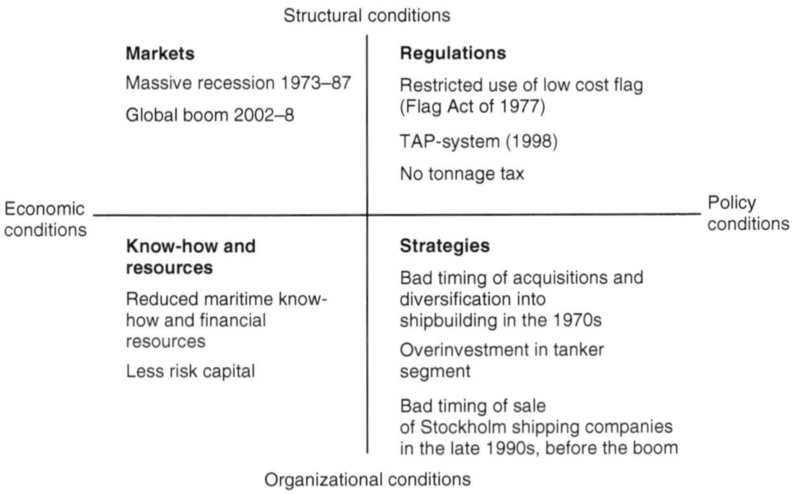

Figure 4.4 Relationships between spatial and economic, structural, policy and organizational conditions, with illustration of explanatory factors

national regulation, and changing Swedish governments took a critical stand towards Swedish shipping, hampering the competitive position of the industry. Declining shipping markets and negative regulation forced Swedish shipping managers to reconsider their corporate strategies. In some cases and in all the main segments (container, oil and dry bulk shipping) the final result was an exit from shipping altogether. Finally, declining markets, disadvantageous regulations and failed strategies caused depletion in the pool of know-how and resources. This did not happen overnight, but with the retirement of the industry's old players after 2000, lack of know-how became a restraining factor for Swedish shipping.

Notes

1. The data on the Swedish fleet and employment in the mid- and late 1950s originate with Rinman (1956, pp. 187–210).
2. For such views see Hermansson (2006), Rinman and Brodefors (1982) and *Svensk Sjöfarts Tidning* 25 (2002), pp. 117–19.
3. Interview with Per Sjöberger, Swedish Shipowners' Association; see also Aspden (1995, pp. 84–5).
4. See, for example, *Svensk Sjöfarts Tidning* 25 (2001), p. 117 and Lennerfors, 2009.
5. Näringsdepartmentet (2001, p. 39). Sjöfartsverket has still only approved the Philippine education system, which means that there are only Filipinos sailing on Swedish-flagged ships under the TAP system. By 2008 around a thousand people were working under the TAP system.
6. See *Svensk Sjöfarts Tidning* 25 (2001), pp. 117–19.
7. For examples of the criticism, see Sveriges Redareförening (2005, pp. 4–10; 2007, p. 6; 2008, pp. 4–6; 2009, pp. 4–5). The lack of a tonnage tax was also a favourite topic in the editorial of *Svensk Sjöfarts Tidning* in the 2000s, see, for example, 13 (2004), p. 11; 19 (2006), p. 11; 1 (2007), p. 11; 5 (2009), p. 11; 8 (2009), p. 11.
8. See *Svensk Sjöfarts Tidning* 10 (2009), pp. 20–1.
9. See, for example, the reports from Rederi AB Transatlantic (1988), pp. 3–4 and (1989), pp. 2–5), as well as Poulsen (2007, 2010), Sjögren et al. (submitted) or Broeze (2002).
10. See, for example, Broström (2008), Møller-Maersk (2009) or *Svensk Sjöfarts Tidning* 11 (2009) pp. 34–6.
11. See Friberg (2007) or *Svensk Sjöfarts Tidning* 7 (2009), pp. 154–77 for a list and brief description of Swedish shipping companies in 2009.
12. Another new player with an old name. The Rederi AB Transatlantic of the 2000s engaged in niche shipping and is not to be confused with liner shipping company Rederi AB Transatlantic from the twentieth century.
13. See Lorange (2009), Wijnolst and Wergeland (2009) and Stopford (2009). On liner shipping, see also Brooks (2000).

14. See Poulsen (2007, 2010) on the important role played by technical organizations in Göteborg shipping companies in the development of new types of container and ro-ro ships during the 1960s. Similarly, Wallenius's technical organization played a crucial role in the development of deep sea ro-ro ships; see Björklund et al. (1984).
15. Swedish newbuilding programmes were published in *Svensk Sjöfarts Tidning*, various years.
16. For the case of Saléninvest, see Sjögren (1999a) and Lennerfors (2009).

5
Finnish Shipping – A Nordic Exception?

Jari Ojala and Yrjö Kaukiainen

The Finnish economy has for centuries been dependent on seaborne transport. In some periods, such as the mid-nineteenth century and the 1970s, Finland also emerged as an important shipping nation in international cross-trades. In the mid-1970s, Finnish tonnage was the sixth largest in the world in per capita terms – just after the Scandinavian countries (Karonen, 1992; Kaukiainen, 2008b). Nevertheless, compared to the other Nordic countries, it was a minor player in international shipping and, subsequently, it has fallen even further behind. In 1987, for example, the freight earnings of Finnish shipping were about one-fifth of those of Norway and about one-third of those of Denmark and Sweden (Ojala and Saarto, 1992, p. 27).

Finland's geographical position at the far end of the Baltic Sea has often been regarded as a disadvantage for shipping. Indeed, it is possible that the modest size of the typical Baltic ships – which probably came about as a result of the limited volume of the market rather than the shallowness of the fairways and ports – was a disadvantage in ocean cross-trades. This cul-de-sac geography was particularly pronounced as long as Finland's next-door neighbour was the Soviet Union, whose economy depended extremely little on foreign trade. This 'backwater' position, however, was not such a bad thing for the country's export and import shipping, because it kept foreign competition at a tolerable level. In this respect, there has been a fundamental change since the collapse of the Soviet system. Particularly, after the turn of the millennium competition in the Baltic Sea trades has greatly intensified.

When speaking of Finnish shipping one should take into account that it is part of a wider maritime cluster that includes different kinds of maritime activities, from shipping and logistics to shipbuilding and shipping services. In this cluster, shipping itself is only one element, but an important one. As in Sweden, the shipbuilding industry was relatively important. However, unlike in Sweden, it has remained so for Finland. In the early 2000s, Finland was still among the ten largest shipbuilding countries in the world. The whole cluster's share of Finnish total exports was around 12 per cent, and shipyards and subcontracting firms were notable employers – although the yards have passed into foreign ownership (Uola, 2001; Pylkkänen et al., 2002; Viitanen et al., 2003; Karvonen et al., 2008). However, unlike in the other Nordic countries, there have not been any deep cross-ownership structures between shipbuilding and shipping industries. This article will therefore not analyse the entire Finnish maritime cluster.

Another notable feature of the structure of Finnish shipping has been its high share of passenger trades, in particular after the introduction of passenger-car ferries around the turn of the 1950s and 1960s. In actual tonnage, the Finnish passenger vessels were not exceptional compared with Denmark and Sweden. However, given the much smaller total tonnage, their relative impact was important. In particular, cargo or ro-ro (roll-on roll-off) ferries have been important since the 1970s, which can be seen in the relatively high global share of Finnish tonnage in this particular niche (see also Chapter 6; Kaukiainen, 2009, 2010)

Though there are some similarities between the development of Finnish shipping and that of the other Nordic countries, there are also notable differences. Above all, shipping did not gain the same kind of significance in Finland's post-war economy and society as it did in the other Nordic countries. Furthermore, Finland's total tonnage was in absolute terms significantly smaller than, for example, that of Denmark and Norway. In the Finnish case, the initially limited position has subsequently decreased even further. Thus, the key question in this article is why Finland seems to present a rather different case in shipping when compared to the Scandinavian countries.

The article will first present an overview of the development of Finnish tonnage. This will be followed by an analysis of shipping in Finland's economy and politics and a brief discussion of the strategies of Finnish shipping companies followed by concluding remarks. The article is primarily based on previous literature, especially on Kaukiainen (2008b, 2010) if not otherwise noted.

Finnish merchant tonnage 1960–2010

General development

The post-war growth of Finland's economy was also experienced in shipping. Tonnage grew rapidly, surpassing pre-war levels in 1953, reaching one million tons in 1966 and two million by 1975. Finnish-flagged tonnage peaked in 1981, at some 2.5 million tons (see Table 5.1 and Figure 5.2 below). From 1950 to 1980 the average annual growth rate of Finnish shipping was around 5 per cent – that is, somewhat higher than the average for the OECD countries. Although the capital, Helsinki, remained the most important home port for shipping, much faster growth was recorded in the autonomous province of the Åland Islands, which increased its share of Finnish total gross tonnage from 15 per cent in 1950 to 26 per cent in 1980 and 32 per cent by 2009. Åland's share has grown particularly high in passenger tonnage, representing 62 per cent of the Finnish fleet of such vessels in 2009 (Sundberg, 1998; Karlsson, 2007; Kaukiainen, 2008b, pp. 420–4; Merenkulku.fi, 2010).

To a large degree the rapid growth of the 1960s and early 1970s was based on the fact that shipping was able to attract capital from outside its traditional networks. Forest industry firms, in particular, engaged in the shipping business to secure – and optimize – their own export transports. The most notable example was Enso-Gutzeit, which was the founder and also the biggest shareholder of the Finnlines company. However, since shipping was found to offer reasonably good rates of return, the forestry industry firms – and even a number of other industrial firms – increased their interests. This led them towards the international

Table 5.1 Finnish-owned tonnage, 1960–2005 (1,000 grt/gt)

	Finnish flag	Other flags	Total	Other flags, %
1960	800	–	800	–
1965	991	–	991	–
1970	1,371	–	1,371	–
1975	2,048	–	2,048	–
1980	2,350	–	2,350	–
1985	1,650	400	2,050	20
1990	1,090	1,500	2,590	58
1995	1,580	1,770	3,350	53
2000	1,670	1,080	2,750	39
2005	1,580	1,030	2,610	39
2008	1,663	1,160	2,823	41

Source: Based on data from Kaukiainen (2008: 422 and 495) and Finnish Official Statistics.

cross-trades and, subsequently, even to investments in passenger tonnage (Kaukiainen, 1991, 1993, 2008b, p. 423; Karonen, 1992).

On the other hand, this period of growth was also a time of a fairly rapid transformation. Finnish shipping – indeed the whole Finnish economy – developed from low cost to high cost. For centuries Finnish shipping companies had been competitive in international markets as a result of low-cost strategies, which were based on both low capital costs – either by using second-hand vessels or new craft built inexpensively in domestic low-cost shipyards – and low labour costs. A sharp turning point was reached at the end of 1945, when the Finnish Seamen's Union compelled the employers to sign a labour agreement for foreign-going tonnage. This agreement was basically similar to that in Sweden, and it introduced the change from the two-watch system to the three-watch system. Subsequently, weekly working hours were further reduced. Finally, in 1980 – six years after the Swedes – Finnish seamen managed to conclude the 'most expensive labour agreement of all time', which increased their time off so much that shipping companies had to hire two alternating crews for individual vessels (Soukola, 2003).[1]

Shipping companies tried to fight these rising manning costs by building increasingly modern labour-saving ships. Thus, not only labour costs but also capital costs were increasing. To some extent, this strategy was successful. It was also supported by the fact that many industrial countries did not yet allow free movement of capital, that is, flagging-out of ships to the so-called 'convenience' registers. The prospects, however, turned gloomier during the 1970s when the oil crises triggered a slump in the tanker trades. This crisis then spread to other shipping sectors (Ojala, 2010).

The shipping crisis was global, caused by an imbalance between supply and demand. Globally, the supply of tonnage exceeded demand by about 15 per cent in the late 1970s, and in the tanker market there was even more excess capacity. As a remedy, Western shipowners tried to cut their costs by flagging out tankers and other bulk tonnage to convenience registers or other low-cost countries. The OECD countries owned 65 per cent of world tonnage in the 1970s and 45 per cent in the late 1980s; Great Britain, the Netherlands – and all the Nordic countries – were particularly hard hit (Laine, 1986, pp. 4–6; Forsskåhl, 1986, p. 13; Kaukiainen, 2008b, p. 487).

During the crises Finnish-flagged tonnage fell from 2.5 million tons in 1981 by one million grt., or 40 per cent, over a period of only six years. This, in turn, diminished the income from shipping: the freight earnings of ships registered in Finland fell by 24 per cent from

1984 to 1988. Earnings from cargo tonnage fell by about 42 per cent, though the passenger fleet still provided decent incomes. Cross-trade earnings fell during the same period to one fourth, as flagging out was especially important for tonnage engaged in cross-trades (Kurki, 1990).

However – as can be seen in Table 5.1 and Figure 5.2 – the volume of Finnish-owned tonnage did not diminish as dramatically because the tonnage of the ships flagged out to low-cost registers was greater than the tonnage that was sold. For example, in 1990 a total of 1.5 million grt. of Finnish-owned ships were sailing under various Flags of Convenience (FoCs), so the total capacity owned by Finnish shipping companies was about the same as in 1981. In the 1990s a kind of recovery took place. Both the tonnage flying the Finnish flag and Finnish-owned tonnage under foreign flags increased; the total Finnish-owned tonnage actually peaked around 1995 (Kaukiainen, 2008b, p. 500).

The sudden drop in the tonnage flying foreign flags between 1995 and 2000 (Table 5.1) is explained by the bankruptcy of the Ålandia Tanker Company, whose ships were registered in the Bahamas (Kaukiainen, 2008b, p. 500). Since then the tonnage flying foreign flags has not grown, but an increasing proportion of it has been registered in other EU countries. In early 2000 that proportion was around 55 per cent, of which Sweden's share was more than half. This development suggests that Finnish companies have founded subsidiaries in West European countries that have 'better' tonnage taxation laws or more liberal manning regulations· As far as passenger-car ferries were concerned, Sweden was attractive because its manning regulations have been slightly more liberal. On the other hand, because of the Finnish–Swedish agreement of pilotage, which allows the use of onboard officers as so-called 'lines' pilots instead of regular pilots, flagging out to other countries would have been less attractive (Kaukiainen, 2008b, p. 502).

The percentage of ships flagged out usually reflects the structure of the fleet in high-cost countries; relatively inexpensive tonnage, such as tankers and bulk carriers, were generally transferred to cheaper registers, while passenger ships and more sophisticated cargo carriers remained. Thus, in the 1980s Norway flagged out 50 to 60 per cent of its tonnage, and in Sweden the share was around 40 per cent. In Finland the corresponding figure exceeded 50 per cent, mainly because the Åland Islands were the leader even in this respect: owners flagged out some 70 per cent of their tonnage while the share in mainland Finland was around 50 per cent (Kaukiainen, 2008b, p. 495; Laine, 1986, pp. 9–11).

Export-led growth

The development of the Finnish fleet has traditionally been closely linked with the country's own export trades, but during the post-war period it has increasingly been linked to imports as well. As can be seen in Figure 5.1, the share of domestic ships in the export trades has increased substantially since the mid-1950s. This increase was partly caused by a conscious strategy adopted by the major export industries – especially the forest industries – and the state. As Finland had lost a large share of its shipping volume during the war – and immediately after it as war reparations to the Soviet Union – there was an urgent need to build up capacity. This was primarily done by purchasing second-hand vessels from abroad. The volume of export shipping also increased at the same time. However, most of the exports going to the Soviet Union were carried by rail (Andersson, 2005; Eliasson, 2005; Malmberg and Stampehl, 2007).

Traditionally, Finnish imports did not demand as much cargo space as exports. However, in the 1950s and 1960s the gap narrowed to the point where the volume of imports actually exceeded that of exports. Since the new imbalance was mainly caused by increasing oil imports, and tankers could not be used for carrying Finnish export goods, it did not solve the old structural problem.

The share of domestic tonnage in the export trades was around 35 per cent in the 1950s, around 51 per cent during the 1960s, peaked around 60 per cent at the turn of the 1970s and 1980s, thereafter diminished to 39 per cent in the 1990s, and to 20 per cent in the first years of

Figure 5.1 Share of domestic (Finnish-flag) tonnage used in Finland's seaborne import and export trade, five-year averages, 1956–2005 (%)

Note: The chart is based on data from Kaukiainen (2008a, pp. 444 and 529).

the new millennium (see Figure 5.1). In terms of import trades there was not such a dramatic decline in the share of domestic vessels carrying goods: in 2005 around 43 per cent of the volume of imported goods was carried on domestic ships. In imports, however, the oil tankers of the state-owned oil company Neste explain this share (Kuisma, 1997). According to government recommendations, the export share of domestic tonnage should have been around 40 and of imports 50 per cent – these recommendations were justified by the need for security of supply (Kurki, 1990). One outcome of the flagging-out of tonnage from the early 1980s onwards was that the tonnage under the Finnish flag was increasingly used in the Finnish export and import trades only, while tonnage that had been transferred to foreign flags was deployed for international cross-trades. In fact, the latter ships could not even come to Finnish ports, as they would have been blockaded by the labour unions (Soukola, 2003; Kaukiainen, 2008b, p. 469).

The shares of Finnish-flagged tonnage in the foreign trade shipments do not, however, reveal the whole picture. Since the 1980s, Finnish liner companies have operated with a substantial amount of tonnage chartered from foreign companies (some of these vessels in fact belonged to their foreign subsidiaries). In the 1990s and continuing into the early 2000s, such tonnage amounted to about one million tons, equivalent to around 60 per cent of Finnish-flagged shipping. Thus, it is clear that Finnish shipping companies have controlled a higher proportion of export and import transports than the official figures suggest (Karvonen et al., 2008, pp. 71–2).

Although Finnish shipping has for centuries been closely linked with the country's own export and import trades, carrying freight between other countries has also been a common, or at least a secondary, occupation. As long as both labour and capital costs were low, the ships could quite easily be deployed in international cross-trades. For example, in the 1930s some 35 per cent of total shipping income was earned in such business. Interestingly, cross-trades regained their importance after the Second World War, in spite of the ongoing transition of Finnish shipping to a high-cost mode. Between 1965 and 1980, the share of cross-trades amounted to about 30 per cent of all Finnish shipping income, and no less that 40 per cent of tonnage was mainly engaged in shipping between foreign ports.[2] However, during the shipping crisis, these shares dropped abruptly, as cross-trade tonnage was typically flagged out.

Since 1995 foreign-flagged cross-trade tonnage has actually diminished: now there is a fleet of only eight 100,000-ton tankers. In consequence, the Finnish shipping sector – both Finnish-owned as well as Finnish-operated ships – has concentrated almost exclusively on short-sea traffic on the Baltic and North Seas. The only exceptions from this pattern are a ro-ro line to North Spain (Finnlines), a container feeder connection between West Europe and the Eastern Mediterranean (Containerships Ltd and its Turkish daughter company, Contaz), and a long-term contract for oil transports from the North Sea area to Greenland (Neste Shipping). Recently, the short-sea specialization has been further strengthened by the growth of Russian seaborne trade since the turn of the millennium. Accordingly, the Baltic trade has witnessed a constant growth, offering possibilities not only to Finnish shipping companies but to the logistics industry as a whole (Viitanen et al., 2003; Karvonen et al., 2008). Such prospects also explain why some Finnish shipping companies have recently been acquired by foreign firms.

Structural changes

Passenger vessels' share of Finnish capacity increased throughout the first part of the period peaking in the early 1990s. The share of tankers peaked in the 1970s and it has declined ever since. The most dramatic decline, however, occurred in the fleet of dry cargo vessels. In the early 1960s, such vessels constituted two-thirds of the capacity, a share that had declined to around one-third of the tonnage by the year 2008. However, the classification of 'dry cargo' has been changed in the statistics, so these figures are not fully comparable. Furthermore, if the tonnage registered abroad were included in these figures, the shares of tankers and dry cargo vessels would be somewhat higher in the 1990 and 2000 figures. Nevertheless, even some passenger vessels were flagged out.

Until 1980 the structure of Finnish tonnage did not differ hugely from that of the international fleet (Tables 5.2 and 5.3). In both 1970 and 1980, Finland's tanker tonnage represented a greater proportion of the total than was the case internationally, and the bulk fleet remained relatively small, but the overall picture did not show much difference. As both tankers and dry bulk vessels were flagged out in the 1980s, with the exception of the tanker fleet of the national oil company Neste, their relative shares naturally decreased. Thus, in 2001 tankers constituted 41 per cent of world tonnage, but just 21 per cent of the Finnish-flagged fleet. Passenger ships showed the greatest difference when compared with the Nordic or world fleets: globally their share in 2001 was only 0.7 per cent, while in the Finnish tonnage such ships made up no less than 30 per cent. Furthermore, Finland's geographical position imposes some special demands: 50 per cent of Finnish ships were in the highest

Table 5.2 Share of different ship types in the Finnish fleet, based on tonnage, 1960–2008 (per cent)

	1960	1970	1980	1990	2000	2008
Passenger vessels	4	8	10	39	31	36
Tankers	30	51	48	27	23	24
Other vessels	66	41	42	34	46	40
All vessels	100	100	100	100	100	100

Table 5.3 Share of different ship types in the Finnish fleet, based on the number of ships, 1960–2008 (per cent)

	1960	1970	1980	1990	2000	2008
Passenger vessels	14	18	38	59	60	64
Tankers	5	11	10	8	6	4
Other vessels	80	71	52	32	34	32
All vessels	100	100	100	100	100	100

Note: Tables 5.2 and 5.3 are based on the Finnish Official Statistics. Please note that only tonnage registered in Finland is included in these figures.

ice class (IA Super) and 30 per cent in the second highest class (IA) in 2001 (Viitanen et al., 2003; Karvonen et al., 2008).

Like the shipping companies of other Nordic countries, Finnish companies also invested heavily in tankers, especially from the mid-1960s onwards. When first the oil crises and then the shipping crises hit, a number of companies had just ordered new tanker tonnage. The largest tankers in the Finnish fleet were only used in international cross-trades, simply because the draught of these vessels was too great to pass the Danish channels. The first Finnish-owned tankers that could not sail to the Baltic with full cargo were launched during the turn of the 1960s and 1970s. The shipping companies Neste and Sally were particularly eager to acquire these supertankers during the 1970s (Kaukiainen, 2008b, p. 431). Tankers were also the first to be flagged out during the shipping crises.

The large share of passenger ships has been a Finnish speciality. In 2001, for example, the Finnish Silja Line was the tenth-largest ferry operator in the world and Viking Line the thirteenth-largest. However, in terms of bed capacity, Silja was the second largest and Viking the third-largest in the same year. The Finnish shipbuilding industry has also specialized in the construction of passenger ferries and cruisers: Finland was the third-largest exporter of passenger vessels in the world in 2000, with an export value of US $1 billion (Viitanen et al., 2003, pp. 113 and 126).[3] The ferries owned by Finnish companies were first used between Finland and Sweden to carry goods, people, and cars. The number of passengers onboard these ferries rose from some six million annually in the early 1980s to about ten million by the early 1990s (Karvonen et al., 2008, p. 75). Some Finnish companies also invested in passenger ships in other geographic regions. Regular lines were opened between Finland and Germany, and some ships were even used in the English Channel. These attempts mainly failed; the ferry lines between Finland and Sweden remained, though the end of duty-free shopping after Finnish entry into the European Union closed down a number of lines, especially in Northern Finland. However, because of special EU permission, duty-free sales remained on Stockholm lines if ships stopped in the Åland Islands. Furthermore, regular ferry lines were opened between Finland and Estonia even during the Soviet period – this regular traffic was dominated by Soviet ships (in practice by Estonians). After Estonian independence, these shipping routes proved to be the most popular, and Finnish capital was also involved in this business. The number of passengers on these routes rose from one million annually in the early 1990s to an annual level of five to six million at the turn of the millennium. At the same time, the number of passengers on Finnish–Swedish lines decreased to eight million. Tax-free sales were for decades among the driving forces behind the passenger shipping between Finland and Sweden. As such sales on these routes ceased because of EU legislation – with the exception of ferries visiting Åland Islands – the routes between Finland and Estonia provided compensation (Andersson, 2005; Eliasson, 2005; Malmberg and Stampehl, 2007; Karvonen et al., 2008).

Finnish shipping has lagged behind its Scandinavian neighbours in terms of container movements. In 1975, for example, a total of around 60,000 (TEU) containers were loaded and discharged in Finland. In the same year the figure for Sweden was over 200,000 and for Denmark about the same; this level was exceeded in Finland only in the late 1980s (Kaukiainen, 2008b, p. 436, 2010, p. 192; Karvonen et al., 2008, p. 160). However, Finnish companies had invested in liner ships that could also carry containers as early as in the late 1960s (Karonen, 1992). Nevertheless, in Finland the container business did not begin to grow rapidly until the early 1990s. In 2004 Finnish ports, with about 1.3 million TEU, were already recording slightly more container lifts than Swedish ports, with 0.9 million, and Danish, with around 1.0 million (Kaukiainen, 2010).

The reason that containers were adopted quite slowly in Finnish shipping was related to the fact that containers did not suit Finnish export goods, such as paper rolls and sawn wood, particularly well. Finnish shipping companies, therefore, favoured other technologies, most notably ro-ro ships. Moreover, Finnish harbours had been developed to support ro-ro rather than container traffic (Teräs, 2002; Kaukiainen, 2008b, p. 436). In the Baltic, cargo ferries offered good returns on invested capital, so these ships were favoured by Finnish shipowners. The first ships with ro-ro technology were ordered by a Finnish company in the late 1960s. The technology made a rapid breakthrough as it was particularly well suited to the shipment of forest industry exports. Therefore, by 1973 there were already 15 ro-ro ships in the Finnish fleet (Kaukiainen, 2008b, p. 433; Karonen, 1992).

The post-war era also witnessed other structural changes in Finnish shipping. Specifically, a low-cost country, which had expanded on the basis of second-hand vessels, developed into a high-cost country with up-to-date craft. While in the 1950s over 80 per cent of the vessels in the Finnish fleet were over 20 years old, this share diminished to one-third in the 1960s and to 8.5 per cent in 1980. At the same time, the average ship size almost trebled from 1220 to 6300 grt (Kaukiainen, 2008b, p. 426). During this period, for the first time even the northernmost ports of the country were kept open by icebreakers throughout the winter. This increased winter traffic as a proportion of total traffic from 18 per cent in the 1930s to around 40 per cent in the 1970s (Kaukiainen, 1993). The first oil refinery was opened in Finland in the 1950s, which in turn led to the import of crude oil shipments and tanker business.

Labour vs capital costs in shipping: what caused the crises?

The shipping crises of the 1970s and 1980s were an international phenomenon. Nevertheless, the effects of the crises were not the same everywhere. There were notable differences even between the Nordic countries. Denmark, for example, suffered less than Norway and Sweden (see also Kaukiainen, 2008b, p. 478).

In Finland it was debated whether these crises had escalated on account of domestic, endogenous, factors. The most important of these were increased labour and capital costs. The Labour Union stressed that the crisis had been made more severe because of increased capital costs, caused by managerial failure and poorly timed investments. Shipowners, in contrast, argued that increased domestic labour costs were exacerbating the crisis, especially as a result of the negotiations at the end of the 1970s. Both parties, however, agreed that external influences in the international markets were the key determinants in the crisis. Both labour and capital costs were already relatively high in Finland when the crises hit. Furthermore, state subventions to the Finnish shipping industries were not as substantial as in many other countries (Forsskåhl, 1986; Vainio, 1986).

Seamen's wages rose at about the same pace as those in manufacturing industries during the period. This was because demands for time off meant that more men were needed to fill each vacancy on board. This did not mean that the number of men on board at any given time increased: in fact, this number decreased, but the number of men on the wages bill went up. Hence, labour costs in Finnish shipping were rising throughout the 1970s. By the early 1980s Finland was one of the most expensive countries: manning costs were equal to those in Sweden, but were, for example, double those of Greece and three times those of Liberia. Even in Norway and in Britain the costs were considerably lower. Only two major shipping nations, the United States and Japan, had higher costs than Finland. The change from being a low- to a high-cost country had happened within a few decades. Indeed, in the 1930s labour costs in Greece had been higher than those in Finland. According to Kaukiainen (2008b, pp. 475–569), the costs of Finnish shipping were higher than those of other Nordic countries in the early 2000s.

The proportion of new vessels in the fleet can be used as an indirect measure of the level of investment in new capacity. In the Finnish merchant fleet this increased from the mid-1950s to the mid-1970s, though perhaps not dramatically. One should, however, bear in mind that, at the same time, the average size of new ships increased, which also led to cost increases in absolute terms per ship. Nevertheless, the cost per ton might be expected to decrease as the average tonnage increases. The proportion of vessels over 20 years old diminished during the same period from 76 per cent to 39 per cent. However, the proportion of old vessels increased again to 60 per cent by 1987, as new ships, in particular, were flagged out to low-cost countries. The new ships were also technically more advanced than the old ones, but new technologies practically always mean increased costs. This can be observed especially with the investments in the high-cost passenger vessels that actually limited companies' opportunities to invest in other types of vessels – simply because of lack of capital. Operating new vessels could also be more profitable, as some costs were decreasing. For example, fuel costs decreased between 1961 and 1973 from 10 per cent to 6 per cent of overall costs, and loading costs from 15 per cent to 12 per cent. At the same time, however, the cost of manning as a proportion of total costs rose from 20 per cent to 25 per cent. The increased labour costs were caused not only by higher salaries, but also, as already mentioned, by labour agreements, which increased overall manning ratios by requiring, in practice, two alternating crews. Indeed, labour regulations also increased capital costs. In 1948, new regulations had ordered two-man cabins on board but by 1976 every seaman had the right to his or her own cabin (Kaukiainen 2008b, pp. 471 and 526).

There were notable differences in capital and labour costs for different ship types. When the shipping crisis hit, tankers represented the largest proportion of Finnish merchant fleet (Tables 5.2 and 5.3). Though the capital cost per ton in tankers was reasonably low in comparison with other ship types, the total capital costs were still significant. The reason that the shipping companies chose to invest in tankers was obvious: this trade was growing fast and offered lucrative rates of return – until the first oil crisis transformed the market in the mid-1970s. During this period of expansion, the oil transport business went through a process of rapid and profound restructuring and specialization. Previously, tankers had usually been either owned or chartered by oil companies. Around the same time, Japanese and European demand for crude oil matured, so the days of continuous growth were over. Quite naturally, the oil crises of the 1970s finally triggered this inevitable development and led to pressures for developing more energy-efficient technologies as well as to finding substitutes for oil (Lennerfors, 2009; Stopford, 2009, pp. 435–7).

As the number of crew on board per ton was low in large tankers, one can argue that shipping companies deliberately emphasized capital rather than labour costs (Table 5.4). However, what happened after the crisis does not lend support to this line of thought. As the proportion of passenger vessels, measured by both number and tonnage, increased, so did manning costs, since the number of personnel per ton is much higher for passenger vessels. Finnish passenger ferries are, however, hardly comparable to deep-sea tonnage in terms of labour costs. First, most of their personnel are different from those on the cross-traders, as all kinds of service personnel are included: the ferries are more like hotels than like other types of ship. Second, as these ferries were primarily used in trade between Finland and Sweden, it should be remembered that this business was regulated and practically impossible to enter for foreign tonnage. Thus, the shipping crises did not affect these trades as

Table 5.4 Different ship types' share of total labour costs, per cent

	1972	1980	1990
Passenger vessels	35	35	71
Tankers	24	16	12
Other vessels	42	48	17
All vessels	100	100	100

Note: Based on data from The Seafarers' Pension Fund (Merimieseläkekassa). Flagged-out tonnage and foreign ships hiring Finnish sailors are not included in the figures. Labour force from continental Finland and Åland Island are summarized. Total labour costs include salaries and other costs induced for hiring labour. The Seafarers' Pension Fund (MEK) kindly offered the raw data for the authors to analyse. The fund is an authorized pension provider that handles statutory earnings-related pension provision for seafarers, awarding and paying seafarers earnings-related pensions under the Seafarers' Pensions Act (MEL). For more information see www.seafarerspensionfund.fi

dramatically as other lines of shipping businesses – which is the major reason for the heavy investments in passenger shipping in Finland.

One could even argue that as newly built passenger vessels are included, the capital costs were rising. As can be detected from Table 5.4, passenger vessels' share of total labour rose from one-third to more than two-thirds. The tankers' share of the costs declined steadily, while the share of dry cargo vessels was reduced only after 1980.[4] In 1990 the flagged-out tonnage represented some 5 per cent of total labour costs, while its share of tonnage was 58 per cent. Thus, one can argue that the cost savings were achieved by flagging out tonnage.

Shipping in the Finnish economy and Finnish politics

Falling freight, growing economy

Sea transport is closely linked to developments and fluctuations in the international economy and trade. The growth of production, whether as a result of industrialization, globalization or other factors, usually increases the need for the transport of raw materials, together with semi-finished and consumer products. In this type of transport, ships have throughout history been the most efficient way to carry products over long distances as well as short runs. The linkages between economic growth and shipping are, therefore, among the classic discussions in economic history, analysing, for example, whether freight rates, shipping productivity development, or tonnage development can be used as proxies to study more general economic growth (North, 1958, 1966; Hausman, 1987; Harley, 1988; Tenold and Nordvik, 1996; Kaukiainen, 2009; Stopford, 2009).

The decline of freight rates has been a significant feature of the past 200 years. In the late eighteenth century freights from the Baltic could easily double the price of goods carried. By the mid-nineteenth century the freight share of some products – such as timber – had already diminished to 10 per cent, which was still a quite typical freight share in the early 1970s. During the last decades of the twentieth century and early years of the third millennium, this freight share has diminished further to some 3 to 3.5 per cent of the value of the products. Freight rates have declined to one-sixth over a period of 150 years. At the same time, the total volume of shipping has increased significantly: in the early twenty-first century it was one hundred times greater than in the mid-nineteenth century (Kaukiainen, 2008b, 2009). This development has affected not only shipping, but the global economy as a whole. That is, the global economy and multinational corporations can gain competitive advantages from the reduced costs of shipping and transport.

For countries dependent upon the global economy but located far away from major markets and population centres, falling transport costs are particularly important. Finland is a typical case. The Finnish economy witnessed a rapid, export-led growth during the post-war period; the average annual growth in gross domestic product (GDP) was 4.1 per cent from 1946 to 1969 and 3.3 per cent from 1970 to 1989. The corresponding figures in Sweden, for example, were 3.3 and 1.9 per cent respectively, albeit from a higher initial level. GDP growth was reduced from the early 1990s falling to some 1.4 per cent for the period 1990 to 2003 (Maddison, 2001; Hjerppe and Jalava, 2006). The Finnish economy tripled in size from the 1940s to the 1970s and grew some 50 per cent during the 1970s. The fact that this growth was highly related to the export trades was reflected in the demand for cargo space. The bulk of Finnish foreign trade has always been carried in ships. In 2001, for example, 91 per cent of exports and 68 per cent of imports were seaborne (Viitanen et al., 2003; Kaukiainen, 2008b, p. 412).

As Figure 5.2 shows, the tonnage growth of Finnish shipping clearly exceeded the growth of total GDP during the 1970s. Indeed, this was a booming period for Finnish shipping, a fact that was related not only

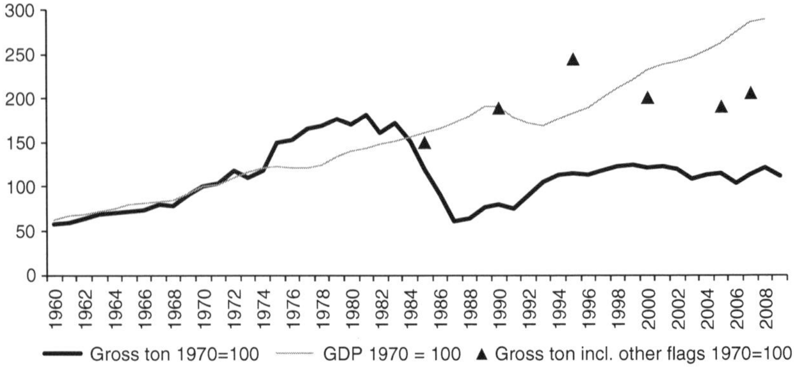

Figure 5.2 Tonnage and GDP indices, Finland, 1960–2009 (1970=100)

Note: The figure has been constructed on the basis of the following sources: Finnish Official Statistics; Kaukiainen (2008); Maddison (2001) and Maddison datasets at http://www.ggdc.net/maddison/

to the increase in exports and imports, but also to the rising cross-trade share. This share was around 30 per cent at the time, recovering to pre-war levels for the first time. Though the tonnage expansion was particularly strong in the 1960s and 1970s, only in the latter decade did it exceed growth in overall GDP (Kaukiainen, 2008b, p. 424). Before this period, throughout the 1960s, tonnage growth and GDP growth were strongly correlated.

The effects of the great shipping crises can clearly be seen in Figure 5.2, which shows a drop in tonnage in the early 1980s. This drop, however, may not be as dramatic as it seems. The tonnage that had been flagged out was still owned by Finnish shipowners, but does not show up in statistics (see also Table 5.1). Indeed, when the flagged-out tonnage is included, one can clearly see from Figure 5.2 that tonnage growth was more rapid than GDP growth, even during the recession years of the early 1990s. It was not until the turn of the millennium that Finland's rapid economic growth exceeded the growth in tonnage.

In the period from 1951 to 2008 tonnage growth outperformed GDP growth in 25 years out of 58 – even if the vessels that were flagged out are excluded. Indeed, even after the great shipping crises, from 1988 onwards tonnage growth outperformed GDP growth in nine years out of 21. This latter period, though, is very diverse. It includes the most severe economic downturn in Finnish history since the war, but also the period of relatively high GDP growth rates around the turn of the millennium.

The growth of the Finnish economy has been dependent on the export trade throughout the post-war era. In the late 1940s foreign trade was around 15 per cent of GDP. By the late 1970s, this share had increased to 25 per cent. The volume of Finnish exports in 1994 was 16 times larger than in 1948, and the volume of imports 11 times larger (Pihkala, 2007). This growth was, in particular, a result of the growth in export of the forest industries, which made up some 70 to 80 per cent of the value of Finnish exports at the peak (Kuisma, 2009; Jensen-Eriksen, 2007). However, other lines of business were also important in exports, most notably in the metal industries and, from the 1980s, electronic equipment. Though the Soviet Union, and lately Russia, played an important role in Finnish exports, throughout the post-war period some 80 to 90 per cent of Finnish exports still went to Western markets (Hjerppe, 1989, p. 159). The transport of goods to these Western markets was dependent on seaborne trade, so shipping has played a particularly important role in the economic development of the country.

The direct share of shipping in Finnish GDP was around 1.5 to 1.6 per cent in the 1950s and 1960s, but had diminished to around 0.5 per cent by the beginning of the new millennium (Ojala and Saarto, 1992; Kaukiainen, 2008b, p. 13). Shipping was thus a marginal activity in comparison to the Finnish economy as a whole. There were, however, significant variations between the different parts of the country. In the autonomous Åland Islands, the shipping industries in the early third millennium still constituted around one-third of GDP and provided 15 per cent of employment (Karlsson, 2007, p. 15).

Institutional environment

Like the other Nordic countries, Finland is a small open economy, which is dependent upon foreign trade (Fellman, 2008). The smallness and openness of the country creates disadvantages of scale – especially as the export share of GDP has traditionally been rather high. To compensate for these disadvantages, efficient domestic – political – institutions are needed (Mokyr, 2006). In the Finnish case, corporatist policies and consensus on the needs of the main export industries have been dominant features of the post-war era (Karlsson, 2007). Finnish shipping has, therefore, never gained an important position in political decision-making, as it has, for example, in Norway. Instead, shipping has been seen as either a supporting line of business for the major export industries or a part of the larger maritime cluster, stressing especially shipbuilding industries. Here we can see clear similarities to the situation in

Sweden and to some extent in Norway, especially during the 1970s and 1980s (Kurki, 1990).

As far as government policy was concerned, taxation was the most commonly used to provide a better operational environment for Finnish shipping. Right after the war and until 1991, shipowners were allowed extra-large write-offs from their net results, provided that such deductions were reinvested in shipping (Kaukiainen and Leino-Kaukiainen, 1992, p. 191). The actual details of tax reliefs varied a little over time: in 1977, for example, an additional three-year allowance was granted for new craft purchased from Finland. This was an arrangement intended to support the operations of Finnish shipbuilding industry, and there were government guarantees for new building loans for the shipping companies (Lastikka, 1983, pp. 224–44). However, when the so-called parallel register of foreign-trading Finnish tonnage was founded, the earlier write-off support was removed. This, in fact, immediately reduced shipping investments and produced the distinct turn in the development of Finnish-owned tonnage that can be seen in Figure 5.2.

Another significant feature of the position of shipping in Finnish domestic (economic) policies is the relative weakness of the bargaining power of the shipowners. This, in turn, is related to the fact that the shipowners were far from being a united group during the post-war era. As Lastikka (1983, p. 26) states, the Finnish Shipowners' Association, for example, was until the end of the 1970s a passive and reactive player rather than one that bargained proactively. The interests of the major forest industry companies, in their roles as shipowners, lay primarily in securing the shipments of export industries rather than in shipping as such. In time, import industries also became engaged in shipping, most notably the oil company Neste, which became an important player through its tanker ownership. Neste was a state-owned company, which created even more mixed interests (Kuisma, 1997). The other shipping companies were also quite diversified, including those operating in the autonomous Åland Islands. These Åland-based shipowners had their own regional interests and their own association, though they maintained close co-operation with the Finnish Shipowners' Association (Kurki, 2003; Karlsson, 2007, pp. 74–5). The Finnish Shipowners' Association was an active player, but especially in the 1970s most of its time was consumed by labour market policy issues (Lastikka, 1983). Even in the early third millennium the diverse interests of the industry were noted as an obstacle to the further development of Finnish shipping (Vainio and Kajander, 2002).

The possibilities for Finnish shipping were, nevertheless, widely discussed in different government bodies from the late 1960s onwards, together with the shipowners and labour unions. After the shipping crises a special committee was set up to discuss the challenges of shipping, including members from all stakeholders. The work of this special committee was pivotal in the recession years in the early 1990s, as its suggestions were taken seriously and were put into effect – perhaps due to the fact that one of the committee members, Esko Aho, was elected as Prime Minister of Finland in the early 1990s (Kurki, 1990).

One of the issues discussed in this committee was double and open registries of the kind that had already been introduced in Norway and in Denmark. The Finnish authorities, however, did not see the use of open registries as a solution for the challenges of Finnish shipping around the turn of the 1980s and 1990s, but instead proposed to give direct subsidies to the shipping companies. The setting up of an open registry was seen as a long-term objective for Finnish shipping. The economic recession, however, changed the situation dramatically. In 1991, therefore, a law on a parallel registry of foreign-going tonnage was given. This law was eagerly opposed by the Seamen's Union and the outcome was a compromise when compared to similar laws in many other countries. The Finnish registry was not as open as Norway's, but more like that adopted in Sweden around the same time: only Finnish ships engaged in foreign traffic could be entered in this new registry. In addition, it was required that at least half of the seamen on board should be Finnish nationals (from 2003, EU/EFTA nationals) if the ship was sailing to or from Finland. In cross-trades between third countries, there were no restrictions on nationality. The law was passed after tripartite negotiations between the ministerial cabinet and the shipowners' and seamen's associations. Part of the deal was an overall diminishing of labour costs – basically, reducing wages – and compensation from the state in the taxation of seamen. By 2000, 63 per cent of the Finnish-flag tonnage was in this double registry (Wasström, 2000; Soukola, 2003, pp. 355–7).

Nevertheless, the role played by the open registry in the growth of Finnish tonnage was rather modest, though some of the out-flagged Finnish tonnage did indeed return. At the same time, the passenger and ro-ro fleets appeared to grow faster than they actually did, merely because of new (1969) international measurement regulations which increased the gross tonnage of passenger ships by 30 to 50 per cent and ro-ros by more than 100 per cent. This particularly affected the ship types that were most common in Finland at the time (Kaukiainen, 2008b, pp. 498–500).

Plans that were suggested in a committee report back in the late 1980s and in other official documents reveal rather interestingly the motives of the authorities and other actors in promoting shipping in Finland (Kurki, 1990). These motives are in line with policies in a number of other countries, with the exception, perhaps, of traditional shipping countries like Norway and Denmark (see, e.g. Ojala and Saarto, 1992). Interestingly, the same motives were more or less repeated in a renewed maritime strategy for Finland in 2003 (Vainio and Kajander, 2002, 2003).

First, the key aim, as noted earlier, of Finnish government policies throughout the post-war period was to secure the domestic import and export trades, thus, in turn, securing the interests of the export and import industries. The possibilities offered by cross-trading between third countries as a source of income for Finnish shipping and economy have usually been underestimated in government reports (Kurki, 1990; Ojala and Saarto, 1992).

Second, the authorities emphasized the special characteristics of Finnish shipping: the winter conditions and the shallow waters of the Finnish archipelago. Because of these, it was thought necessary to secure a healthy proportion of shipping in domestic hands, thus, ensuring the ongoing benefits of experience of working in these conditions. Interestingly enough, environmental considerations were not even mentioned in discussions in the 1980s; they surfaced only after Russian transit traffic in the Gulf of Finland expanded after the Soviet collapse. Related to these special conditions, maintenance support performance was repeatedly mentioned in the political agenda, in particular during discussions about the internationalization of the ownership of ships transporting Finnish exports and imports. This discussion was strongly affected by historical experiences from the Second World War and the Finnish Civil War (1918). Integration into Western markets has further amplified this development (Paavonen, 2008). The 1989 committee report, for example, noted that 'security supply' reasoning was noted in 'all Western economies' when discussing the future of shipping (Kurki, 1990, p. 26).

The third major argument was related to more general economic matters such as shipping's contribution to the balance of payments and GDP (Kurki, 1990). Shipping's share of GDP was, however, rather insignificant in Finland, as noted above (Ojala and Saarto, 1992).

Fourth, the role of shipping as employer was noted both in public discussion and in political debate. In Finland the number of seamen, however, has been relatively low compared to other Nordic countries;

nevertheless, the point was emphasized by the Finnish Seamen's Union in particular, which has traditionally taken a strong line on this because of its strategically important position in the Finnish economy (again, primarily through its indirect role in the export trades). Until the 1980s, this union tended to be eager to strike, and even to block vessels' access to harbours if they found conflicts of interest in the operations of the vessel. For example, in 1980 a seamen's strike lasted about two months. This particular strike resulted in the introduction of Swedish-type labour systems, with two alternating crews for most ships, into Finland, and the concomitant substantially increased labour costs. (Lastikka, 1983, p. 224; Kurki, 1990; Ojala and Saarto, 1992).

Fifth, the effect of shipping on the other sectors of the Finnish economy and society – in addition to the export industries – was mentioned in government reports, usually stressing the role of the shipbuilding industry. In fact, Finnish shipbuilding was not intimately connected to domestic shipping: Finnish companies bought ships from foreign shipyards as well. More importantly, the markets for the Finnish shipyards were in most cases foreign. In addition to shipbuilding, the role of education and the importance of keeping shipping know-how in Finland for the future were also stressed in these discussions (Kurki, 1990).

Finnish membership of the European Union from 1996 onwards also challenged domestic shipping policies. The competitiveness of shipping companies has been a major concern both for the Finnish and the EU authorities throughout the 1990s and the first decade of the third millennium. Environmental issues, together with overall safety questions, gained more emphasis in the discussion.

Tonnage taxation has been widely debated in politics and public discussion (Karlsson, 2007). In 2002, a law on tonnage taxation was issued that made it possible for shipping firms to adopt a tonnage tax instead of normal income taxation (as was already the case in many EU countries). This was, however, so unattractive a law that only one small company took up the option. Discussion on more competitive tonnage taxation was resumed after 2005 and in October 2009 the government presented its proposal to parliament, which accepted it. This law was then submitted to the European Commission for approval, which by early 2011 had not yet been granted.

Particularly important for Finland have been the EU discussions on short-sea shipping, as the majority of the Finnish-owned fleet has been engaged in these trades throughout the Finnish membership period. Among EU countries national shipping clusters have been subsidized by national governments, and this has caused a lot of debate among the member countries (Wasström, 2000; Vainio and Kajander, 2002).

Shipping company strategies

Table 5.5 shows that the Finnish shipping company population experienced a number of changes during the period. Only Finnlines kept its position in all three of our sample years; 1965, 1980, and 2003.

Table 5.5 Finland's seven largest shipping companies 1965, 1980 and 2003 (1,000 gross tons)

1965	**Finnlines**	**130**
	SHO-FÅA	115
	Wihuri & Vaasan l.	49
	Etelä-Amerikan linja	43
	United Owners	25
	Bore	22
	Silja	20
	Total	404
1980	Neste	619
	Sally	391
	Finnlines	357
	Henry Nielsen	352
	SHO-FÅA	237
	Lundqvist	97
	Etelä-Suomen l.	62
	Total	2,115
2003	**Finnlines**	873
	Neste Shipping	658
	Lundqvist Red.	458
	Silja Line	347
	Viking Line	212
	Engship	129
	Bore Group	114
	Total	2,791

Note: Based on data from Kaukiainen (2008). For 1965 only tonnage used in liner trade foreign shipments is included, and for 2003, tonnage registered under both Finnish and foreign flags, as well as time-chartered tonnage, is included.

However, it should be noted that the ownership and organization of this company changed a number of times during the period.

Though the basis of Table 5.5 varies slightly from year to year, it still reveals a lot about the changes in the Finnish shipping industry. First, tonnage grew and became increasingly concentrated in the hands of the big players. Second, several new companies emerged: the most notable being Neste and Sally in the tanker business in the 1980 list, and Silja and Viking in the passenger line business in the 2003 data. However, as operating line companies, the latter two date back to the 1960s. Third, even though the list includes a number of changes, there are still companies that existed both in the first and in the last of the sample years. Nevertheless, as a result of ownership and strategy changes, companies with the same name in two or more samples can in fact be 'new' companies. Fourth, the number of shipping companies in Finland has been relatively small in comparison with the other Nordic countries, and the tonnage per company has been lower than in the Scandinavian companies.

Shipping was a lucrative line of business from the Second World War until the great shipping crisis, so it is no wonder that investments were made in buying and building new capacity. As stated before, some of the owners came from the Finnish export industries that sought opportunities to secure their own foreign trade shipments. Shipping was a part of their strategy for related diversification and vertical integration. The forest industry companies were primarily interested in short-sea shipping to secure exports to their main European markets (though, in the case of Enso-Gutzeit, US markets were served as well). Consequently, only a handful of companies were engaged in the global cross-trades. Even Finnlines was among them, which, in addition to North American lines, also managed ships engaged in global tramp trades. At the end of the 1960s and into the 1970s some of these vertically integrated shipping companies diversified further to unrelated businesses such as cross-trades and passenger shipping (Karonen, 1992). Even the national oil company, Neste, was vertically integrated in shipping.

When compared with the Scandinavian countries there was one notable difference in this respect: Finnish shipbuilding and shipping companies were not vertically integrated. There was, however, close co-operation between shipping and shipbuilding companies throughout the period, for example, when developing new types of ro-ro ships. This co-operation created challenges, particularly in the late 1980s when one of the largest shipbuilding companies, Wärtsilä Marine, went bankrupt (Kaukiainen, 2008b, pp. 428–516).

The 1970s witnessed the end of the traditional low-cost strategy as a result of increased capital and labour costs. This change in shipping strategy from low to high cost occurred faster in Finland than in all the other Nordic countries. Specialization was the key in the newly adopted high-cost strategy. Strategies of specialization in Finnish shipping can, however, be traced back to the 1950s when the passenger-car ferry trade started to expand. This trade experienced a rapid growth that continued until the 1990s; since then only the ferry lines between Finland and Estonia have grown significantly. In the 1970s those between Finland and Sweden produced some 10 per cent of the total income in Finnish shipping, but this number subsequently increased to almost 40 per cent (Kaukiainen, 2008b, p. 460).

Some other specialized lines of business also emerged in the 1960s, such as Erikson Reefer lines that operated worldwide (Kaukiainen, 2008b, p. 446). Tankers were the next wave of specialization following the international trend of the late 1960s. After 1970, Finnish cross-traders were increasingly engaged in a tanker sector that soon witnessed challenges. Specialization within ferries and ro-ros has, however, been the dominant strategy in Finnish shipping since the 1970s.

Finnish shipping companies were not able to adapt to the decreasing freight earnings caused by the shipping crisis. It was estimated in the mid-1980s that, essentially, no Finnish shipping company could survive by concentrating on commodity shipping. Indeed, diversification was considered to be the only feasible solution (Forsskåhl, 1986, p. 14). This was very clear to companies that were owned by other industries (like Finnlines and Transfennica), but others had to consider new approaches – usually to change to passenger traffic and try to get the value added from tax-free sales (Viitanen et al., 2003; Andersson, 2005; Karvonen et al., 2008).

There were also other strategic adaptations. Some shipping companies concentrated on low-cost shipping and flagged-out tonnage. Others chose high-cost specialization within certain niche markets, for example, to serve the Finnish forest industries with specialized ro-ro vessels. Such ships were not the most competitive in global shipping markets, as the annual growth of trade in forest product shipments, at around 1.3 per cent per annum, was rather modest in the period 1985 to 2005. This trade, however, does not include paper transport (Stopford, 2009, pp. 458–66). One clear strategy was to decrease the capital risk by chartering-in tonnage. This happened especially in liner companies: for example, in 2003 over 40 per cent of the Finnlines fleet consisted of chartered vessels. Thus, the equity ratio of the companies increased from 16–17 per cent to 40 per cent, as less of the companies' own capital was tied to the tonnage. At the same time, however, profitability in terms of return on capital decreased (Kaukiainen, 2008b, pp. 531–2). One consequence of the crisis was that a number of owners withdrew from shipping. As the rate of return fell, the forest industry companies, for example, lost their interest in shipping and outsourced these businesses, in many cases by selling the vessels and shipping companies abroad (Kaukiainen, 2008b, p. 481). Only one of them, UPM Kymmene (UPS Seaways), still manages its export and import transports with a dozen chartered ships.

Some other diversified shipping companies continued within the business, the most notable being the national oil company Neste with its tankers, but even this company made a partial move from owning to chartering. Many of these ships were also used in international cross-trades, mainly in the Baltic and North Sea areas.

Conclusion

Table 5.6 summarizes the main features of Finnish shipping in the period 1960 to 2010. This sector in Finland was affected by markets and by institutions; its organizational forms were created to provide solutions to the constraints created by these structures. The main question posed in this chapter has been why Finland's shipping industry seems to have been rather different from that of other Nordic countries.

We argue that the answer to the question can be found, first, in the general structure of the Finnish economy, especially, in the important role played by the major export industries. Therefore, the core *market* for the Finnish shipping has been the carrying of the export – and import – trades for Finnish industries – even though cross-trades have frequently also played an important role. Finland changed exceptionally quickly from a low-cost to high-cost economy, not only in shipping but in other industries too, so companies in all lines of business were forced to adapt to this change relatively rapidly.

Second, we argue that the *institutional environment* of Finland was not favourable, mainly due to the fact that the industry played a relatively weak role in the economy. While in the political arena shipping was seen as a vital part of society, its role was still understood more as supporting export industries and as part of a larger maritime cluster. Indeed, within this cluster, it was shipbuilding, not the shipping industry, which played a more important role as an employer and as an export industry.

Table 5.6 Finnish shipping in 1960–2010, major determinants

Main features	**1960s–1970s Growth**	**1980s Shipping Crises**	**1990s–2010s Recovery**
Markets	Finnish exports, rising cross trades, tanker business, passenger shipping	Passenger shipping Increasing importance of short-sea shipping Market differentiation between flagged-out and Finnish flag tonnage Specialized niches	Specialized niches, passenger shipping
Organization	Diversified (related and unrelated), forest industry as owner	Flagged-out tonnage with foreign subsidiaries	Specialization, increasing separation of owning and managing, foreign ownership
Institutions	Domestic security of exports and imports Conflicting interests between shipowners and labour union increased	Primacy of shipbuilding industry in the cluster, export industry dominance	Fading domestic influence Liberalization of capital movements, competition within EU Unfavourable taxation and (domestic and EU) legislation

Third, we argue that the *organization* of Finnish shipping reflects the markets and institutions described above. The number of shipping companies has traditionally been relatively low – indeed, the Finnish economy seems always to have been more landward than seaward oriented. Furthermore, shipowning was dominated for a long time by large industrial corporations to whom shipping was just another diversified line of business that supported their core business areas.

Fourth, we argue that *specialization*, especially towards passenger shipping, began quite early, namely around the turn of the 1950s and 1960s. The technological breakthrough, first of passenger ferries and then of ro-ros, suited Finnish markets particularly well. Both, in turn, were related to factors in the general development of the Finnish economy, such as migration to Sweden, increased time for holidays and increased trade with nearby areas, as well as to the needs of the major export industries.

Fifth, we argue that though in a *Nordic* perspective Finnish shipping might look modest or even a failure, in a *global* setting it is a quite typical shipping nation: an export-oriented country with relatively large tonnage carrying its own volume-demanding import and export trades. With a modest role in global cross-trading, it has been an exception in the Nordic context. However, after the shipping crises, development in Finland and Sweden has grown increasingly similar, mainly because in both countries economic policies have tended to disregard the interests of shipping.

However, even in Finland the corporate structures of shipping have recently been following the example of manufacturing industries, with increasing division of labour between shipowning, management, and operation – 'subcontracting' as well as 'outsourcing'. With greater integration within the EU, flagging-out of tonnage, and foreign ownership, it has become increasingly difficult to define in an unambiguous way the 'actual' size of Finnish merchant tonnage. Nevertheless, we can claim that, at the moment (2011), shipping firms with an official domicile in Finland operate and control a fleet which clearly exceeds the tonnage that actually flies the Finnish flag.

Notes

1. This characterization was originally presented with regard to the Swedish labour agreement of 1974, which in principle was similar to the Finnish one of 1981; see Rinman and Brodefors (1982, p. 237).
2. Note that such ships also carried cargoes to and from Finland.
3. In total shipbuilding exports, Finland ranked tenth in 2000. In passenger shipbuilding, Italy and France surpassed Finland in 2000.
4. Changes in formulating statistics means that 'dry cargo' vessels include all types of other vessels.

6
Nordic Shipping: A Statistical Overview

Espen Ekberg

Introduction

This chapter provides a broad statistical overview of the development of Nordic shipping in the period from 1960 to 2008. The general objective is descriptive rather than explanatory, aiming for a general presentation of the main trends in the development of shipping in the various Nordic countries during this period. In addition, the chapter offers an explicit comparison between the Nordic countries and between Nordic shipping and developments internationally.

The presentation focuses on three overall aspects. First, it outlines changes in the size of the separate Nordic fleets and the Nordic fleet combined in terms of overall tonnage growth, showing development and growth rates over time, and compares this to international trends. In the second section, the development in the market composition of the Nordic fleets and the Nordic fleet combined are explored. Contemporary international shipping is a complex industry, characterized by increasing specialization and segmentation. Numerous separate markets occupied by specially built tonnage have replaced the traditional two-tiered structure of liners and tramps (Stopford, 2009). The section shows how the Nordic fleets have responded to this trend, showing in what segments Nordic shipowners are primarily engaged, how this engagement has changed over time and points to similarities and differences between Nordic shipowners in this respect. Third and finally, the chapter traces a few main development trends in the industry structure of Nordic shipping. It analyses changes in the number of companies operating in the industry within each country, as well as the average share of tonnage held by these companies.

Overall the chapter points to the complexity and divergent development traits of Nordic shipping in the years during and after the shipping crisis of the 1970s. In Chapter 1 of this book, the notion of Nordic shipping as a distinct category was challenged. The country chapters have shown that the history of Nordic shipping during the upheavals of the shipping crisis and the subsequent years of intensified globalization is indeed quite varied. The statistical analysis presented in this chapter confirms this impression. While there are obvious common traits in the development of Nordic shipping during the period, the variations in overall fleet development, in the market composition of the fleets as well as in the overall structure of the various Nordic shipping industries, are most revealing.

Nordic shipping – general overview

This first section provides a presentation of the overall tonnage development of Nordic shipping and the rate of growth within the various Nordic countries between 1960 and 2008.[1] It also compares the development in Nordic shipping with overall trends at the international level during the same period.

Table 6.1 shows the overall tonnage development of Nordic shipping combined as well as that of the separate Nordic countries and for the world fleet, measured in gross tons.[2] As the table reveals, both for the Nordic region taken together and for the individual countries. the overall story is one of growth. Combined, the size of the fleet more than trebled. The relative position of Nordic shipping in world shipping did, however, decline quite markedly during the period. The reason is simply that while the size of the Nordic fleet trebled, the world fleet increased sixfold.

It is also noticeable that for some nations, the fleet actually contracted quite substantially in certain periods. For example, in the period between 1975 and 1985, the size of the Norwegian fleet almost halved while the Swedish fleet more than halved. The Swedish fleet also continued to contract until 1990. From 1980 to 1990, and especially from 1985, the Finish fleet also experienced a substantial decline, as did the Icelandic, if at a much slower pace. On these grounds it is no surprise that the Nordic fleet combined also contracted substantially during the 15-year period from 1975.

Despite these general trends, differences between the individual countries are substantial. Most prominent is the strong growth of the Danish fleet from the mid-1980s onwards, and especially in the few years since

2005. During the period taken as a whole the Danish fleet increased more than tenfold. Furthermore, we see that despite growing much slower than the Danish fleet, the Norwegian-owned fleet remained the largest of the Nordic fleets, while the Danish fleet overtook the Swedes to become the second largest.

Table 6.2 further clarifies the trends depicted in Table 6.1. It shows the average annualized growth rate of the different Nordic fleets as well as for the Nordic fleet and the world fleet combined.

We see that the growth of the Nordic fleet lags behind that of the world fleet. An interesting exception is the period from 1985 to 1995, when the Nordic fleet grew significantly faster than the world fleet. In part, this may have to do with ships returning to the Norwegian and Danish registries after the establishment of NIS and DIS.[3] It probably also has to do with a temporary revival of both Finnish and Swedish shipping, growing at annual rates of more than 20 per cent during the period 1990 to 1995. As we recall, while the overall story of Swedish shipping from 1960 to 2008 was one of decline, the industry experienced a temporary expansion in the late 1980s and 1990s, with several new companies developing a substantial business operating tankers and dry bulk carriers. In addition, the Finnish fleet experienced a temporary revival during this period, with a particular growth in passenger ferries.[4] We can also see clearly the substantial growth of the Danish fleet, especially during the last period. Finally, it is noticeable that the Swedish fleet was, in relative terms, the fleet hardest hit by the shipping crisis of the 1970s and 1980s, decreasing by 8.2 per cent at an annual rate. In absolute terms, the loss of 11 million gross tons of shipping capacity experienced by the Norwegians (as shown in Table 6.1) was of course the most dramatic.

The consequences of the different growth rates of Nordic and world shipping, and also of the different Nordic countries, in terms of market shares, are shown in Table 6.3.[5]

Perhaps the most noticeable point shown by this table is the prominent position held by Nordic shipowners in world shipping in the mid-1960s. At this point they alone owned almost a sixth of the entire world fleet of merchant ships. At the same time, we see how this strong market position was gradually eroded during the shipping crisis of the 1970s and 1980s, only to revive somewhat in the period up to 2008. From a peak of 14.7 per cent market share in 1965, Nordic shipping's share of world shipping declined to a 6.15 per cent low in 1985, returning to a new peak at 11.79 per cent in 2000, before decreasing again, ending at 8.55 per cent in 2008. Again, the differences between the

Table 6.1 Tonnage development of Nordic shipping, 1960–2008 ('000 gt)

	1960	1965	1970	1975	1980	1985	1990	1995	2000	2005	2008
Denmark	2,270	2,562	3,314	4,478	5,390	4,942	5,188	8,599	13,589	15,204	24,204
Finland	714	1,009	1,397	2,002	2,530	1,974	1,069	3,011	2,298	2,071	2,273
Iceland	25	129	119	154	188	180	177	–	190	452	486
Norway	11,203	15,641	19,347	26,154	22,007	15,339	23,429	31,333	39,670	33,442	35,090
Sweden	3,747	4,290	4,921	7,486	4,234	3,162	2,775	9,251	7,995	6,200	7,341
Nordic	17,960	23,632	29,098	40,274	34,350	25,597	32,638	52,194	63,743	57,369	69,394
World	129,770	160,392	227,490	342,162	419,911	416,269	423,627	473,890	540,675	657,049	811,709

Table 6.2 Average annualized growth-rate of Nordic shipping tonnage, 1960–2008 (per cent)

	1960–65	1965–70	1970–75	1975–80	1980–85	1985–90	1990–95	1995–00	2000–05	2005–08
Denmark	2.45	5.29	6.20	3.78	–1.72	0.98	10.63	9.56	2.30	16.76
Finland	7.16	6.72	7.45	4.80	–4.84	–11.54	23.01	–5.26	–2.06	3.14
Iceland	38.53	–1.55	5.29	4.04	–0.85	–0.42	–	–	18.90	0.50
Norway	6.90	4.34	6.21	–3.39	–6.97	8.84	5.99	4.83	–3.36	1.62
Sweden	2.74	2.78	8.75	–10.77	–5.67	–2.58	27.23	–2.88	–4.96	5.79
Nordic	5.64	4.25	6.72	–3.13	–5.71	4.98	9.85	4.07	–2.08	6.53
World	4.33	7.24	8.51	4.18	–0.17	0.35	2.27	2.67	3.98	7.30

Table 6.3 Nordic shipping's share of world tonnage, 1960–2008 (per cent)

	1960	**1965**	**1970**	**1975**	**1980**	**1985**	**1990**	**1995**	**2000**	**2005**	**2008**
Denmark	1.75	1.60	1.46	1.31	1.28	1.19	1.22	1.81	2.51	2.31	2.98
Finland	0.55	0.63	0.61	0.58	0.60	0.47	0.25	0.64	0.43	0.32	0.28
Iceland	0.02	0.08	0.05	0.05	0.04	0.04	0.04	–	0.04	0.07	0.06
Norway	8.63	9.75	8.50	7.64	5.24	3.68	5.53	6.61	7.34	5.09	4.32
Sweden	2.89	2.67	2.16	2.19	1.01	0.76	0.66	1.95	1.48	0.94	0.90
Nordic	13.84	14.73	12.79	11.77	8.18	6.15	7.70	11.01	11.79	8.73	8.55

Nordic countries are clearly detectable. For example, while the share of the Norwegian fleet more than halved from its peak in 1965, the Danish share almost doubled in the same period. Also, the Swedes lost out substantially as their market share was reduced to a third of its 1960 peak.

As indicated in Chapter 1, even if the Nordic shipowner's share of the world fleet has declined somewhat since its heyday in the 1960s, the position of shipping relative to the Nordic countries' overall demographic and economic importance in the world remains remarkable. In 2008 the Nordic share of world population was 0.4 per cent, while the region's share of world GDP was 1.4 per cent.[6] At the same time it owned 8.5 per cent of world shipping tonnage. The relative importance of the maritime sector within the Nordic economies thus remains undisputable.

Overall tonnage development, however, tells only part of the story of Nordic shipping in the period. As has already been noted – and also well illustrated in the chapters for each country – a major trend in the development of the post-war shipping market, at least from the 1970s onwards, was the increasing specialization of the world fleet. From being dominated by a few types of general ships, the world fleet diversified into numerous different types of specialized ships. These operated in separate markets, causing an increasing segmentation of the shipping industry. Nordic shipowners often stood at the forefront of this development, developing new ship types and facilitating the growth of new, specialized seaborne trades. As a result the fleet gradually became characterized by a high share of advanced vessels. One consequence of this is that the relative decline of the fleet recorded by the tables above probably appears somewhat exaggerated. As Nordic shipowners shifted their investment from large tankers and dry bulk carriers into smaller, specialized tonnage, the recorded size of the fleet relative to that of other nations declined quite substantially. However, since specialized ships are generally much more expensive per ton than bulk ships, the true economic significance of the fleet relative to other nations probably declined much less (see the appendix at the end of this chapter). An interesting question to ask, therefore, is exactly how this development came about. In what segments did Nordic shipowners primarily operate in their heyday in the 1960s and how did this market positioning change during and after the shipping crisis of the 1970s and 1980s? Moreover, were there any marked differences between the shipowners of the various Nordic countries in the ways they developed their fleets? These questions are central to the next section.

Market specialization in Nordic shipping

Until 1950 the basic structure of the shipping industry was not very different from what it had been a century earlier. On the one hand there were cargo liners, transporting general cargo on a scheduled basis, and on the other, the so-called tramp ships operated in the spot market, taking all kinds of raw materials and other cargo not carried by the liners.[7] This traditional two-tier structure would change substantially in the second half of the twentieth century. As noted in Chapter 1, at least three major transformative processes can be detected. The first was the massive growth in the size of tankers and dry bulk carriers, often referred to as the 'bulk revolution'. These vessels took over the transport of all bulk cargo such as oil, grain, coal and ores.[8] The second major change was the containerization of the general cargo, or liner market, the so-called 'container revolution'.[9] The third was the development of specialized shipping: the development of ships purpose-built to carry only one or a few types of cargo, the most important being chemicals, liquid gas, unit-load cargoes (such as cars, forest products and high and heavy cargo), refrigerated foods and passengers.[10] The overall consequence of these transformations was that the shipping market became diversified into a number of separate segments, each operating according to its own industrial logic and employing ships specialized for one or a few specific cargoes.

How did this development affect Nordic shipowners? The purpose of this section is to determine the segments in which they were primarily operating and also how their market positioning has changed over time. A further important goal is to detect similarities and differences in the market positioning of shipowners from the various Nordic countries. First we look at the Nordic fleet as a whole, before looking in more detail into the experiences of the Nordic countries separately.[11]

The Nordic fleet

In which segment of the shipping market is the Nordic fleet primarily engaged? Figure 6.1 answers this question by showing the composition in 2008 of the Nordic fleet, estimated on the basis of tonnage distribution. As indicated by the table, the largest segment in the Nordic fleet in 2008 on this basis was the crude oil segment, followed by container ships, chemical tankers, dry bulk ships and roll-on roll-off (ro-ro)/car carriers. While Nordic shipowners operate in many of the new, specialized segments, the 'traditional' crude oil and dry bulk segments

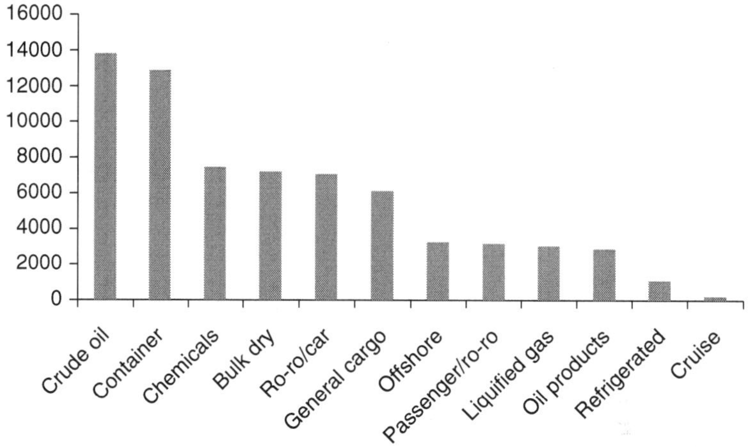

Figure 6.1 Composition of the Nordic fleet in 2008 ('000 gt)

together continued to make up a substantial proportion of the fleet. A first impression may thus seem to be that not much had happened in terms of specialization in the Nordic fleet. Looking more closely at the historic development in the composition of the fleet, however, reveals a strong trend away from tankers and bulk carriers towards specialized trades. Table 6.4 provides the details, showing how the composition of the Nordic fleet developed from 1975 to 2008.

From this overview it is clear that the trend has been away from tankers and dry bulk carriers. As late as 1975 these ships made up more than 80 per cent of the entire Nordic fleet. By 2008, 33 years later, their share had dropped to 30 per cent. During the same period container ships, as well as specialized ships such as ro-ro/car carriers, chemical ships, liquefied gas carriers, oil products tankers and offshore service ships had increased their share of the fleet quite substantially. In 1975 container ships made up less than 1 per cent of the Nordic fleet, while specialized ships together accounted for less than 5 per cent. By 2008 container ships made up almost 20 per cent of the fleet while specialized ships accounted for about 37 per cent.

As already mentioned, estimates of the importance of various segments in a given fleet based on gross tonnage figures tends to overestimate the economic importance of bulk ships while underestimating the importance of specialized ships. The following figure therefore presents the composition of the Nordic fleet estimated in 'compensated gross tons' (cgt).[12]

Table 6.4 Development in the composition of the Nordic fleet (per cent)

	1975	1980	1990	2000	2008
Liquefied gas	1.1	2.1	4.5	4.4	4.9
Crude oil	49.0	52.3	36.8	35.0	19.9
Oil products	–	–	4.8	1.6	4.1
Chemicals	0.9	2.0	3.0	6.4	10.7
General cargo	11.6	11.7	3.3	8.2	8.8
Bulk dry	31.5	23.0	24.6	12.4	10.4
Container	0.8	1.9	4.7	9.3	18.5
Refrigerated	–	–	0.9	1.7	1.5
Ro-ro/car	0.4	0.9	3.4	11.0	10.2
Passenger/ro-ro	2.2	3.4	4.9	3.5	4.6
Cruise	–	–	–	2.8	0.3
Offshore	0.2	0.3	0.5	2.4	4.7
Total	**97.7**	**97.5**	**91.5**	**98.7**	**98.1**

Clearly, what we see in Figure 6.2 is that when estimated on the basis of cgt, the trend towards increased specialization is further confirmed. The largest segment in Nordic shipping by this measure is the container segment, but the specialized segments achieve a much more prominent position, while the relative importance of bulk ships, particularly tankers, is reduced. Another fairly large segment by this measure is the general cargo carrier. An obvious reason is, of course that these are generally small ships operating in niches where scale economies are less relevant and where the trend of substituting smaller ships with fewer and larger ships has been less prominent than in other segments.[13] A less obvious, but still very important second reason is that the category 'general cargo ship' includes ships of the open hatch type, known as 'open hatch bulk carriers'. As we shall see, this is a segment that has grown substantially within the Norwegian fleet. In fact, the growth of the general cargo segment within Nordic shipping is fully accounted for by the Norwegians, the major reason being the growth in the open hatch bulk segment.

Overall, an analysis of the fleet composition of the Nordic fleet and its development since 1975 shows that the fleet has become substantially more diversified. From being extremely reliant on tankers and bulk

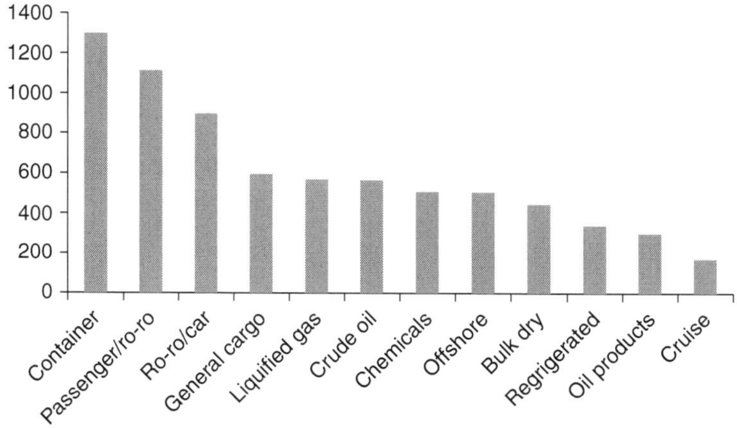

Figure 6.2 Composition of the Nordic fleet in 2008 ('000 cgt)

carriers, Nordic shipowners have increasingly explored alternative market segments. Most prominent is the growth in specialized segments such as gas and chemical carriers, car carriers and offshore ships. The effect is that the Nordic fleet in 2008 comprises a high share of technologically advanced tonnage. This trend towards increased specialization was, as previously shown, a general trend in international shipping. The question remains, then, whether the development seen within the Nordic countries merely reflected this overall trend or whether it is possible to detect some specific features of the Nordic experience. Figure 6.3 gives some indication of the answer. It shows the combined market share of Nordic shipping in 12 different market segments and compares it with the overall market share of Nordic shipowners in world shipping, estimated by gross tonnage.[14] The graph identifies those segments in which the Nordic fleet has a disproportionate share of the world market as compared to its overall share of the world fleet, thus revealing the markets in which the shipping companies of the Nordic countries are primarily engaged.

In general, what the graph shows is that, compared to their overall market share, Nordic shipowners in 2008 were over-represented in some selected specialized niches, most prominently chemicals, refrigerated cargo, ro-ros (all categories including car carriers and passenger ro-ros) and offshore marine services, while they were under-represented in the dry bulk segments, in crude oil and in a few of the more specialized niches.

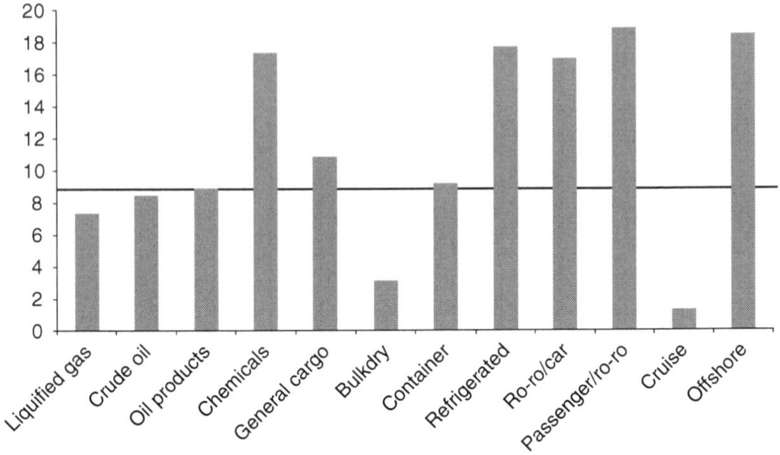

Figure 6.3 Nordic share of the world fleet and some segments in 2008 (per cent)

Table 6.5 Development in Nordic share of world fleet in some segments (per cent)

	1975	1980	1990	2000	2008
Liquefied gas	14.5	9.7	13.7	14.3	7.4
Crude oil	13.1	10.3	9.3	17.2	8.4
Oil products	–	–	–	4.3	9.4
Chemicals	36.6	30.6	27.6	23.8	17.5
General cargo	6.6	4.8	2.1	9.8	11.4
Bulk dry	14.8	7.2	6.0	5.2	3.1
Container	5.3	5.7	5.2	9.8	9.2
Refrigerated	–	–	4.0	15.7	18.0
Ro-ro/car	28.4	16.3	14.3	26.0	17.2
Passenger/ro-ro	19.4	15.2	22.9	17.7	19.6
Cruise	–	–	–	22.6	1.3
Offshore	5.6	6.7	5.9	19.1	20.3
Total market share	**11.8**	**8.2**	**7.7**	**11.8**	**8.5**

How has this picture changed over time? Table 6.5 shows the historical development of Nordic shipowners' share of the world fleet in the selected segments. Clearly, they have reduced their share of the world fleet in traditional segments such as crude oil and dry bulk, while their relative position in specialized segments such as offshore shipping, refrigerated cargo and product tankers has been substantially strengthened. The same is true for the container segment, even if the relative strengthening here has been less pronounced. A second interesting feature revealed by the table is the very strong positions held by Nordic shipowners in the ro-ro/car, chemicals, cruise and liquefied gas segments in the early part of the period. For example, in 1975 more than a third of the total world tonnage of chemical tankers was in the hands of Nordic shipowners. They also owned more than a quarter of the ro-ro/car carrier fleet and almost 15 per cent of the liquefied gas carrier segment. When separate figures for the cruise segment were revealed for the first time in 2000, it turned out that one- fifth of this tonnage was owned by Nordic shipowners. This clearly indicates that Nordic shipowners played an important role as innovators in these specialized trades. At the same time, the gradual decline in the relative positions held in all the segments shows how the dominant position once held could not be sustained as these specialized markets matured.[15] As far as the massive decline in the cruise segment is concerned, this has a simple explanation: after 2000 most of the tonnage owned, primarily by Norwegian citizens, was fully or partly sold to foreign owners. A third and final observation is the stable and strong relative position held by Nordic shipowners within the passenger/ro-ro business. Throughout the period covered about a fifth of the total tonnage of such ships has been in the hands of Nordic shipowners.

A perhaps even more revealing picture of the composition of the Nordic fleet relative to the world fleet is presented in Table 6.6. Instead of showing the shares held by Nordic shipowners in selected segments it directly compares the composition of the Nordic fleets with the composition of the world fleet (excluding the Nordic countries). Hence it shows to what extent Nordic shipowners have been over- or under-represented in certain segments compared with the composition of the world fleet, and how this has changed over time.

The basic finding revealed by this table is that Nordic shipping during the period 1975 to 2008 has moved from being over-represented in tanker and dry bulk shipping, to being over-represented in specialized tonnage. Hence, compared with the overall development in the world fleet, the trend towards increased specialization has been particularly strong within the Nordic countries. To simplify the argument, it could be said that Nordic shipowners own a higher share of specialized tonnage than the average shipowner in the world and a smaller share of the dry bulk and tanker tonnage. They also own a slightly higher share of container ships. Finally, for reasons already noted, while Nordic

Table 6.6 Development in the composition of the Nordic fleet and world fleet (excluding Nordic) (per cent)

	1975		1980		1990		2000		2008	
	Nordic	**World**	**Nordic**	**World**	**Nordic**	**World**	**Nordic**	**World**	**Nordic**	**World**
Liquefied gas	1.1	0.8	2.1	1.7	4.5	2.4	4.4	3.5	4.9	5.1
Crude oil	49.0	43.2	52.3	40.7	36.8	29.8	35.0	22.5	19.9	20.2
Oil products	–	–	–	–	4.8	1.2	1.6	4.9	4.1	3.7
Chemicals	0.9	0.2	2.0	0.4	3.0	0.6	6.4	2.7	10.7	4.7
General cargo	11.6	21.8	11.7	20.0	3.3	12.7	8.2	9.8	8.8	6.4
Bulk dry	31.5	24.1	23.0	26.4	24.6	32.0	12.4	30.1	10.4	30.2
Container	0.8	2.0	1.9	2.8	4.7	7.3	9.3	11.4	18.5	17.1
Refrigerated	–	–	–	–	0.9	1.7	1.7	1.2	1.5	0.6
Ro-ro/car	0.4	0.1	0.9	0.4	3.4	1.7	11.0	4.2	10.2	4.6
Passenger/ro-ro	2.2	1.2	3.4	1.7	4.9	1.4	3.5	2.2	4.6	1.8
Cruise	–	–	–	–	–	–	2.8	1.3	0.3	1.9
Offshore	0.2	0.4	0.3	0.4	0.5	0.7	2.4	1.3	4.7	1.7
Total	**97.7**	**93.8**	**97.5**	**94.5**	**91.5**	**91.4**	**98.7**	**95.2**	**98.1**	**98.1**

shipowners were under-represented in the general cargo segment in 1975 they are clearly over-represented in this segment by 2008.

However, this overall picture of the composition of the Nordic fleet and its development over the 30-year period since 1975 hides important variations in the specialization strategies of various Nordic shipowners. To illustrate some of these differences, the following subsections present some selected data for each individual Nordic country. The analysis begins with the position and development of the Danish fleet.

The Danish fleet

The Danish merchant fleet experienced the largest overall tonnage growth of all the Nordic countries during the period 1960 to 2008. As we have seen, growth was particularly fast in the latter part of the period, and from 1985 onwards Danish shipping almost trebled its share of world tonnage. Naturally Danish-owned shipping also increased its share of total Nordic tonnage quite substantially during this period. While Danish citizens owned 11 per cent of the Nordic fleet in 1965, by 2008 their share had increased to 35 per cent. Figure 6.4 provides a summary of the market composition of the Danish fleet in 2008 and shows the segments in which this growth primarily occurred.

As is clear from the graph, by 2008 Danish shipping was primarily a container fleet. About 50 per cent of the fleet, estimated in gross tons, consisted of container ships. In addition, traditional segments such as

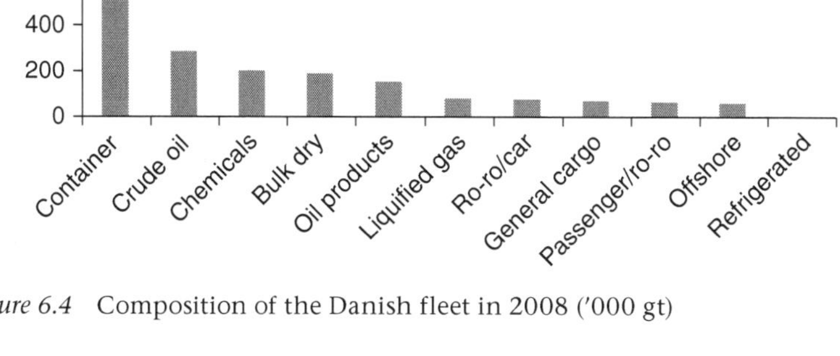

Figure 6.4 Composition of the Danish fleet in 2008 ('000 gt)

dry bulk and tankers continued to play a prominent role. Apart from chemicals and product tankers, specialized shipping, by contrast, seemed to occupy a less important role among Danish shipowning firms. The growth of Danish shipping from the 1980s onwards therefore seems to have been concentrated quite substantially in very few segments, with containers by far the most important. Looking at the historical development of the fleet, this impression is largely confirmed (see Table 6.7).

The most striking finding from this table is of course the substantial decline in the importance of crude oil, general cargo and dry bulk ships (and partly also of passenger/ro-ros) and the parallel growth of the container fleet. In 1975 bulk (wet and dry) and general cargo ships alone made up almost 90 per cent of the fleet. In 2008 their share had shrunk to roughly 20 per cent. During the same period, container ships had increased their share from a minuscule 4 per cent share to roughly 50 per cent. As far as the specialized segments are concerned, growth has been confined largely to chemical ships and product tankers, even if their share has declined somewhat from a peak of 10 per cent in 1990. Gas tankers and offshore service ships have also become more important niches in Danish shipping but their total shares remain fairly low, at 3.4 and 2.6 per cent respectively. This general picture is further

Table 6.7 Development in the composition of the Danish fleet (per cent)

	1975	1980	1990	2000	2008
Liquefied gas	0.7	0.9	2.5	3.4	3.4
Crude oil	48.3	52.1	28.9	22.1	11.8
Oil products	–	–	10.1	3.0	6.5
Chemicals	0.7	0.1	0.3	5.9	8.3
General cargo	26.0	17.9	4.5	4.2	3.1
Bulk dry	12.3	11.9	4.6	8.3	7.9
Container	4.0	9.1	25.5	38.6	49.8
Refrigerated	–	–	1.6	2.5	0.2
Ro-ro/car	0.0	0.0	6.0	6.8	3.3
Passenger/ro-ro	5.3	4.5	7.2	2.0	2.8
Cruise	–	–	–	0.0	0.0
Offshore	0.3	0.03	0.7	2.0	2.6
Total	**97.4**	**96.5**	**91.9**	**98.8**	**99.7**

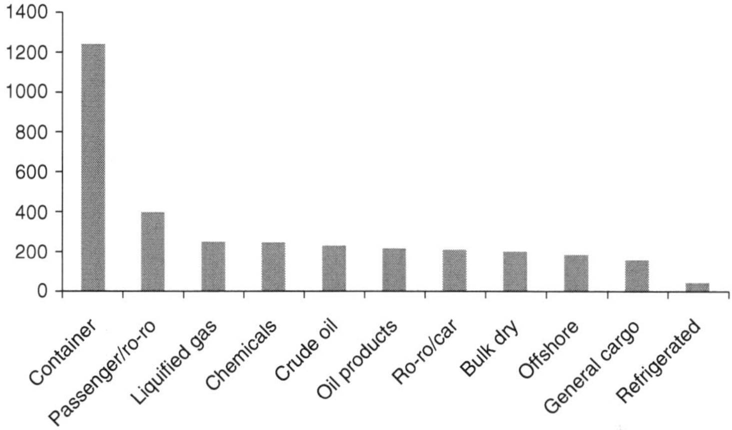

Figure 6.5 Composition of the Danish fleet in 2008 ('000 cgt)

confirmed when estimating the composition of the Danish fleet by the alternative cgt measure.

Figure 6.5 shows that container ships remain the most important ship type, while the relative importance of crude oil tankers and dry bulk ships decreases. The smaller specialized ships, the most prominent being the passenger/ro-ros, strengthen their relative position. On the whole, however, these changes are fairly minor and the overall picture presented by this figure is that the Danish fleet by 2008 was dominated by its large fleet of container ships. Looking at the fleet in an comparative international perspective underlines the substantial position held by Danish shipping in the container segment. Figure 6.6 shows Danish shipowners' share of the world fleet and of some segments in 2008 by tonnage.

Again, the position of container ships in the fleet is underlined. In fact almost 9 per cent of the world container fleet is owned by Danish interests. Oil products, chemicals, passenger/ro-ros and offshore marine services are further segments in which Danish shipowners hold market positions that are stronger than their overall position in world shipping. Hence, apart from its dominance in the container segment, in comparative terms the Danish fleet is primarily a specialized fleet.

How has the international market position of the fleet developed in a historical perspective? The most general finding is, of course, that Denmark during the period from 1990 onwards strengthened its relative position in world shipping, from 1.2 to 3 per cent. As we recall, among the Nordic countries Denmark was the only country experiencing a

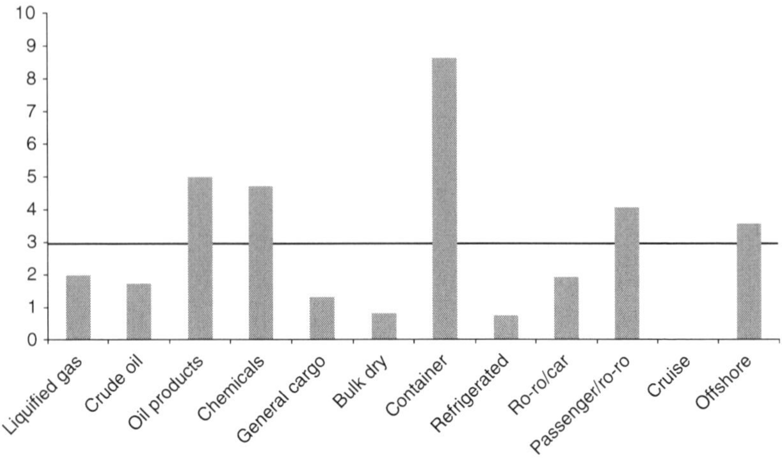

Figure 6.6 Danish shares of world fleet and some segments in 2008 (per cent)

growth in their share of total world shipping tonnage. How did this growth come about? From Table 6.8 it is clear that the growth was largely caused by a substantial expansion of the container segment, but also specialized segments such as offshore, gas and, especially, chemicals increased their relative position.

At 3 per cent, the Danish fleet, as defined by the nationality of the owner, is ranked as the ninth-largest fleet in the world. But the adequacy of estimating the position of national fleets in world shipping on the basis of the nationality of the owner may be problematic.[16] Shipping is no longer only about owning ships. Shipowners often outsource the operation of their ships to other companies. There has therefore been the development of a substantial number of ship management companies, operating ships on behalf of owners often of a different nationality. This is a development that has been particularly embraced by Danish shipping companies. In Table 6.9 two alternative ways of estimating the size of a country's shipping fleet that capture this development are presented. It compares the market share of Danish shipping based on the *owner's country of residence* with market shares based on the *operator's country of residence*.

As is clear from the table, compared to the traditional ownership estimate, the position of the Danish fleet in world shipping according to these alternative estimates strengthens quite substantially. Hence, while Norway is by far the largest fleet in the Nordic region when estimated on the basis of the traditional nationality of owner criterion, the

Table 6.8 Development in Danish share of world fleet and some segments (per cent)

	1975	1980	1990	2000	2008
Liquefied gas	1.0	0.7	1.2	2.3	2.0
Crude oil	1.4	1.6	1.2	2.3	1.7
Oil products	–	–	8.5	1.6	5.2
Chemicals	3.1	0.2	0.5	4.7	4.7
General cargo	1.7	1.2	0.5	1.1	1.4
Bulk dry	0.6	0.6	0.2	0.7	0.8
Container	2.9	4.4	4.4	8.7	8.6
Refrigerated	–	–	1.2	4.9	0.8
Ro-ro/car	0.0	0.0	4.0	3.4	1.9
Passenger/ro-ro	5.1	3.2	5.4	2.1	4.2
Cruise	–	–	–	0.0	0.0
Offshore	1.0	0.1	1.2	3.4	3.9
Total market share	**1.3**	**1.3**	**1.2**	**2.5**	**3.0**

Table 6.9 Control of world tonnage in 2009 ('000 gt)

	Split by owner's country of residence		**Split by operator's country of residence**	
Rank	**Country**	**Fleet**	**Country**	**Fleet**
1	Japan	123.512	Japan	105.829
2	Greece	80.074	Greece	64.377
3	Germany	73.228	China	51.404
4	China	57.290	United States	46.541
5	South Korea	27.082	**Denmark**	41.112
6	Great Britain	24.221	South Korea	39.585
7	United States	23.554	Singapore	37.467
8	**Denmark**	23.218	Great Britain	33.285
9	Norway	21.467	Germany	32.752
10	Hong Kong	21.378	Hong Kong	26.694

Danes overtake the Norwegians when the estimate is based on where the owner actually lives. Even more remarkable is the change when the fleet size is estimated on the basis of the operator's country of residence. By this estimate, Danish shipping ranks among the top five leading maritime nations in the world, while neither the Norwegians nor any of the other Nordic countries are even close to the top ten list. While this way of estimating the importance of shipping in a country is still quite unconventional, the figures say a great deal about how the strategic focus of Danish shipping firms has shifted substantially towards the activity of operating ships.

The Finnish fleet

Apart from Iceland, Finland is the smallest shipping nation within the Nordic region. In 1960 only about 0.5 per cent of the world tonnage was in the hands of Finnish shipowners, as compared to the Norwegian share of more than 8 per cent and an average Nordic share of 3.4 per cent.[17] As a share of the Nordic fleet, the Finns owned 4 per cent. By 2008 the share was 3 per cent.

While small in comparative terms, the growth rate of Finnish shipping during the 1960s and 1970s was the strongest within the entire Nordic region. As revealed by Table 6.2, between 1960 and 1980 the annualized growth rates of Finnish shipping outpaced those of all the other Nordic countries, often by a substantial margin. From the 1980s onwards, however, higher than average growth was replaced by higher than average decline. The consequence was that by 2008 the Finnish fleet was actually smaller than it had been in 1980. While all the other Nordic fleets had expanded in absolute terms during this period, the Finnish fleet had contracted.

Figure 6.7 provides details of the composition of this contracted fleet. The data shows that the Finnish fleet is concentrated in three major segments: passenger ro-ro ships, crude oil carriers and ro-ro/car carriers. Another notable feature is the minuscule role played by dry bulk carriers. Even if the relative position of such tonnage is generally overestimated in comparisons based on gross ton figures, it appears as a very small fraction of Finnish shipping in this overview. So how has this fleet composition developed over time? Table 6.10 provides a picture.

The first notable feature is the very strong position of crude oil carriers in 1975, making up almost 60 per cent of the entire Finnish fleet. In fact, none of the other Nordic fleets had such a high concentration in tankers, the share of the Nordic fleet combined being just below 50 per cent.

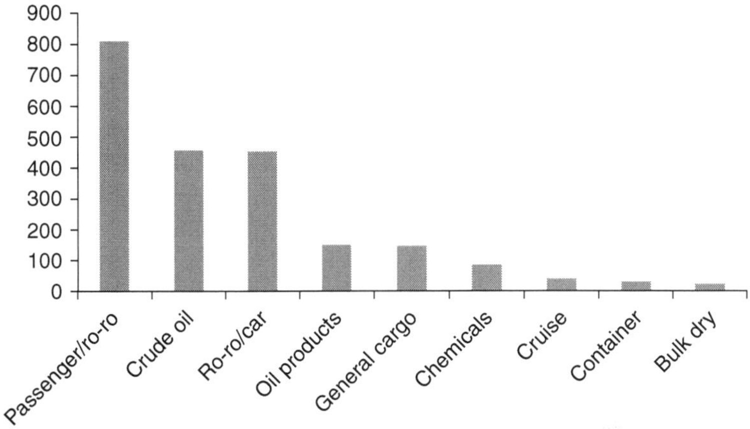

Figure 6.7 Composition of the Finnish fleet in 2008 ('000 gt)

Table 6.10 Development in the composition of the Finnish fleet (per cent)

	1975	1980	1990	2000	2008
Liquefied gas	0.3	0.1	1.9	1.9	0.0
Crude oil	56.9	47.5	15.1	23.5	20.2
Oil products	–	–	7.8	0.4	6.6
Chemicals	0.1	0.1	0.8	1.2	3.7
General cargo	24.3	21.1	8.9	3.9	6.4
Bulk dry	7.7	21.2	11.3	3.9	1.0
Container	0.2	0.2	0.0	0.0	1.3
Refrigerated	0.0	0.0	0.0	1.3	0.0
Ro-ro/car	0.5	0.0	15.3	20.8	19.9
Passenger/ro-ro	7.5	7.3	29.8	38.4	35.5
Cruise	–	–	–	1.3	1.8
Offshore	0.1	0.2	0.0	0.2	0.0
Total	**97.7**	**97.6**	**91**	**97.0**	**96.4**

A substantial decline in the relative position of this segment is further evident and by 2008 only about a fifth of the Finnish fleet was made up of tanker tonnage. Again, comparing Finland's development with the overall Nordic experience, the decline in the relative position of Finnish tanker tonnage was in fact more substantial. By 2008 both the Finnish fleet and the Nordic fleet combined held a tanker share of about 20 per cent.

A second notable feature is the parallel decline in the general cargo and dry bulk segments. Both these segments held substantial positions by the end of the 1970s, but from then on their role was greatly diminished. A third feature is the expansion of the passenger/ro-ro and car/ro-ro segments. The car/ro-ro expansion is exclusively explained by a strong growth in the use of flexible ro-ro tonnage, and not an expansion into specialized car carrying.[18] As noted in Chapter 5, ro-ro ships were well attuned to Finnish export needs – the forest industry being the most important – and were thus more and more widely used.[19] Also substantial is the expansion in passenger/ro-ro ships, although this segment was already fairly important in 1975. This fleet is essentially made up of conventional car and passenger ferries. Indeed, as noted in Chapter 5, some of the world's largest passenger ferry operators are owned by Finnish interests. Many of these are situated in the Åland Islands, operating scheduled services primarily within the Baltic Sea and across the Gulf of Finland and the Gulf of Riga. Finally, it may be noted that some Finnish shipowners also seem to have found a successful niche in the transport of oil products. At 6.6 per cent, this specialized segment was the fourth largest in Finnish shipping in 2008, estimated in traditional tonnage terms.

The dominance of the passenger/ro-ros in Finnish shipping, as well as the strong position also held by cargo-carrying ro-ro ships, is further underlined when we look at the composition of the fleet according to cgt. The results of this exercise is shown in Figure 6.8. As one would expect, compared with the conventional tonnage view, the dominant position of the passenger/ro-ro segment is further underlined from this perspective. The relative position of the crude oil carrier, by contrast, is becoming much less pronounced. Moreover, on this estimate the cargo ro-ros have become the second largest segment in Finnish shipping. Nevertheless, as in the Danish case, the picture emerging is of a merchant fleet highly dominated by one particular segment, in this case the car/passenger ferries.

How does this composition look from an international perspective? Figure 6.9 shows the Finnish shares in 2008 of the world fleet and of some segments, estimated in conventional tonnage terms.

Again, the impression is confirmed of a fleet dominated by passenger/ro-ros. Moreover, the figure shows that the Finnish fleet of passenger/ro-ros in fact makes up a substantial proportion of the total world fleet

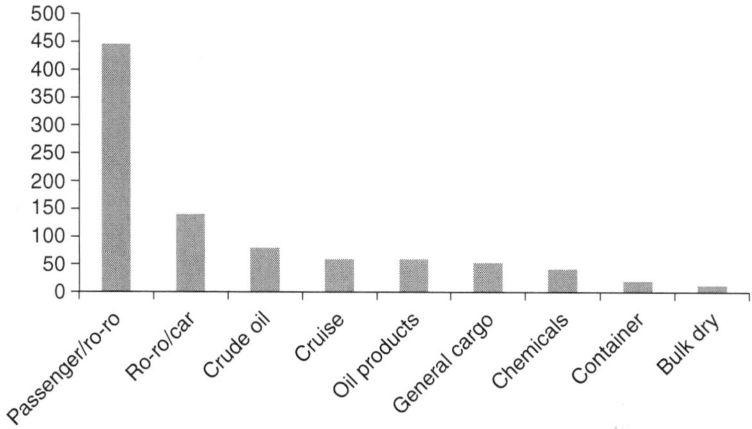

Figure 6.8 Composition of the Finnish fleet in 2008 ('000 cgt)

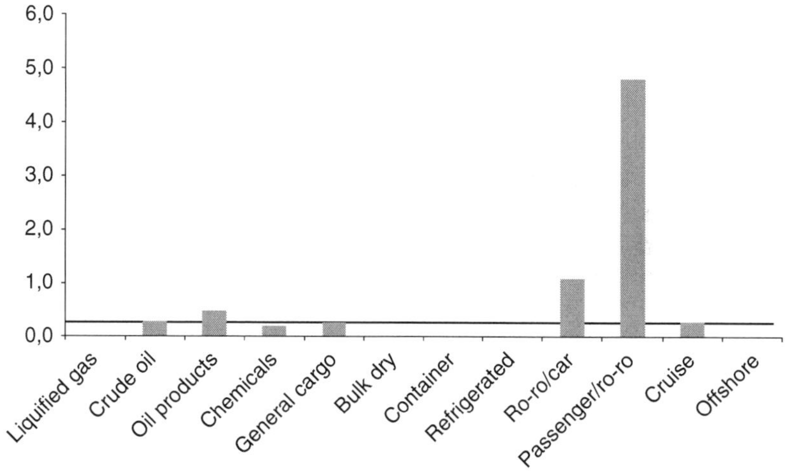

Figure 6.9 Finnish shares of world fleet and some segments in 2008 (per cent)

of such ships. While the Finnish fleet taken as a whole owned less than 0.5 per cent of the world fleet in 2008, it owned 5.5 per cent of the passenger/ro-ro fleet. In line with earlier findings, we can also see that the Finnish fleet is quite well represented in the cargo-carrying ro-ro market. Finally, the more recent development of a substantial Finnish fleet of oil products tankers is also evident.

Table 6.11. Development in Finnish share of world fleet and some segments (per cent)

	1975	1980	1990	2000	2008
Liquefied gas	0.2	0.05	0.2	0.2	0.0
Crude oil	0.8	0.7	0.1	0.4	0.3
Oil products	–	–	1.4	0.0	0.5
Chemicals	0.3	0.1	0.2	0.2	0.2
General cargo	0.7	0.7	0.2	0.2	0.3
Bulk dry	0.2	0.5	0.1	0.1	0.01
Container	0.1	0.03	0.0	0.0	0.02
Refrigerated	–	–	0.01	0.4	0.0
Ro-ro/car	1.8	0.0	4.6	1.8	1.1
Passenger/ro-ro	3.3	2.4	4.6	7.0	5.5
Cruise	–	–	–	0.4	0.3
Offshore	0.2	0.3	0.0	0.05	0.0
Total	**0.6**	**0.6**	**0.3**	**0.4**	**0.3**

How, then, has the international market position of the Finnish fleet developed in a historical perspective? The answer to this question is revealed in Table 6.11.

Clearly, since the shares are so small, most changes in market position are minor and difficult to interpret, but there are some trends that can be detected. First, the international market position of the Finnish passenger/ro-ro fleet seems always to have been fairly strong. From a starting point at 3.3 per cent in 1975 it reached a peak in 2000 at 7 per cent, before being reduced to 5.5 per cent by 2008. Second, Finland's position in cargo-carrying ro-ro ships has also been fairly strong during the period, the peak year in this segment being 1990.[20] While still an important segment in Finnish shipping the trend has clearly been one of decline since that point. Finally, the oil products segment, a new, important part of Finnish shipping, also seems to have seen its heyday around 1990.

By and large, the development of Finnish shipping since 1960 is largely a story of general fleet decline. After experiencing the most substantial expansion of all the Nordic fleets during the 1960s and 1970s, the fleet actually contracted from the 1980s onwards. The one important exception to this trend is represented by the car and passenger ferries. A substantial part of Finnish shipping today is concentrated within this segment, and the companies owning and operating these ships are among the largest of their kind in the world.

The Norwegian fleet

The Norwegian-owned fleet is the largest within the Nordic region. Consistently throughout the period covered here, Norwegian owners have owned more than half of the Nordic fleet in tonnage terms, and for long periods more than 60 per cent. However, in terms of tonnage growth the picture is more mixed. After peaking in 1975 the shipping crisis took a hard toll on the Norwegian fleet, and by 1985 it had been reduced by more than 40 per cent. At that point a new period of expansion began, and by 1990 the fleet had almost regained its 1975 size, continuing to grow until 2000, when a new, short period of contraction started. New growth was again achieved from 2005 to 2008.

The overall experience of Norwegian shipping in the period after the shipping crisis was on this basis fairly positive. As we have seen already, compared to the growth of Danish-owned tonnage, the Norwegians lagged behind. However, while the Danish growth was confined largely to one particular segment – container shipping – the Norwegian fleet expanded in a large number of niches. Many of these were technologically sophisticated, specialized niches, and the capital needed to finance the expansion was substantial. A first impression of this development is provided in Figure 6.10, showing the composition of the Norwegian fleet in 2008, estimated in tonnage terms.

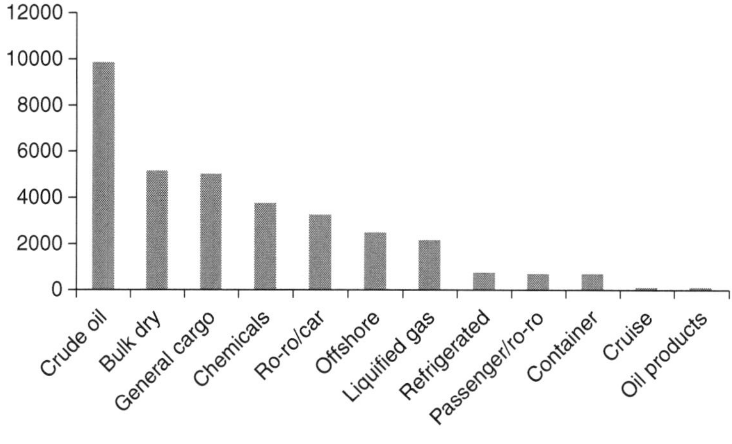

Figure 6.10 Composition of the Norwegian fleet in 2008 ('000 gt)

The figure clearly reveals that the old strongholds of Norwegian shipping, the dry bulk carriers and the tankers, still hold an important position in Norwegian shipping. The relative size of the crude oil segment is particularly impressive when estimated in conventional tonnage terms. It is at the same time evident that the fleet is broadly spread across a large number of specialized segments. In fact, the Norwegian fleet is the only Nordic fleet operating ships in all the 12 segments selected for this overview. Niches such as chemicals, ro-ro/car, offshore service ships, liquefied gas and reefers all hold substantial positions. The historic development of this fleet structure is shown in Table 6.12, where we can see clearly how the importance of the bulk segments has decreased substantially in the period from the mid-1970s, while specialized segments have radically improved their relative position.

By the early 1970s the Norwegian fleet, much like those of the other Nordic countries, was strongly dominated by tankers and dry bulk carriers. In 1975 these segments alone accounted for 86 per cent of total Norwegian tonnage. The comparable figure for the world fleet as a whole was 67 per cent (see Table 6.7), while the combined Nordic fleet consisted of 80 per cent tanker and dry bulk tonnage. From then on, however, the development of the Norwegian fleet started to diverge

Table 6.12 Development in the composition of the Norwegian fleet (per cent)

	1975	1980	1990	2000	2008
Liquefied gas	1.4	3.0	5.6	5.8	6.2
Crude oil	51.2	54.9	42.5	39.3	28.0
Oil products	–	–	3.6	1.0	0.4
Chemicals	1.2	2.8	3.6	6.1	10.7
General cargo	7.1	6.1	2.6	10.8	14.3
Bulk dry	35.2	27.4	31.1	16.2	14.7
Container	0.2	0.3	0.6	1.6	2.0
Refrigerated	0.0	0.0	0.8	1.8	2.2
Ro-ro/car	0.5	0.6	1.2	8.1	9.3
Passenger/ro-ro	0.8	2.3	1.3	1.2	2.1
Cruise	–	–	–	4.4	0.4
Offshore	0.2	0.4	0.6	3.0	7.1
Total	**97.9**	**98.2**	**93.6**	**98.9**	**97.4**

quite substantially from the experiences of the other Nordic fleets. First, the decline in the traditional bulk trades was not as marked in Norway as it was in the other Nordic countries. While the overall tonnage share of the Danish and Finnish bulk fleet (wet and dry) declined by almost 70 per cent, and the Swedish by almost 90 per cent, the relative position of the Norwegian bulk fleet was only halved. By 2008 the bulk fleet still made up more than 40 per cent of the Norwegian fleet, compared to less than 20 per cent in the Danish case, just above 20 per cent in Finland and 10 per cent in Sweden. More importantly, the expansion of the Norwegian fleet was not limited to one or a few segments but was spread across a large number of segments, As the table reveals, a substantial number of niches strengthened their relative position during the period covered. The consequence was that by 2008 the Norwegian fleet was by far the least concentrated of the Nordic fleets.

The spread of Norwegian shipping across a large number of niches, many of which are specialized, becomes even more revealing when the fleet is estimated in cgt. This has been done in Figure 6.11.

As the figure clearly shows, the fleet is indeed spread across a large number of segments, and if a cgt measure is used, the relative position of the specialized niches becomes even stronger. An exception may seem to be the general cargo segment, this being the second largest in Norwegian shipping. But, as already noted, the strong position of this segment is to a large extent explained by the fact that it includes 'open hatch bulk carriers', which is one of the largest specialized niches

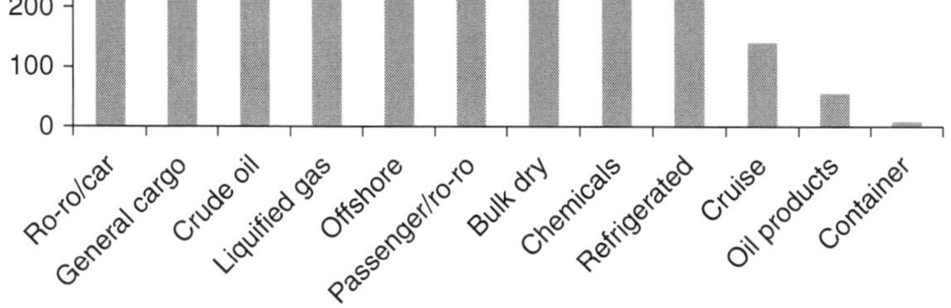

Figure 6.11 Composition of the Norwegian fleet in 2008 ('000 cgt)

within Norwegian shipping (Stokseth, 1992; Tenold, 2009c). Another large segment is specialized car carriers. Norwegians – and, as we shall soon see, Swedes – have been dominant players in this market since its early beginnings in the mid-1960s. Two of the five companies dominating the car-carrying industry today, Wallenius Wilhelmsen and Höegh Autoliners, have a substantial Norwegian ownership. The leading position of the car ro-ro segment does therefore not come as a surprise. It is also well known that Norwegian-owned companies hold substantial market shares within segments such as liquefied gas and chemicals (Svendsen, 1992; Murphy and Tenold, 2008). A less studied, but still very important feature revealed by the figure, is the strong position – also from a Nordic perspective – of offshore service ships. Using a cgt measure, offshore supply ships, which are very small vessels compared to most cargo-carrying ships, is the fifth-largest segment in Norwegian shipping. While not evident from this figure, the strong position of offshore ships represents a significant shift in Norwegian shipping towards offshore services.

In the Norwegian case we have managed to obtain additional data on the composition of the fleet. These are data from the Norwegian Shipowners Association on the estimated market value of the fleet, divided by ship type, in the period from 1987 to 2006. These are effectively indirect estimates of which segments in the fleet have attracted the highest shares of total investment; perhaps the best estimate of the importance of different segments in a national fleet. Figure 6.12 provides the details for 2006.

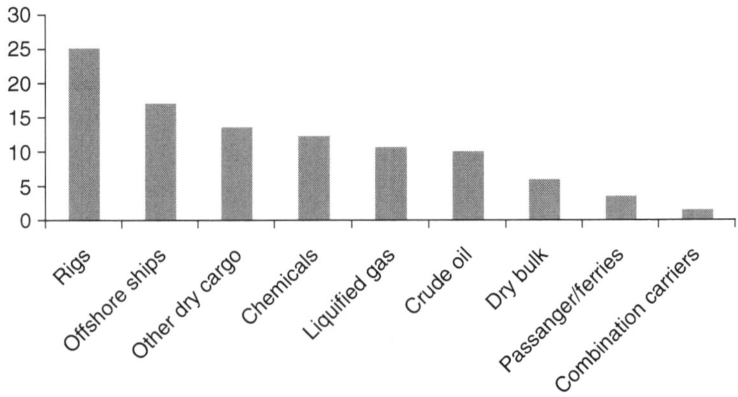

Figure 6.12 Composition of the Norwegian fleet in 2006, by value (per cent)

While the ship-type categories used here differ somewhat from the categories used by Lloyd's, the overall message is clear. The most important segments of Norwegian shipping in 2006 were related to offshore services and included mobile rigs and offshore service ships.[21] Together these two segments accounted for 42 per cent of the total market value of Norwegian-owned shipping in 2006. Recognizable also is the strong position of chemicals and liquefied gas shipping, as well as other dry cargo ships, mostly represented by various specialized segments such as open hatch and car carriers. The position of bulk carriers, by contrast is much less pronounced on this measure, with crude oil carriers, combination carriers and dry bulk carriers together valued at about 18 per cent of the total market value of Norwegian shipping in 2006.

From the specific features of Norwegian shipping and their development in a Nordic perspective it is interesting to relate the Norwegian fleet composition and its development since 1975 to overall trends in the international shipping market. Figure 6.13 depicts the now familiar picture of the fleet's share of the world fleet and some segments.

In line with earlier findings, the figure shows a substantial over-representation in a number of specialized segments, the most prominent being offshore services, reefers, chemicals and cars. As a result of its strong position in open hatch bulk carriers the fleet is also quite substantially over-represented in the general cargo segment but only

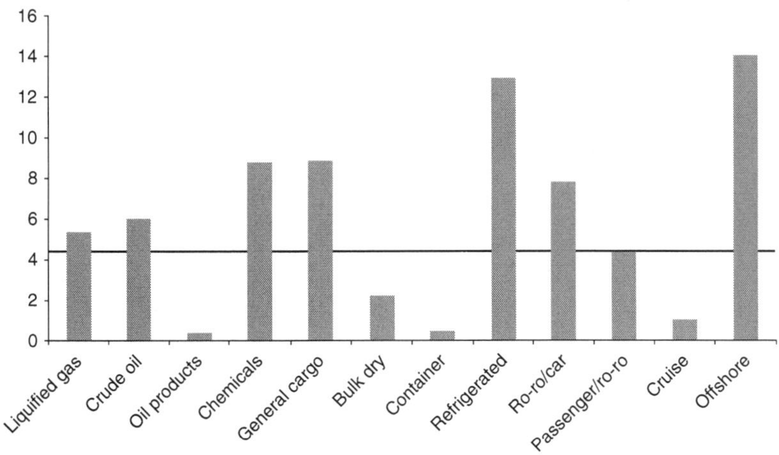

Figure 6.13 Norwegian shares of world fleet and some segments in 2008 (per cent)

Table 6.13 Development in Norwegian share of world fleet and some segments (per cent)

	1975	1980	1990	2000	2008
Liquefied gas	12	9	12.3	11.8	5.4
Crude oil	8.9	6.9	7.7	12.0	6.0
Oil products	–	–	13.6	1.6	0.4
Chemicals	32.5	27.4	24.3	14.0	8.8
General cargo	2.7	1.6	1.2	8.2	9.3
Bulk dry	10.8	5.5	5.5	4.2	2.2
Container	0.8	0.6	0.5	1.0	0.5
Refrigerated	–	–	2.8	8.5	13.1
Ro-ro/car	26.2	11	3.8	11.9	7.9
Passenger/ro-ro	4.6	6.7	4.4	3.6	4.5
Cruise	–	–	–	22.1	1.0
Offshore	4.2	5.1	4.7	15.0	15.4
Total market share	**7.6**	**5.2**	**5.5**	**7.3**	**4.3**

slightly so in the tanker segment. The old stronghold of bulk dry shipping – the Norwegian dry bulk fleet was arguably among the world's largest in the mid-1960s – has, however, been lost (Fon, 1995). Finally, Table 6.13 shows how this relative market composition has developed over time.

Perhaps the most striking feature of this table, not visible by earlier measures, is the development trends in some of the specialized niches, especially chemicals and ro-ro. In 1975 Norwegian owners completely dominated these segments, controlling a third and a quarter of the world fleets respectively. Also, the Norwegian presence in the transportation of liquefied gas was strong from the very beginning. All these segments remained important in Norwegian shipping in 2008, but the market shares have been reduced quite significantly. We also know that Norwegian shipowners were early innovators in the cruise segment and, as the table reveals, in 2000 they actually owned more than a fifth of the world's cruise fleet (Martinussen, 1992; Vadseth et al., 2000). But since then large parts of this fleet have been sold off and ownership has been spread. The growth of the offshore fleet is also marked, especially from the 1990s onwards. In the course of 15 years, the Norwegian-owned share of the world fleet trebled, making Norway the second-largest owner of offshore service ships in the world, the US being the largest. Even more marked is the growth of the reefer fleet, expanding from 2.8 to more than 13 per cent of world tonnage. Finally, we may note the decline in the international position of the Norwegian dry bulk fleet. At more than 10 per cent in 1975, the fleet was still one of the world's largest, but by 2008 its position in world shipping was much less pronounced.

The composition of the Norwegian fleet is characterized by a continued high presence in tanker shipping as well as a broad involvement in a number of specialized segments. In contrast to the other Nordic fleets, which had concentrated much of their tonnage in one or a few segments, Norwegian shipowners continue to operate ships in a number of different ones. These shipowners, moreover, tend to hold dominant positions within their international markets. Therefore, in segments such as liquefied gas, chemicals, open hatch, ro-ro/car, carrying offshore supply and mobile rigs, some of the world's largest companies are fully or partly owned by Norwegian interests. To the extent that the Norwegians have tended to focus on a single segment, offshore related services have indeed become the new backbone of Norwegian shipping, at least if ownership of mobile rigs is included.

The Swedish fleet

Finally, we move on to the Swedish fleet. As we recall, Sweden was the fleet hardest hit by the shipping crisis of the 1970s and 1980s. By 1985 more than half of the fleet had been lost. A short revival then followed before the fleet again experienced a decline from 1995 onwards. By 2008, the Swedish fleet was still smaller in absolute terms than it had been during its historic peak in 1975. As highlighted in Chapter 4, the contemporary history of Swedish shipping is indeed a history of overall decline.

The general impression of a stagnating Swedish merchant marine does not imply, however, that the Swedish shipping fleet did not experience some interesting developments in the period from 1975 to 2008. Quite to the contrary, of all the Nordic fleets, it is probably the Swedish fleet that has seen the most substantial change in its market composition since 1975. Let us first take a look at the composition of the fleet in 2008, as seen in Figure 6.14.

The first striking feature of this graph is, of course, the strong position of the ro-ro/car segment. As already indicated, Swedish shipowners, Wallenius being by far the most prominent, were at the forefront

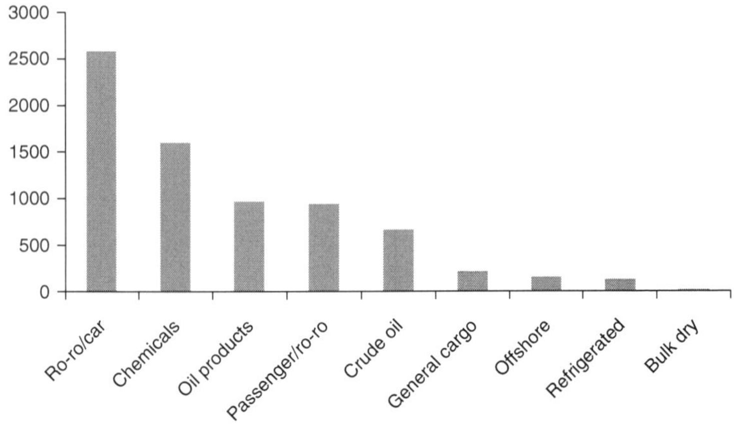

Figure 6.14 Composition of the Swedish fleet in 2008 ('000 gt)

in the development of car carrying as a specialized shipping segment, and have managed to remain one of the biggest players in the world. Hence, the development of the ro-ro/car fleet is an obvious success story in the recent history of Swedish shipping. Some success has also been achieved in niches such as chemicals, passenger/ro-ros and oil products. Tanker shipping and dry bulk carriers, by contrast, seem to play a very small role in Swedish shipping.

Looking at the composition of the fleet 33 years earlier, a very different picture emerges. The details are provided in Table 6.14. Obviously, within the period from 1975 to 2008, Swedish shipping has experienced a more or less complete reversal of its position. Like the other Nordic countries, in 1975 the Swedish fleet was completely dominated by tankers and dry bulk carriers. Together, these constituted almost 80 per cent of the entire fleet. From then on, however, the tanker fleet was radically reduced while the dry bulk fleet simply collapsed. For the tanker fleet, a revival was seen between 1990 and 2000, but subsequently a large proportion of this fleet was sold to foreign owners.[22] Hence by 2008 less than 10 per cent of the fleet was made up of bulk carriers (wet and dry). None of the other Nordic countries experienced a similar collapse in its fleet of tankers and dry bulk carriers.

In parallel with this development, a number of new segments increased their importance in Swedish shipping. First, we see a strong growth in passenger/ro-ros, reaching a peak in 1990 before again reduceing quite substantially. However, the position of this segment in 2008 remains quite strong. As we shall soon see, this is indeed one of the few

Table 6.14 Development in the composition of the Swedish fleet (per cent)

	1975	1980	1990	2000	2008
Liquefied gas	0.5	0.0	0.0	0.0	0.0
Crude oil	40.5	44.2	14.5	39.3	9.2
Oil products	–	–	4.8	3.0	13.2
Chemicals	0.1	1.6	3.3	10.6	21.7
General cargo	14.7	26.1	3.7	3.5	3.0
Bulk dry	37.1	16.4	13.8	3.3	0.2
Container	1.3	1.7	3.2	0.2	0.0
Refrigerated	0.0	0.0	0.0	1.4	1.8
Ro-ro/car	0.0	2.3	12.4	29.4	35.1
Passenger/ro-ro	4.0	5.1	21.8	7.9	12.8
Cruise	0.0	0.0	0.0	0.0	0.0
Offshore	0.03	0.5	0.1	0.6	2.1
Total	**98.3**	**97.8**	**77.5**	**99.2**	**99.2**

segments in Swedish shipping that has largely managed to sustain its overall position in world shipping, despite the trend of overall decline. Oil products and chemicals have also gradually become important Swedish segments. In 2008 oil products constituted 13.2 per cent of the Swedish fleet while chemicals constituted a third of the fleet. In contrast with the Norwegians, Swedish shipowners did not take part in the early development of the chemicals trade, but they gradually managed to get a foothold, and by 2008 the chemical segment had in fact become (relatively) more important for Swedish shipping than for Norwegian shipping.

The most striking development is, however, the ro-ro/car experience, which alone made up more than a third of the Swedish fleet by 2008. It appears from the table that the Swedes, again unlike the Norwegians, established their position in the ro-ro/car trade at a later date, and did not play an important part in the early development of the fleet. But as already noted, it is well known that Swedish shipowner Wallenius dominated the world transport of cars in the 1950s and 1960s.[23] So why, then, are no car carriers registered under Swedish ownership in 1975? This may be explained by the fact that most of Wallenius' ships in 1975 were not pure car carriers (PCC) but rather combined car/bulk carriers, so were probably registered as dry bulk carriers.[24] From 1975 onwards, however, the ro-ro/car segment gradually increased its proportion of Swedish tonnage to become the leading niche in tonnage terms by 2008.

The strong position of car carriers, but also of other specialized segments, and the minuscule role of bulk and general cargo carriers is confirmed when the composition of the fleet is estimated in cgt terms. This is done in Figure 6.15.

As the figure reveals, car carriers continue to hold a dominant position. The largest segment by this measure is, however, the passenger/ro-ros. Like the Finnish case, this fleet is largely made up of passenger ferries. Such ships are expensive to build per ton, so the investment needed to build a passenger ferry is substantially larger than for most other vessels of a similar size. Therefore, while the passenger ro-ro fleet may not seem that important when estimated in tonnage terms, its true economic significance remains substantial.[25]

Looking at the Swedish fleet from an international perspective underlines the strength of the passenger segment, a well as that of the ro-ro/car carriers. Figure 6.16 shows the details.

As can be seen, more than 6 per cent of the world's ro-ro/car tonnage and almost 6 per cent of ro-ro/passenger tonnage is Swedish-owned. Compared to a share below 1 per cent for the fleet as a whole, these segments stand out as the most important remaining strongholds of Swedish shipping. It is also evident that, despite clear tendencies to

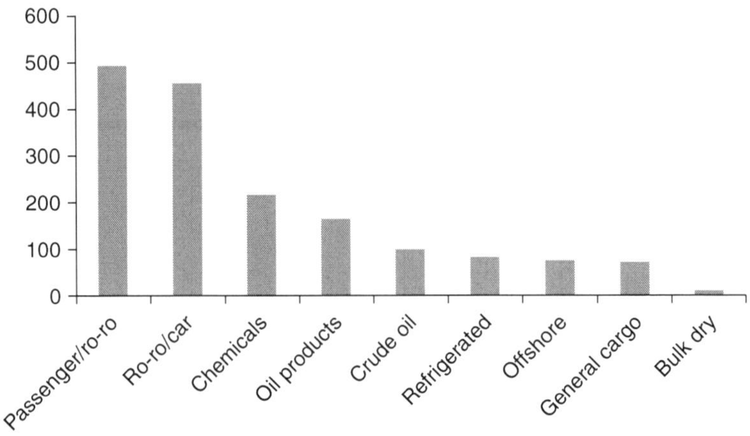

Figure 6.15 Composition of the Swedish fleet in 2008 ('000 cgt)

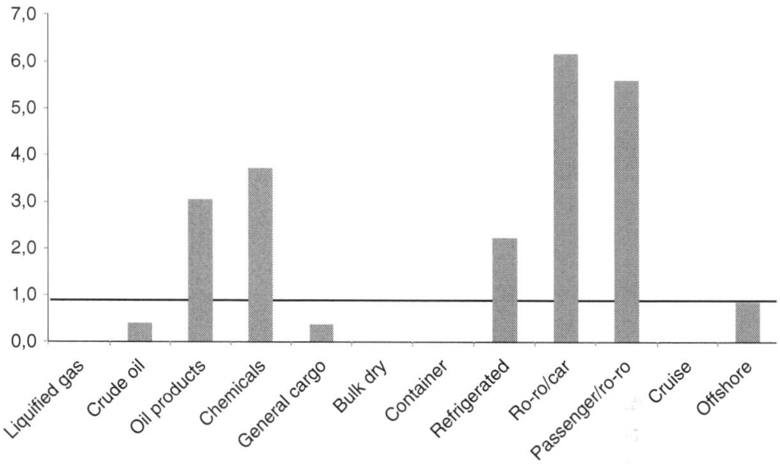

Figure 6.16 Swedish shares of world fleet and some segments in 2008 (per cent)

decline, Swedish shipowners in 2008 still owned almost 4 per cent of the world's fleet of chemical tankers, about 3 per cent of the oil products tankers and more than 2 per cent of the world's reefer fleet. Looking at how this international market position developed historically further confirms that while the overall history of Swedish shipping is clearly one of decline, important exceptions do exist. The details are shown in Table 6.15.

It is clear, looking at the total market share figures, that decline is the overall trend for Swedish shipping, with shares dropping from more than 2 per cent in 1975 to less than 1 per cent by 2008. The decline in segments such as crude oil and dry bulk is also substantial. At the same time, however, within several specialized segments, Swedish shipowners have managed to secure market shares, in some instances substantial ones. Within passenger/ro-ro ships, Sweden's market position has been largely defended. Within car carrying, market shares have also been fairly stable and at times even increasing.[26] Even more impressive is the growth in chemical transport and oil products. From 1975 to 2008 the Swedish-owned share of the world fleet of chemical tankers quadrupled, while Swedish owners also managed to gain more than 3 per cent of the market for product tankers and 2 per cent of the reefer market.

While Swedish shipping has declined substantially in overall tonnage terms from its heyday in the 1960s and early 1970s, the detailed statistics presented here reveals that the contemporary history of shipping

Table 6.15 Development in Swedish share of world fleet and some segments (per cent)

	1975	1980	1990	2000	2008
Liquefied gas	1.3	0.0	0.0	0.0	0.0
Crude oil	2.0	1.1	0.3	2.4	0.4
Oil products	–	–	2.1	1.0	3.2
Chemicals	0.7	3.0	2.6	4.9	3.7
General cargo	1.6	1.4	0.2	0.5	0.4
Bulk dry	3.2	0.6	0.3	0.0	0.0
Container	1.6	0.6	0.3	0.2	0.0
Refrigerated	0.0	0.0	0.0	1.8	2.3
Ro-ro/car	0.4	5.3	4.5	8.7	6.2
Passenger/ro-ro	6.4	2.8	8.6	5.0	5.8
Cruise	–	–	–	0.0	0.0
Offshore	0.2	1.2	0.1	0.6	0.9
Total market share	**2.2**	**1.0**	**0.7**	**1.5**	**0.9**

in Sweden also contains some apparent successes. Most prominently, while declining in traditional tanker and dry bulk segments, Swedish owners have remained dominant players in the world market for car carriers and passenger ferries, and at the same time developed strong positions within chemical shipping, oil products shipping and refrigerated shipping.

The company structure of Nordic shipping

Our analyses of both the overall tonnage development of Nordic shipping and the development of the market composition of the Nordic fleet, during and after the shipping crisis of the 1970s and 1980s, showed significant differences between the Nordic countries. To some extent, the same can be said about the development of the company structure of Nordic shipping. This section analyses that development in the shipping companies operating in the industry within each Nordic country and the average tonnage held by these companies.

From the general literature we know that the shipping industry of the post-Second World War period was characterized not only by increasing specialization, but also by increasing concentration. From being dominated by numerous small companies often operating only one or a few ships, an increasing amount of tonnage was gathered together in large companies. This was part of a general industrialization of shipping, where the objective of exploiting economies of scale, both at the company level and in ship operation, played an increasing role (Stopford, 2009). We also know, however, that from around the mid-1990s onwards this trend towards larger, integrated companies was partly reversed as many shipping companies started to outsource important parts of their activity to specialized firms. One of the most striking examples of this trend was the rise of the ship management companies, specializing in the commercial operation of ships on behalf of external shipowners.

The development in the company structure of Nordic shipping largely confirms this two-stage process, even if the centralization process began at different times in the different Nordic countries. As Figure 6.17 shows, in both Norway and Denmark the number of shipping companies actually continued to rise after 1960. From 1970 onwards however, the trend is clearly one of increasing centralization. In the Nordic fleet as a whole, the number of companies was reduced from 717 in 1970 to 421 in 2000, a reduction of more than 40 per cent. The trend was now similar across the different Nordic countries. In all the countries the number of companies was reduced substantially and the rate of decline was roughly the same.

From 2000 onwards, however, the trend is reversed. The number of shipping companies starts to increase again. Most prominent is the growth

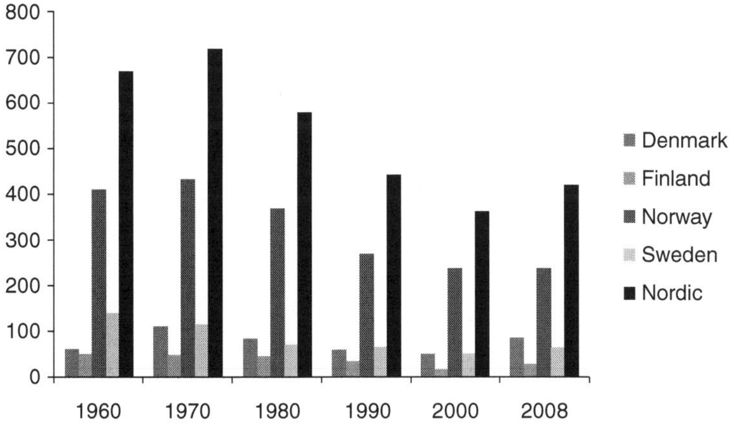

Figure 6.17 Number of shipowning firms in Nordic shipping, 1960–2008

in the number of Danish companies, increasing from 51 in 2000 to 86 in 2008, or by almost 70 per cent. As has been highlighted many times already, apart from the continued growth of the shipping giant Maersk, the substantial growth in Danish shipping during the 1990s and 2000s was to a large extent related to the expansion in the country's ship management business. While Danish citizens owned about 24 million tons of shipping capacity in 2008, more than 40 million tons were actually operated from Denmark. Finland's shipping industry also experienced a quite substantial increase in the number of companies operating within it, as did the Swedes. In Norway, however, the number of companies remained stable.

A second observation to be made from the chart is the high number of shipowning companies operating from Norway, compared with the rest of the Nordic countries. Consistently throughout the period covered Norway hosted more than four times the number of shipping companies of any other Nordic country.[27] In fact, in some years Norway hosted more than twice as many companies as the rest of the Nordic countries combined. Does this large number of companies mean that Norwegian shipping has generally been less concentrated than the other Nordic countries? The simplest way of estimating this is to look at the average share of tonnage owned by each company within the various Nordic countries. This has been done in Figure 6.18, our final figure.

Clearly, on this basis Norwegian shipping is not less concentrated than the shipping industries of the other Nordic countries. On the

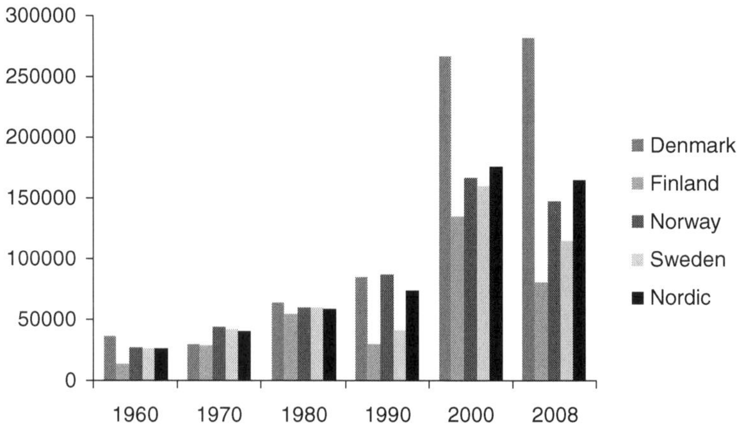

Figure 6.18 Average tonnage owned by Nordic shipowners, 1960–2008

contrary, it has consistently remained among the most concentrated in terms of the average size of the tonnage held by each shipping company. The second striking feature revealed is the substantial increase in the average size of tonnage held by Danish shipping companies, especially from 1990 onwards. By 2000 Danish shipping was by far the most concentrated of the Nordic fleets by this estimate. While the average Nordic shipowner owned 161,000 gross tons of shipping room, the average Danish shipowner owned 266,000 gross tons. This trend was further strengthened between 2000 and 2008. Despite the substantial increase in the number of shipping companies operating from Denmark, average tonnage levels continued to increase, while decreasing in the other Nordic countries.[28]

Appendix – Contemporary shipping statistics and Nordic shipping

The statistical analysis presented in this chapter draws its data from two main sources. The most important is *Lloyd's Register of Shipping Statistical Tables/Lloyd's World Fleet Statistics*.[29] Lloyd's statistical data are commonly regarded as among the most reliable and comprehensive sources for statistics on international shipping. Their fleet statistics have been published annually since 1878 and today contain analyses by ship type, size and age, propulsion, dimensions, ships launched and completed as well as time series on the development of merchant fleets by nationality of owner, country of registry and ship type.[30] In the present chapter, statistics from Lloyd's were the source for data on tonnage developments as well as for developments in the market composition of the Nordic fleet. The second main source is the *Yearbook of Scandinavian Shipowners and Ship Management Companies*, published annually since 1936.[31] This offers a substantial body of data on Scandinavian shipowners, including complete fleet lists and the country and city from which the company operates. From 1994 onwards it also contains data on ship management companies, reflecting the recent growth of such specialized businesses within shipping.[32] These data were used as the source of information on changes in the company structure of Nordic shipping.

The purpose of the analysis was to detect trends, similarities and variations in the development of the merchant fleets of the Nordic countries, as well as for the Nordic region combined. This is, for several reasons, not as straightforward a task as it may seem. At the most general level, it must be recognized that even contemporary shipping statistics are often hampered by inaccuracies. Since not all ships in the world are registered with Lloyd's, the fleet statistics developed by Lloyd's has to be supplemented by existing national sources. Hence, the list is in part a second-hand list. This introduces a number of potential sources of minor error; for example, ship data obtained from national statistics will often not show up in international statistics until a year or two after they have been registered nationally. National statistics may also rely on ship classification systems that differ from those used by Lloyd's. Translating between different classification systems is another obvious source of inaccuracies. When considering the development of the fleets of the various Nordic countries, the observant reader will recognize some fairly substantial differences between the data presented in this chapter, which are based on Lloyd's, and data presented in the chapters on each country, which are often based directly on national sources. While the overall trends are generally not affected by such differences, there may be quite substantial variations in the registered size of a given ship segment or its relative position vis-à-vis other segments, in a given year.

Other problems are caused by changes in how the shipping industry itself has evolved over the years and the difficulties of taking this into account in the statistics. As highlighted in the introduction, the last 40 to 50 years of the shipping industry have been marked by increasing complexity on at least two dimensions.[33] First, the definition of what 'shipping' actually is has become increasingly blurred. Traditionally shipping was linked to the activity of owning and operating merchant ships. Today, however, many shipping companies (a) own ships without operating them, (b) operate numerous ships, without owning them, or (c) operate some ships that they own and some ships that they do not. This is linked to an overall trend whereby the traditional, integrated shipping firm is being replaced by specialized firms focusing on one or a few aspect of the value chain; as expressed by Lorange (2009), 'owning ships, using ships, operating ships or innovating around ships'. A consequence of this development is that it becomes increasingly difficult to define the actual size and importance of the shipping industry in a given country. It is just not obvious what activities or types of companies should be included in the definition of 'shipping'.

This difficulty is compounded by a second complexity, namely that the *nationality* of a given shipping activity also has become increasingly difficult to define. As we have seen, Nordic shipowners operate their ships through companies registered in a number of different countries.

These companies are often publicly listed and hence owned by shareholders of various nationalities. The ships these companies own and/or operate are often build by foreign yards, financed by foreign equity and fly flags of various nationalities, and the crews actually running the ships often come from a number of different countries. Hence the challenge when analysing statistically the size, structure and development of the shipping industry of the Nordic countries is not only to define the activity of shipping, but also to decide according which criteria a given shipping activity may be regarded as, say, Swedish or Finnish.

This problem of nationality became even more difficult from the 1970s and 1980s onwards when most countries liberalized their ship registry rules and more and more companies chose to flag out their ships to open registers, the so-called Flags of Convenience (FoCs). This development posed a major challenge for the statistical determination of the size of a given nation's shipping industry. This had traditionally been based on the size of the country's registered shipping tonnage: the only information needed for assessing the importance of shipping in a country was the total tonnage of ships registered in that country. But as more and more ships were registered outside the country from which the ship was actually owned and operated, this way of collecting data gave an increasingly inaccurate picture of the actual importance of shipping in a country. As a consequence, from the early 1990s, Lloyd's introduced an alternative estimate based on the nationality of the shipowners. Instead of (or, actually, in addition to) recording the country where a ship was registered, the nationality of the owner of the ship was also recorded. This method provided very different results from the traditional 'country of registry' formula. For example, on the basis of registry, it would seem that by 2008 Panama was by far the largest shipping nation in the world, followed by Liberia, the Bahamas and the Marshall Islands. When estimated on the basis of ownership, however, none of these countries was even close to reaching the list of the 20 largest shipping nations in the world. The four largest by this measure were Japan, Greece, Germany and China, in that order.[34]

Using Lloyd's as the main source, the analysis has followed the definitions of fleet nationality used here. This means that for the period from 1960 to 1990 the importance of shipping in a given country is defined by the size of the fleet registered in that country. For the period after 1990, its importance is defined by the size of the fleet owned by the citizens of that country, irrespective of where these citizens live or where the ships and the companies they own are registered.[35] This also implies that the definition of shipping as an economic activity is limited to the act of owning ships. An obvious weakness with such a definition is that it excludes all tonnage that is controlled or managed by a given country's shipowners, but not owned by them. Within a Nordic context, this is particularly problematic in the case of Denmark since, as we have seen, a substantial part of the growth in the Danish shipping industry in the last 20 years has been based on growth in so-called ship management companies. These are companies that operate a number of ships without actually owning them. However, very limited data exist on the growth and importance of such companies, and we have therefore chosen to stick with the ownership criteria. The importance of the ship management sector is, however, reflected partly in the specific data presented in Chapter 3, as well as in the data series on Scandinavian ship owning and ship management companies presented in the last section of this chapter.

A third complicating factor when estimating on a statistical basis the importance of shipping in a country relates to how we measure the *size* and *composition* of a fleet. The standard measurement of ship size is gross tons (gt) and the total size of a fleet or a shipping segment is typically defined by the total gross tonnage of all the relevant ships. But this estimate is not as straightforward as it may seem. Estimating the size of a country's shipping industry in terms of gt may in fact prove to be a quite inaccurate measure of the actual importance of shipping in that country. It may also give a skewed picture of the relative significance of different segments within the total fleet, because of what gt actually measures. A ship's gt is calculated by measuring the total volume of all enclosed spaces of the ship, from keel to funnel to the outside of the hull framing, and by applying a standard formula.[36] Hence, gt is not a estimate of the ship's weight or of the total weight of cargo it can carry, but of cubic capacity. More importantly, gt cannot provide an accurate estimate of the actual cost of a ship, or its 'value...per unit of tonnage'.[37] That is, a large, technologically 'simple' ship costs less to build per ton than a smaller, technologically advanced ship. Put differently, the cost of building a standard bulk carrier is much lower per ton than the cost of building an advanced liquefied natural gas (LNG) tanker. This implies that the actual investment needed to build a gross ton of LNG tanker capacity is higher than that needed to build a similar ton of bulk-carrying capacity. Estimating the size of a fleet with a high proportion of advanced tonnage by gross tonnage will therefore underestimate the true economic significance of that fleet compared to one consisting of less technologically advanced tonnage. While a fleet dominated by specialized vessels may seem small in gt terms, the actual investment needed to finance such a fleet may be substantial. As the chapters for each country have shown, the Nordic fleet is generally characterized by a high share of advanced vessels, so using only a regular gt measurement will tend to underestimate the importance of Nordic shipping in world shipping in economic terms. Gt measurements will, of course, also misrepresent the relative importance of different ship types *within* a national fleet. Simply put, using a standard gt measure will tend to underestimate the importance of the relative more costly specialized tonnage and overestimate the economic performance of bulk and (to some degree) container tonnage.

To some extent, this problem has been tackled by applying a standard conversion method known as the compensated gross tonnage system (cgt). This system was originally developed by international shipbuilding associations in co-operation with OECD to estimate, on the basis of gross tonnage figures, the actual work content of a ship: the work needed to produce a gross ton of a given ship type. Indirectly, however, the measure also estimates the cost per ton of building a given ship and hence also the investment needed to build the ship. Converting the gross tons of a fleet into cgt therefore provides us with a better impression of the true economic significance of a fleet, relative to other fleets, as well as the actual importance of various ship segments within it.[38]

The best way of estimating the importance of shipping in a country, as well as the relative importance of different shipping segments within that country, would probably be calculations based on investment levels. Ideally one would want figures on the levels of investment in shipping, both at the aggregate level, and also disaggregated to total investments in various ship types or shipping segments. We have, however, not been able to collect a complete sample of such figures for the present publication. Some indirect estimates for the Norwegian shipping industry, showing the development in the market value of the various segments within the Norwegian fleet were, however, obtained and presented in the analysis.

In many respects, the statistical analysis presented in this chapter is necessarily flawed, with minor inaccuracies and potential pitfalls. However, by making all the possible problems and shortcomings of the data clear to the reader, and by offering alternative calculations and measurements where possible, we nonetheless believe the analysis offers the best possible view of the main trends in Nordic shipping in the period from 1960 to 2008.

Notes

1. I have included Iceland in the general overview, but do not provide a separate analysis of the composition and the structure of the Icelandic shipping industry. The data on Denmark includes the fleet of the Faroe Islands. A through discussion of the data and the general challenges of contemporary shipping statistics are provided in a separate appendix at the end of this chapter.
2. Unless otherwise stated, all tonnage data are estimated in gross tons.
3. In 1990 the size of national shipping fleets was still estimated on the basis of country of registration. While NIS, established in 1987, was an open registry and hence open for ships of all nationalities, ships registered there were counted in the statistics as Norwegian (NIS). It is evident that many of the Norwegian ships that had fled their national flag during the shipping crisis, now returned to NIS. The same was the case with the Danish flag (although DIS, established in 1988, was not an open register). See Chapters 2 and 3 for details.
4. It should be noted that since both Finnish and the Swedish shipping companies increasingly registered their ships under foreign flags, the extremely high growth rates recorded between 1990 and 1995 has in part a statistical explanation. In 1990 the size of the fleets was defined by country of registry while in 1995 it was defined by the nationality of the owner. We know that a revival in both Swedish and Finnish shipping occurred in the late 1980s, but since most of the ships were registered abroad this expansion was not recorded in the statistics – that is, not before 1995, when the size of the fleets was defined not by total tonnage registered in Sweden and Finland but by the total tonnage owned by Swedish and Finnish citizens. While it may seem from the figures in Table 6.2 that Swedish and Finnish shipping declined substantially from 1985 to 1990, only to see substantial growth in the next five-year period, the actual development in Swedish-and Finnish-owned shipping was probably more one of slow revival from the mid-1980s onwards. See Chapters 4 and 5.
5. A similar figure is presented in Chapter 1.
6. See Chapter 1.
7. Of course, by 1950 quite a few specialized tankers were in operation, but the total fleet of tankers still represented only a small fraction of the world fleet. For an overview, see Stopford (2009).
8. For a study of the growth of tanker tonnage, see Ratcliffe (1985). For the dry bulk fleet, see Fon (1995).
9. For studies (of various quality) tracing this development, see Burg (1969), Drewry (1978), Broeze (1998a, 2002), Cudahy (2006), Donovan and Bonney (2006) and Levinson (2006).
10. See Stopford (2009).
11. Unlike the time series in the previous section, the series presented here starts in 1975. The reason is simple. Before 1975 Lloyd's statistical tables (or any other statistics) only reported separate data for a few types of specialized ships. Before 1970 the only distinction made was between different means of propulsion (motor or steam) and the material from which the hull was built (steel, iron or wood/composite). From 1970 onwards Lloyd's provided a more detailed overview of national fleets divided into ten different

segments. But many of the segments that eventually came to dominate world shipping were very small at this point, many were not included at all, some of the segments having separate categories in 1970 were gradually phased out while others were irrelevant to the present study (for example, fishing vessels). Hence 1975 is the first year from which it makes sense to start a serial study of market segmentation over time. In the data presented, 'fish-catching' and 'other fishing' vessels have been excluded, as well as a number of minor segments such as 'passenger/general cargo', 'passenger', 'other dry cargo', 'towing/pushing', 'tugs', 'dredgers', 'ice-breakers', 'live-stock carriers' and 'other activities'. In 2008 these segments together made up about 3 per cent of the total world fleet in tonnage terms.

12. Compensated gross tonnage (cgt) is a specific tonnage measurement developed by international shipbuilding associations in co-operation with the OECD. The purpose is to estimate on the basis of gross tonnage figures the actual work content of a ship, that is, the actual work needed to produce a gross ton of a given ship type. A broader description is provided in the appendix.
13. The average size of a Nordic general cargo carrier in 2008 was roughly 8000 gt. In comparison, the average oil tanker exceeded 90,000 gt while the average ship size for the fleet combined was close to 20,000 gt.
14. For a similar type of presentation of Norwegian shipping separately, see Tenold (2010).
15. For a detailed analysis of how this development unfolded within chemical shipping and also, in part, for the open hatch bulk segment, see Murphy and Tenold (2008) and Tenold (2009a).
16. For instance, the ranking according to owner's nationality differs from a ranking according to the owner's country of residence. See the appendix for a broader discussion.
17. Note that this is a rough estimate, as it has not been weighted by the size of the different Nordic countries.
18. Detailed overviews of the ownership structure of the world's car carrying fleet in the 1970s is provided by Drewry shipping consultants; see Drewry (1977). The first of the flexible ro-ro ships were launched in the late 1960s and were employed both in smaller line trades and as tramps. In addition to rolling cargo they could normally also take containers on deck. For many shipowners they offered a more flexible alternative to full containerization. For overviews, see Drewry (1980, 1985).
19. It should be noted that the figures for 1975 and 1980 are uncertain and may be too small. Lloyd's records only three ro-ro car ships in the Finnish fleet in 1975 and none in 1980. According to other sources, however, the ro-ro fleet had already reached 13 ships by 1973 (see Chapter 5). This discrepancy is certainly a puzzle, but is probably explained simply by differences in how the ships have been categorized. See the appendix for more information.
20. The zero tonnage recorded for 1980 is, however, a puzzle. It may, of course, simply stem from incorrect registration.
21. Mobile rigs are not defined as shipping in Lloyd's statistics, but have since the exploration of oil and gas started in the North Sea in the early 1970s been an integral part of Norwegian shipping. Most of the companies investing in mobile rigs in the 1970s were owners, and a separate organization was also set up within the Norwegian Shipowners Association to represent the interest of the rig owners. An overview is provided by Karlsen (1992).

22. See Chapter 4. For a broad analysis, see Lennerfors (2009).
23. See Chapter 4 and, for example, Drewry (1977) and Nerheim and Gjerde (1996).
24. According to Drewry, Wallenius by 1977 was 'believed to have over 20 car carriers under his control, of which three...are pure car carriers'. One of these, the *Montmorency* entered service in 1973, and if registered in Sweden, should have appeared in the 1975 data. The other two were supposedly delivered in 1976 – see Drewry (1977). However, according to Wallenius's own version, these two ships – the *Don Juan* and the *Don Carlos* – were in fact the first PCCs in the fleet and entered service in 1975 and 1976, www.wallenius.com (accessed 12.11.10).
25. The majority of passenger ferries are owned by Stena Line, one of the largest ferry companies in the world; it operates routes within Scandinavia, the North Sea and the Irish Sea.
26. Remember that the 1975 figure grossly underestimates the true position of Swedish shipping in the car-carrying segment, as it only includes pure car carriers (PCC).
27. The only exception being Denmark in 2008, which then hosted about a third of the number of companies operating from Norway.
28. As concerns Denmark, it should also be remembered that the figures presented here only includes tonnage owned by Danish shipping companies. If the tonnage controlled by these companies were included the difference would have been even larger.
29. From 1878 to 1991 the data were published under the heading Lloyd's Register of Shipping *Statistical Tables*, from 1992 as *Lloyd's World Fleet Statistics*.
30. It should be noted that printed ship registers were published by Lloyd's well before 1878, but their international reach was more limited then.
31. The publication has changed title several times and was originally called *'Norske skibsrederier: med opgaver over skib i utenriks fart: ledelse, coder, linjer, utenlandske agenter, skibenes byggeår, størrelse, dypgående, fart,* etc.'.
32. The data are collected by the small Norwegian company Selvig Publishing and are 'partly based on replies received from the respective owners and/or from our own editorial research on Internet, from press releases and other sources'; see Selvig and Selvig (2000).
33. See Chapter 1.
34. All of these countries were, however, on the top twenty registry list, Greece being number five, China number nine, Japan number twelve, and Germany number fourteen (figures from *Lloyd's World Fleet Statistics*, 2008).
35. The use of FoCs, at least for Nordic shipowners, was quite limited during the 1960s and 1970s, but started to increase quite dramatically during the 1980s. The consequence in statistical terms is that while the gap between ship registry and actual ownership was minuscule, if increasing slightly during the 1960s and 1970, it became quite substantial during the 1980s. Hence, ideally one would also want data for the 1980s estimating the size of a given nation's shipping fleet on the basis of the owner's nationality. While some scattered evidence does exist, it is too sparse and unsystematic to be applied in a time series. For 1980 the United Nations Conference on Trade and development (UNCTAD) offered an overview of the country or territory of the beneficial owners of open registry fleets, the beneficial owner being

defined as 'the person, the company or organization which gains the pecuniary benefits from the shipping operations' (UNCTAD, 1980). Apart from this, however, all figures on fleet size and fleet size development presented by UNCTAD are based on data supplied by Lloyd's. It is worth nothing that UNCTAD reports the size of national fleets on the basis of ships' 'country of domicile'. This may seem somewhat different from defining the size on the basis of the nationality of the owner, as the country of domicile is supposed to indicate 'where the controlling interest [i.e. parent company] of the fleet is located'. It is, however, unclear how strict the country of domicile definition is followed. As the UNCTAD reports specify: 'in several cases, determining this [the country of domicile] has required making certain judgments. Thus, for instance, Greece is shown as the country of domicile for vessels owned by a Greek owner with representative offices in New York, London and Piraeus, although the owner may be domiciled in the United States'; see (UNCTAD, 2005). This obviously looks quite similar to the definition applied by Lloyd's, based on the 'nationality of the owner'. A possible second alternative source for statistics on fleet development could have been the data developed by the Institute of Shipping Economics and Logistics in Bremen, but this source reports only ship registry/fleet size by flags before 1990, see ISL. As a consequence, we are obliged to accept that the figures for 1985 and 1990 probably somewhat underestimate the actual size of the shipping fleet owned by Nordic citizens.

36. Details are provided in IMCO (1969).
37. Tenold (2001b).
38. The figure is calculated by multiplying the gross tonnage of the ship (or a fleet of similar ships) by an appropriate, ship-specific, conversion factor. For details see OECD (2007). For a short description see Stopford (2009).

7
A Future for Nordic Shipping?

Victor D. Norman

This book has looked at the varied experience of Nordic shipping over the past decades. In this concluding chapter I shall try to use this as a basis for looking ahead. The aim is not to predict what will happen, but to identify issues that could be critical for the future of shipping companies based in the Nordic countries and thus provide a framework which may be useful when assessing the future potential for shipping based in that area.

The fundamental issue, of course, is whether the Nordic countries still have comparative advantage in international seaborne transportation. The British shipping economist Richard Goss once said that Norwegian shipping seemed to him to be a prime example of *comparative* advantage: Norwegians invested in shipping simply because the return on alternative use of Norwegian resources was low. That may have been the case historically. It is not so today and has not been so for a long time. It has been argued that the US shipping industry disappeared because the US became too rich. If so, the outlook for the Nordic shipping industry today should be bleak indeed.

The question, therefore, is whether Nordic shipping, in markets where it competes with companies based in locations which are both cheaper and closer to the main transport routes, can earn sufficiently to compete with domestic sectors in the Nordic countries for resources such as equity capital and key personnel.

It could be that the answer is 'yes' for some segments of Nordic shipping and 'no' for others. Nordic shipping varies – between countries and between regions within countries – and it is not inevitable that all will flourish or all perish. It may be that the Norwegian shipping cluster, with small companies tightly interlinked through the system of brokers and financial institutions that is the backbone of the industry, will be more adaptable than the Danish model, where the backward linkages are internalized in large corporations. Or it could, of course, be the other way around. Similarly, the 'industrial' shipping companies we find in Finland and Western Norway may be more robust than the speculative tramp shipping companies that abound in Oslo. And then again, perhaps not.

The previous chapters have focused on the differences in recent history between the Nordic countries: the sad demise of Swedish shipping, the restructuring force of creative destruction in Norway, Finnish exceptionalism and the remarkable record of corporate professionalism in Denmark.

I shall argue that, despite all this, the similarities between companies within Nordic shipping are more striking than their differences and that it is meaningful to speak about an industry that tends to flourish or struggle in unison.

The most important point of similarity is the one I have touched upon already: the companies are based in high-wage, high-income countries remote from the major trading routes in the world. Another is that these countries have long maritime traditions that are reflected in other industries: engineering, insurance and finance in the Nordic countries have, at least traditionally, had a much stronger focus on the maritime sector than is the case in other countries. A third point of similarity, and the one I shall take as my point of departure, is that Nordic shipping is dominated by independent suppliers of transport services – they are not in-house transport divisions in companies mainly concerned with production and sale of goods.

The question I shall ask, therefore, is whether there is a (profitable) future for independents based in the Nordic countries.

To arrive at an answer, I shall have to make a detour, starting with a more general discussion of outsourcing of water transportation (which is the entire basis for independent shipping companies), moving on to the characteristics and historical profitability of independent companies and the changes that are likely to occur in these in the future. This detour will provide a framework for assessing the future of Nordic independents.

Outsourcing of seaborne transport

There is nothing new about independent providers of shipping services. The term 'outsourcing' was not a common one until the 1980s, but seaborne transportation has been outsourced to independent operators for hundreds of years, and independent shipowners in Scandinavia go back to at least the seventeenth century.

Nevertheless, there is something inherently strange about independent shipping as an outsourced activity. We ordinarily think of outsourcing as a close and reasonably long-term contractual relationship between a producer and a subcontractor. There are plenty of examples of such relationships in shipping – shipping companies specializing in car carriers, liquefied natural gas (LNG) or chemical carriers have typically had long-term contracts with production companies. For many commodities, however – the markets for bulk transportation in particular – short-term contracts are as common as long-term, and in many cases, independent shipping companies take on a larger part of the risks than is common in other forms of outsourcing.

Some might argue that it is misleading to look at bulk shipping (and other forms of tramp shipping) as an outsourced activity: that this is a standardized service that is bought and sold in ordinary markets, without the characteristics and special problems that we typically associate with outsourcing.

As I see it, that is not the case. Historically, most forms of tramp shipping – from the tea clippers to modern tankers – started as in-house transport activities in companies engaged in commodity production and trade. Even international liner shipping has its historical roots in-house (in private trading houses and the British postal service). Economically, tramp shipping is a clear example of outsourcing in the sense that (a) it is the commodity carried, not the transport service itself, which is of value to the final user, (b) the value of the commodity is high relative to the cost of carrying it, so transportation is a small (but important) part of the value chain, and (c) the quality of the transport service (cargo handling and speed) is important, but not always easily observable.

There are three reasons why a firm can benefit from outsourcing. First, independents can be cheaper – because they are located in a low-cost venue; because, being specialized, they can operate more efficiently; because they compete with each other; or possibly for other reasons. Second, independents can provide a benchmark and exert competitive pressure on in-house providers of the same service, thus making the firm's in-house operations more efficient. Third, independents may be able to spread the risks associated with under- or overcapacity in ways that are impossible for in-house operations, thus providing a more favourable risk-return schedule than a production firm can achieve on its own.

These general benefits must be weighed against the agency problems that outsourcing entails: the shipping company will not have the same interests as the charterer when it comes to safety, quality and reliability.

To ensure the service the charterer wants, therefore, he must either spend resources on vetting the company and monitoring the shipping operation, or pay extra to make sure the shipping company has an economic incentive to do a good enough job to keep the contract.

Independent shipping is the rule, not the exception, in international seaborne transportation, so the trade-off between the agency costs and the benefits must generally favour outsourcing. It is instructive to ask why that is so: why are independent shipping services cheap, why do they provide a favourable risk-return schedule, and why do these gains offset the agency problems? The answers may shed important light on the prospects for independent companies based in high-cost countries.

The price of independent tramp shipping services

Let us begin with tramp shipping, that is, those markets (for transportation of oil, bulk cargoes, etc.) that are sufficiently large and standardized to ensure a large number of companies and a high degree of competition, and that are also well-developed markets, both for short- and long-term charters and for second-hand vessels.

We do not have comprehensive data on what charterers have to pay for independent tramp shipping services compared to what it would have cost them to do the job themselves. There are, however, good reasons to believe that freight rates tend to be low relative to the costs to independents of providing the service and the risks they undertake.

First, there is some evidence that independent tramp shipping, historically, has been a losing proposition for the companies involved. The first to point this out was Zannetos (1966), in a pioneering study of the oil tanker market. He demonstrated that tanker shipping was a loss-making activity, in the sense that the expected long-term rate of return in tanker shipping was lower than in alternative investments. Because the market logic is the same in other bulk transport markets, it is likely that these results carry over to dry bulk.

Bulk shipping is not, of course, always a low-profit activity. There have been long periods with reasonably good returns – the 25 years following the Second World War and the years of the wave of globalization in the 1990s are examples. The typical pattern, however, is one of short boom periods followed by long periods of depressed freight rates. According to Bennathan and Walters (1969), this is as it should be. The cost of transport capacity is low relative to the cost of not having it when needed, so the optimum capacity should be higher than the expected transport requirements. Specifically, if we abstract from risk aversion, the optimum capacity is such that the probability of undercapacity relative to the probability of overcapacity should equal the cost of a ton of overcapacity relative to the cost of a ton of undercapacity.

If we take transportation of crude oil as an example, the cost of a ton of undercapacity is the net profit that an oil company would make from a ton of oil which it is unable to carry. With an oil price of US \$100 a barrel, the price per ton is US \$700. Assuming that production costs plus royalties and taxes to the oil producer take 90 per cent of this, we are still left with a net value to the oil company of US \$70 per ton; and thus with a cost to the company of the same amount if oil cannot be delivered because of a shortage of tonnage. The cost of a ton of overcapacity is the capital cost (per dwt per potential voyage) of building a tanker (which is then laid up). A Very Large Crude Carrier (VLCC) has in recent years cost between US \$100 and 150 million, which gives a capacity cost of a little over US \$10 dollars per ton (not) carried between the Persian Gulf and Europe. Thus, the ratio of overcapacity to undercapacity costs is around 1 to 7; so the optimum capacity should give, on the average, one year to undercapacity to every seven years of overcapacity. Figure 7.1 illustrates this argument.

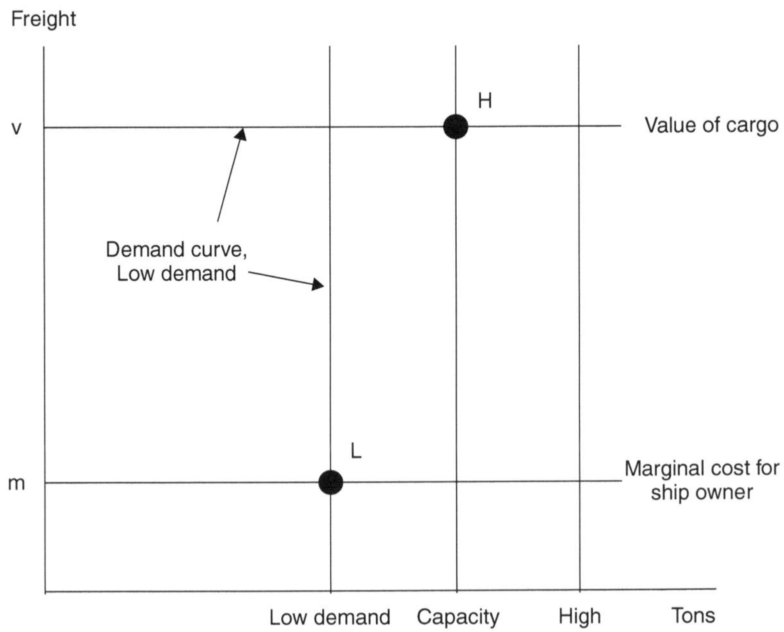

Figure 7.1 The Walters argument

With low demand, the market equilibrium will be met at L. The freight rate will equal marginal cost, and the shipowner profit will be zero. With high demand, equilibrium will be at H. The freight rate will equal the value of the cargo, and the shipowner will make a profit per ton carried of $(v\text{-}m)$.

A risk-neutral shipowner will invest so long as the expected profit per ton is higher than the cost of providing an extra ton of capacity, call it c. In equilibrium, therefore, the capacity will be such that

$$p_{\mathrm{H}}(v - m) = c,$$

where p_{H} is the probability of high demand (i.e. the probability of undercapacity). It follows that the equilibrium capacity will be such that

$$p_{\mathrm{H}} = \mathrm{c}/(v - m).$$

The implication is that tramp shipping is inherently extremely risky. In cases of overcapacity, freight rates will be close to lay-up costs, so there will be zero profits. In cases of undercapacity, shipping companies will capture the entire rent that normally accrues to the charterer. Thus, in the oil transportation example, investment in a tanker is like buying a lottery ticket with a 1 in 8 chance of winning eight times the price of the ticket and a 7 in 8 chance of getting nothing.

This would not be a viable market solution if independent shipowners were risk-averse. To be attractive to shipping investors, the high inherent risk would have to be offset by a correspondingly high-risk premium.

The problem is that shipowners (at least Nordic ones) do not seem to be risk-averse. In a study carried out in 1970, Peter Lorange and I interviewed 17 Scandinavian tanker owners, presenting each of them with a series of hypothetical investments to map their attitudes to risk (Lorange and Norman, 1973). All but one systematically preferred a risky investment to a safe alternative with the same expected return. When we submitted the study to the *Journal of Political Economy*, it was rejected because, as the editor argued, he did not believe the results because 'such investors would not last long'. He was right: nine of the owners went out of the tanker business within ten years.

These shipowners were not oddballs, and some well-known gamblers, such as Hagbart Waage and Hilmar Reksten, were not even among them. A few were regarded as active risk-takers, but the group included many who were seen as prudent and highly professional – Tom Wilhelmsen, Leif Høegh, Sven Salen, Einar Rasmussen, Nils Astrup Sr – to mention a few. The group as a whole had, if anything, an establishment bias.

It should be noted that we also asked the shipowners what their answers would have been had they been subject to liquidity constraints, and we found that all of them would act more conservatively in that case. This was confirmed in a follow-up study by Eckbo (1977). This does not alter the fundamental conclusion: the owners *preferred* risky investments to safe ones – they would *act* differently if they were short of cash, but only because that would constrain their choice sets.

Panel studies should be interpreted with care. One can also argue that there is a selection bias in studies such as ours, where we interviewed shipowners who at the time had been the most successful: among these, there was likely to be an over-representation of owners who had gambled and won. It does not follow that there would be an over-representation of gamblers, however: gamblers who had lost would be as over-represented among unsuccessful companies as lucky ones would be over-represented among the successful ones.

Ultimately, the strongest reason for believing in the result is the reason the *JPE* editor gave for rejecting the paper.

It seems likely, therefore, that Zannetos was right: independent tramp ship owners are willing to offer a service that is inherently unprofitable, at least in the sense that they need not be paid for the very substantial market risk they undertake.

The survival paradox

If tramp shipping is so unprofitable and so risky that it attracts only risk-prone investors, how has the industry survived? Gambler's ruin will eventually overtake even the most prudent investor, but in the case of risk-prone ones, 'eventually' will typically mean 'very soon'.

One answer is that yes, shipping companies tend to face gambler's ruin quite quickly. This is particularly striking in Norwegian shipping, where few companies – even large ones – survive for more than a generation. The period following the shipping crisis in the 1970s provides striking examples of this, with the demise of large, first-generation companies such as Reksten, Waage and Jahre. As shown by Tenold in Chapter 2, one of the most characteristic features of Norwegian shipping over the past decades has been the dramatic change in the composition of firms.

The last 40 years are not unique in this respect. As shown in Norman (2005), there was an equally dramatic change in the company composition of the Norwegian shipping industry from 1914 to 1950: of the 11 largest companies in 1914, four had disappeared by 1950; and of the 11 largest in 1950, four did not exist in 1914 and three had grown from virtually nothing. The numbers are even more striking for small to medium companies. In Bergen, almost half (28 of 62) of the shipping companies in 1920 had disappeared from the ship registry by 1938; and of the active companies in 1938, one in four had been established after 1920.

If this were the entire story, the long-term survival of the industry would have to be explained by a steady influx of new, risk-prone investors to replace those who had gambled and lost. While this is undoubtedly part of the story, it cannot be the only explanation – simply because the exceptions to the short life-span rule are too many and too striking. Companies like Fred. Olsen and Wilh. Wilhelmsen in Norway, or A. P. Møller in Denmark, have been large and robust shipping companies for more than 100 years; and while they have had their shares of high-risk investments, they cannot be characterized simply as risk-prone gamblers.

There are at least two important elements that have to be added to give a complete story.

The first is the profits from intermediation – or from deal-making, to use a more expressive phrase. Running a shipping company is not the same as being a shipping investor. Nordic shipping companies have traditionally invited external equity investors to participate on a project basis in their investments, and the external equity shares have often been higher than those of the company itself or its owners. Many Nordic independents are thus in reality capital market intermediaries as much as investors. Their profits are then as much payment for organizing investment projects and managing vessels owned by others as returns on their own investments. With risk-loving (or tax-leveraged) external investors, such profits can easily be high even if the project itself has a low expected return.

The second element is that asset markets in shipping seem to be inefficient, in the sense that they do not follow a random walk (Norman, 1981). When markets are depressed, vessels (and time charters) are systematically underpriced; when markets are high, they are overpriced.

Inefficient asset pricing is not as surprising as it may seem at first glance. Ordinarily we should expect all available market information to be reflected in asset prices simply because professional traders would buy or sell if prices differed from the expected future value of the assets. That conclusion hinges on the free entry and exit of professional traders. For speculative investments in ships, however, a trader must be able to operate vessels efficiently from purchase to future sale (or find someone else to do that job for him). If good management is in limited supply, which is a reasonable assumption in the short to medium term, the scope for financial traders is limited. Moreover, some of the pure rents from speculation would accrue to those managing the ship from purchase to sale.

The implication is that there are systematic profit opportunities, for companies with management competence and capacity, from good timing of sale and purchase of ships.

This accords well with the conventional wisdom within the industry, which has it that most of the profits made historically come from sale and purchase. That is probably to overstate the point – and a natural consequence of misleading accounting in settings with general inflation and liberal depreciation allowances – but it is nevertheless worth noting. It is also worth pondering, however. The sale and purchase of second-hand vessels is a zero-sum game, so any speculative profit made by one owner is a loss to another. If a major part of the profits made by existing companies comes from good timing of sale and purchase, the implication is therefore that there must be a corresponding loss made by companies which have gone out of business.

The conclusions we can draw from this discussion seem to be (a) that it is possible to survive as an independent shipping company even if the expected, risk-corrected return from shipping investments is low (and lower than in alternative investments), and (b) that those who survive are (i) lucky, (ii) able to earn pure rents from deal-making or (iii) capable of trading on inefficient pricing in shipping asset markets to make systematic profits from good timing. In all three cases, survival is contingent on the death of someone else.

Aside from pure luck, another conclusion is that the profits of the survivors is their return on competence – ability to organize and manage shipping investment projects, ability to operate and charter ships efficiently, and ability to analyse shipping asset markets. This return is a pure rent arising either because there is a shortage of management capacity or because the companies in question have above-average ability to analyse asset markets.

Agency problems and industrial shipping

There are serious agency problems relating to independent shipping. In the 1890s the Norwegian barque *Britannia* loaded a cargo of ice in Risør, Norway for New York. The charter party did not specify which route the ship should take for the Atlantic crossing, so the captain chose the pleasant, southern one via the Azores – and arrived in New York with a cargo of water. The cargo owner refused to pay the agreed freight; the shipowner sued – and won!

Ensuring proper and efficient handling of the cargo is the fundamental agency problem for cargo owners. Traditionally, this has been handled through detailed, standardized charter parties or other contracts. For bulk cargoes such as oil, grain, iron ore and other raw materials, that seems to have been enough. For other goods the problem is more complex. Offshore loading of oil or handling of dangerous (and sometimes unstable) chemicals is so risky and difficult that the cargo owner needs greater assurances from the shipping company than a signature on a standard contract. The typical solution has been a closer relationship – longer-term contracts, more often in the nature of a relationship contract (i.e. a contract that does not specify all details, leaving things open for future dialogue), and sometimes granting the shipping company exclusive rights to carry goods for the cargo owner.

If this sounds very much like what is commonly called industrial shipping, that is because it is. Industrial shipping (sometimes also called niche-market shipping or knowledge-based shipping) is commonly defined as seaborne transportation for cargo owners with special requirements as regards the vessel, the transport service, or customer handling. It is true that transportation of chemicals and cars falls into this category, as does transportation of oil from offshore installations and most other examples commonly given. The problem is that the definition applies equally well to general transportation of crude oil or iron ore (you need an oil tanker or a dry bulk carrier, so you have special vessel requirements) or transportation of general cargo in container ships (you have special transport service requirements, such as frequency and destinations).

It is more fruitful to define industrial shipping as shipping in market segments where the agency problems are so severe that they cannot be handled by ordinary market instruments.

It is often asserted that industrial shipping is more profitable and less risky than tramp shipping. Looking at industrial shipping from an agency perspective makes it easier to understand why that may be true. It could simply be a case of so-called efficiency pricing: the cargo owner may not be able to monitor cargo handling perfectly (or it may be costly to do so). A more attractive alternative may be to offer a high freight rate, but making it clear that the relationship will be terminated at any sign that the quality of the service is not being maintained. This will give the shipping company the necessary incentive to maintain the quality that the cargo owner wants.

There is little doubt that industrial shipping has been a lucrative alternative for some independent shipping companies. It is equally clear that it is not an option for all independents, (a) because the industrial market segments are small relative to total seaborne transportation, and (b) because an efficiency price premium ultimately is payment for quality, and not all independents can provide that quality.

It is also worth noting that industrial shipping tends to become more standardized and transparent over time. Transportation of chemicals, cars and offshore oil was technologically difficult and hard to monitor at the outset. Today the technological and managerial solutions are well established, the monitoring issues are simpler, and the number of companies capable of providing high-quality services is correspondingly large. As a result, the efficiency price premiums needed to ensure high quality have declined.

What about risk? Is industrial shipping a safer haven than tramp shipping? The correct answer is probably 'yes and no'. Industrial shipping may provide companies with safer and more predictable freight earnings than tramp shipping (although many of them face a risk associated with freight volumes that owners of vessels on time charters do not face). They face the same risk associated with newbuilding markets for ships, however, and the risks associated with second-hand values of vessels are, if anything, higher for the owner of highly specialized tonnage than for an owner of a standard tanker or bulk carrier.

The future of Nordic shipping

The detour is completed. It is time to use the framework to assess the future potential of Nordic shipping.

The Nordic countries are, in general terms, in the same position the US was when American shipping declined: domestic economies with high productivity and shortage of manpower and with reasonably good investment opportunities both at home and abroad – and as a result with expensive labour and not particularly cheap capital. If they still have a comparative advantage in shipping, therefore, it is unlikely to be of the Heckscher–Ohlin, relative factor-abundance type. On the contrary, shipping companies based in the Nordic countries will start with a cost handicap.

They can (as most have done already) compensate for this by using Asian crews instead of Nordic ones and by getting cheap capital from the government (through special tax schemes) or from risk-loving private investors. They can also compensate for high costs by capitalizing on inefficient shipping asset pricing, in other words, by being better at timing of sale and purchase than other companies. Finally, they can compensate by cashing in the efficiency price premium paid by cargo owners in industrial market segments.

The problem is that these options may be self-defeating or mutually exclusive.

One of the most marked changes in Nordic shipping – with a few notable exceptions – is the move away from the traditional, fully integrated shipping company which performed all tasks in-house. Instead, we have specialized shipping investment firms, management companies, marketing pools and so on. This fragmentation and specialization is a natural response to the market realities of the last 30 years and the high level of costs in the Nordic countries. Shipping is not unique in this respect – outsourcing and offshoring of non-essential tasks and concentration on the strategic core (or, as economists would prefer to put it, the tasks in which you have your comparative advantage) have been the trend in most industries.

Nevertheless, fragmentation and specialization could be a double-edged sword, for two reasons.

The first, which applies to many industries that respond to competition from Asia by offshoring non-core tasks, is that all tasks may be non-core in the end. In industries such as clothing, shipbuilding and car manufacturing, offshoring to Asia of the most labour-intensive parts of the value chain has typically been the first step in the gradual relocation of most (and in the end all) activities.

The same may well be true for shipping. Nordic companies, who outsourced crewing to Asia in the 1980s, are finding it increasingly difficult to recruit people to technical operation and management, so we see a trend towards moving technical operations to Asia as well. The growth in Asian shipping has, at the same time, made it more attractive to look for partners and other investors there.

The second reason is that to outsource activities from an independent shipping company is to outsource activities that have already been outsourced – from the cargo owner to the shipping company. To do so may be smart, but not necessarily wise. The trend seems to be for cargo owners to become more, not less, concerned about agency problems, particularly as environmental concerns have grown and cargo owners are made accountable for environmental problems in the transport chain regardless of whether transportation is an in-house or outsourced activity. Outsourcing to a company which in turns outsources to an undefined chain of new agents and subagents is unlikely to remain attractive in such a setting.

The troublesome scenario, therefore, is one where the integrated shipping company has problems surviving in the Nordic area because of the cost level, and where the functionally specialized company cannot earn an efficiency price premium because it cannot guarantee high quality for the services that it does not provide itself, and thus must survive in the low-profit, high-risk tramp shipping markets.

The solution is critical mass.

A fully integrated shipping company can survive in the Nordic area by compensating for high costs through greater efficiency. To do so, however, it must be large enough to support top-quality technical, operational and marketing staffs in-house – that is, by developing a self-reinforcing shipping cluster within the company. The most notable exception to the fragmentation trend – A. P. Møller – may be an example of just that.

The rest of the industry must retain critical mass at the industry level: it must be large enough (a) to provide opportunities for profitable intermediation (deal-making), (b) to develop and maintain above-average sale-and-purchase expertise, and (c) to have a sufficiently high influx of new companies to replace the steady flow of gamblers who will lose.

The nice thing about an industrial cluster is that it is self-reinforcing so long as it has critical mass. The sad thing is that it disintegrates rapidly once it is below critical mass. Swedish shipping is an example of the latter. Norwegian and Danish shipping (for different reasons) are still examples of the former.

Bibliography

Abernathy, W. and J. Utterback (1978) 'Patterns of industrial innovation', *Technology Review*, 80 (7), 40–7.

Adland, R. and K. Cullinane (2005) 'A time-varying risk premium in the term structure of bulk shipping freight rates', *Journal of Transport Economics and Policy*, 39 (2), 191–208.

Alderton, T. (ed.) (2004) *The Global Seafarer: Living and working conditions in a globalized industry* (Geneva: International Labour Office).

Alderton, T. and N. Winchester (2002) 'Globalisation and de-regulation in the maritime industry', *Marine Policy*, 26 (1), 35–43.

Andersson, L. F. (2005) *Bilateral Shipping and Trade: Swedish–Finnish experiences in the postwar period* (Umeå: Umeå University).

Aspden, P. (1995) Shipping Law Faces Europe: European policy, competition, and environment: international colloquium held on 16, 17 and 18 November (Antwerp: Maklu).

Bakka, D. Jr (2004) *Vekst gjennom nyskapning* (Bergen: Seatrans DA).

—— (2005) *Skipsfartens bok* – Norges maritime næringer 2006 (Gothenburg: Breakwater Publishing).

Barton, J. R. (1999) ' "Flags of Convenience": geoeconomics and regulatory minimisation', *Journal of Economic and Social Geography*, 90 (2), 142–55.

Benito, G., E. Berger, M. de la Forest and J. Shun (2003) 'A cluster analysis of the maritime sector in Norway', *International Journal of Transport Management*, 1 (4), 203–15.

Bennathan, E and A. A. Walters (1969) *The Economics of Ocean Freight Rates* (New York: Praeger).

Beth, L., A. Hader and R. Kappel (1984) *25 Years of World Shipping* (London: Fairplay Publications).

Bjerrum, C. A. (1993) ØK i uvejr: Da ØKs aktiekapital forsvandt i Stillehavet (Copenhagen: Børsen).

Bjerve, P. J. and O. Myrvoll (eds) (1971) *Økonomi og Politikk* (Oslo: H. Aschehoug & Co.).

Björklund, B., B. Fris and A. Röhl (eds) (1984) *Walleniusrederierna 1934–1984: glimtar ur rederiets historia med anledning av 50-årsjubiléet den 23 november 1984* (Stockholm: Rederi AB Soya).

Bohlin, J. (1989) *Svensk varvsindustri 1920–1975: lönsamhet, finansiering och arbetsmarknad* (Göteborg: Ekonomisk-historiska Institutionen).

Bramsen, B. (1983) *Hundrede år under Dannebrog 1883–1993* (Rungsted: Rederiet Dannebrog).

Brautaset, C. (2002) 'Norsk Eksport 1830–1865', unpublished PhD thesis, Norges Handelshøyskole, Bergen.

Broeze, F. (1998a) 'Containerization and the globalization of liner shipping', in D. J. Starkey and G. Harlaftis (eds), *Global Markets: The internationalization of the sea transport industries since 1850* (St Johns, NL: IMEHA).

Broeze, F. (1998b) 'At sea and ashore: a review of the historiography of modern shipping', *NEHA-Bulletin*, 12 (1), 3–37.

——(2002) 'The globalisation of the oceans: containerisation from the 1950s to the present', *Research in Maritime History*, no. 23 (St Johns, NL, IMEHA).

Brooks, M. (2000) *Sea Change in Liner Shipping: Regulation and managerial decision-making in a global industry* (Oxford: Pergamon).

Brooks, M. R. and P. Ritchie (2006) 'Mergers and acquisitions in the maritime transport industry 1960–2000', *Transportation Journal*, 45 (2), 7–22.

Broström (2008) *Broström Annual Report 2007* (Göteborg: Broström).

Burg, G. v. d. (1969) *Containerisation: A modern transport system* (London: Hutchinson).

Cafruny, A. W (1987) *Ruling the Waves: The political economy of international shipping* (Berkeley, CA: University of California Press).

Campbell, J. L. and O. K. Pedersen (2001) *The Rise of Neoliberalism and Institutional Analysis* (Princeton: Princeton University Press).

Carlisle, R. P. (1981) *Sovereignty for Sale: The origins and evolution of the Panamanian and Liberian Flags of Convenience* (Annapolis, MA: US Naval Institute).

Carter, J. P. (1956) 'The new maritime nations', *The Journal of Business*, 29 (3), 207–15.

Casson, M. (1986) 'The role of vertical integration in the shipping industry', *Journal of Transport Economics and Policy*, 20 (1), 7–29.

Chida, T. and P. N. Davies (1990) *The Japanese Shipping and Shipbuilding Industries: A history of their modern growth* (London: Athlone Press).

Christensen, I. L. and C. Ydesen (2009) 'Staten, individet og styringen' in A. Lundkvist (ed.) *Dansk nyliberalisme* (Copenhagen: Frydendal).

Concordia Maritime AB (various years) *Concordia Maritime AB: Annual report and accounts* (Göteborg: Concordia Maritime AB).

Cudahy, B. J. (2006) *Box Boats: How container shipping changed the world* (New York: Fordham University Press).

Cufley, C. F. H. (1960) *Ocean Freights and Chartering* (London: Staples Press).

Dagens Næringsliv, various issues.

Dahl, C. G. (2003) *Loggbok från kust och hav 2003* (Karlskrona: Canopus förlag).

Danmarks Rederiforening (1949–2010) *Annual Report* (Copenhagen: Danish Shipowners' Association).

——(1984) *Frit hav. Dansk skibsfart i 100 år.* (Copenhagen: Danish Shipowners' Association).

——(1986) *Dansk skibsfarts konkurrencevilkår* (Copenhagen: Danish Shipowners' Association).

—— (1987) *Konkurrencesituationen for dansk skibsfart*: Notat 13/10–87 (Copenhagen: Danish Shipowners' Association).

DeSombre, E. R. (2002) 'Globalization, competition, and convergence: shipping and the race to the middle', *Global Governance*, 14 (2), 179–98.

——(2006) *Flagging Standards: Globalization and environmental, safety, and labor regulations at sea* (Cambridge, MA: MIT Press).

Donovan, A. and J. Bonney (2006) *The Box That Changed the World: Fifty years of container shipping – an illustrated history* (East Windsor, NJ: Commonwealth Business Media Inc.).

Drejer, I., F. S. Kristensen and K. Laursen (1999) 'Cluster studies as a basis for industrial policy: the case of Denmark', *Industry and Innovation*, 6 (2), 171–90.

Drewry, H. P. (1977) *The Growth of the Car-Carrying Fleet* (London: HPD Shipping Publications).
—— (1978) *The Advance of Deep-Sea, Fully Cellular Container Shipping* (London: HPD Shipping Publications).
—— (1980) *The Status of Deep-Sea Ro/Ro Services* (London: HPD Shipping Publications).
—— (1985) *The Market Role of Large Container Ro/Ro Vessels*, vol. 130 (London: Drewry Shipping Consultants).
—— (2006) *Car Carriers: The fast lane of international shipping* (London: Drewry Publishing).
ECON (2010) 'Evaluering av sysselsettingsordningene for sjøfolk', *Econ-rapport 2010–023* (Oslo: Econ Pöyry).
Eckbo, E. (1977) *Risikopreferansen blant noen skandinaviske skipsredere før og etter krisen i tankmarkedet* (Bergen: Institute for Shipping Research).
Ekberg, E. (2011) 'The foray of Norwegian ship-owners into car carrier shipping, 1960–2008', *Research in Maritime History*, 46 (St Johns, NL: IMEHA).
Eliasson, T. A. (2005) *Viking Line i backspegeln* (Mariehamn: Viking Line).
Erhvervsministeriet (1996) *Skibsfinansiering 1986–1995* (Copenhagen: Ministry of Economic and Business Affairs).
Eriksen, E. (2005) *TORM i 115 år. Fra dampskibsselskab til globalt rederi* (Copenhagen: D/S TORM).
Fagerberg, J. (1988) 'International competitiveness', *The Economic Journal*, 98, 355–74.
Falkensteen, J. (1996) *Dampskibsselskabet 'NORDEN' 1871–1996: 125 years on the high seas* (Copenhagen: D/S Norden).
Farthing, B. (1987) *International Shipping: An introduction to the policies, politics and institutions of the maritime world* (London: Lloyd's of London Press Ltd.).
Fearnley and Egers Chartering Co Ltd/ Fearnley's *Review*, various issues, 1960–2009.
Fearnley Consultants (2006) *Legal and Economic Analysis of Tramp Maritime Services*, EU Report comp/2006/D2/002 (Brussels: European Commission Competition Directorate-General (DG Comp)).
Fellman, S. (2008) 'Growth and investment: Finnish capitalism, 1850s–2005s' in S. Fellman, M. Iversen, H. Sjögren and L. Thue (eds), *Creating Nordic Capitalism: The development of a competitive periphery* (Basingstoke: Palgrave Macmillan).
Fon, A. M. (1995) 'En Stormakt i Tørrbulk. En økonomisk-historisk analyse av norsk tørrbulkfart 1950–1973', unpublished PhD dissertation, Norges Handelshøyskole, Bergen.
Forsskåhl, P. (1986) 'Suomen merenkulun nykytila ja tulevaisuus. Kansalliset kehittämismahdollisuutemme' in J. Vainio (ed.), *Merenkulun nykytila ja tulevaisuus* (Turku: University of Turku).
Fougner, T. (2006) 'The state, international competitiveness and neoliberal globalisation: is there a future beyond "the competition state"?', *Review of International Studies*, 32 (1), 165–85.
Frandsen, L. A. (2008) *Svitzer: Safety and support at sea, 1833–2008* (Copenhagen: Svitzer A/S).
Frankel, E. G. (1987) *The World Shipping Industry* (London and New York: Croom Helm).

Frémont, A. (2007) 'Global maritime networks: the case of Maersk', *Journal of Transport Geography*, 15, 431–42.

Friberg, D. D. (2007) *Donsörederierna: från dåtid till framtid* (Göteborg: BAS).

Fritz, M., and K. Olsson (1994) 'Twentieth-century shipping strategies: Broström and Transatlantic, Gothenburg's leading shipping companies' in S. Ville and D. M. Williams (eds), *Management, Finance and Industrial Relations in Maritime Industries: Essays in international maritime and business history*, Research in Maritime History, no. 6 (St Johns, NL, IMEHA), 91–109.

Frontline Ltd (2010) *Annual Report 2009 FRO* (Hamilton: Frontline).

Gardiner R. (ed.) (1992) *The Shipping Revolution: The modern merchant ship* (London: Conway Maritime Press).

Gibson, A. and A. Donovan (2000) *The Abandoned Ocean: A history of United States maritime policy* (Columbia, SC: University of South Carolina Press).

Glenne, B. (ed.) (1997) *Sagaen om Saga* (Sandvika: Saga Petroleum).

Goulielmos, A. M. (1998) 'Flagging out and the need for a new Greek maritime policy', *Transport Policy*, 5, 115–25.

Graae, P. (1966) *Hundrede år på havene: Det Forenede Dampskibs-Selskab 1866–1966* (Copenhagen: DFDS).

Grammenos, C. (ed.) (2002) *The Handbook of Maritime Economics* (London: Lloyd's).

Hahn-Pedersen, M. (1997) *A. P. Møller og den danske olie* (Copenhagen: Schultz).

Halvorsen, T. (2007) *Vi seiler for velstand og lykke* (Oslo: Pax).

Harlaftis, G. (1993) *Greek Shipowners and Greece 1945–1975* (London: Athlone Press).

——(1996) *A History of Greek-owned Shipping: The making of an international tramp fleet, 1830 to the present day* (London: Routledge).

Harlaftis, G. and J. Theotokas (2002) 'Maritime business during the 20th century: continuity and change' in C. Th. Grammenos (ed.), *Handbook of Maritime Economics and Business* (London: LLP).

——(2004) 'European family firms in international business: British and Greek tramp-shipping firms', *Business History*, 46 (2), 219–55.

——(2009) Leadership in World Shipping: Greek family firms in international business (Basingstoke: Palgrave Macmillan).

Harley, C. K. (1988) 'Ocean freight rates and productivity, 1740–1913: the primacy of mechanical invention reaffirmed', *Journal of Economic History*, 48, 851–76.

Hauge, O. H. and G. Stavrum (1991) *John Fredriksen: Uautorisert biografi* (Oslo: Gyldendal).

—— (2005) *Storeulv – En uautorisert biografi om John Fredriksen* (Oslo: Gyldendal).

Hausman, W. J. (1987) 'The English coastal coal trade, 1691–1910: how rapid was productivity growth?', *Economic History Review*, 40, 588–96.

Henderson, R. and N. Clark (1990) 'Architectural innovation: the reconfiguration of existing technologies and the failure of established firms', *Administrative Science Quarterly*, 35 (1), 9–31.

Henriksen, P. (2004) *Anparter af en livshistorie* (Copenhagen: Mercandia).

Hermansson, R. (2006) *Sveriges Redareförening 100 år, 1906–2006* (Göteborg: Breakwater Publishing).

——(2007) *Historien om Stena Bulk* (Göteborg: Breakwater Publishing).
Hjerppe, R. (1989) *The Finnish Economy 1860–1985: Growth and structural change* (Helsinki: Bank of Finland).
Hjerppe, R. and J. Jalava (2006) 'Economic growth and structural change. A century and a half of catching-up' in J. Ojala, J. Eloranta and J. Jalava (eds), *The Road to Prosperity. An economic history of Finland* (Helsinki: SKS).
Hornby, O. (1987) *'With Constant Care...' A. P. Møller: Shipowner 1876–1965* (Copenhagen: Schultz Forlag).
Höwing, F., F. Johansson and T. Polesie (1995) *Kvalitet som strategi: ett rederi växer fram* (Malmö: Liber-Hermod).
Hummels, David (2007) 'Transportation costs and international trade in the second era of globalization', *Journal of Economic Perspectives*, 21 (3), 131–54.
IMCO (1969) International Convention on Tonnage Measurement of Ships.
Industriministeriet (1980) *Skibsfartens økonomiske forhold* (Copenhagen: Ministry of Industry).
——(1987a) *Hvidbog om skibsfartens konkurrencesituation* (Copenhagen: Ministry of Industry).
—— (1987b) *Skibsfartspolitisk Redegørelse 1987* (Copenhagen: Ministry of Industry).
——(1991) *Det Blå Danmark* (Copenhagen: Ministry of Industry).
Innst. S. nr. 167 (1978–9) Innstilling fra den forsterkede finanskomite om støttetiltak for skipsfartsnæringen (Norway: Parliament)
ISL, Shipping Statistics.
Jamieson, A. G. (2003) *Ebb Tide in the British Maritime Industries: Change and adaptation, 1918–1990* (Exeter: University of Exeter Press).
Jensen, N. (1993) *Anpartsbogen 1993/94: Investering i kommanditselskaber, partrederier og I/S'er* (Copenhagen: Børsen).
Jensen-Eriksen, N. (2007) *Läpimurto. Metsäteollisuus kasvun, integraation ja kylmän sodan Euroopassa 1950–1973* (Helsinki: SKS).
Jeppesen, H., S. A. Andersen and H. C. Johansen (2001) *Dansk søfarts historie, vol. 7: 1960–2000. Containere & koncentration.* (Copenhagen: Gyldendal).
Johnson, D. and C. Turner (2006) *European Business*, 2nd edn (Oxon: Routledge).
Karlsen, J. K. (1992) 'The mobile rig industry', *SNF Report 67/92* (Bergen: Stiftelsen for samfunns- og næringslivsforskning).
Karlsson, A. (2007) *Det Åländska sjöklustret. En studie i den ekonomiska tillväxtens entreprenöriella och instutionella förutsättningar* (Marienhamn: Ålands statistik- och utredningsbyrå).
Karonen, P. (1992) *Enso-Gutzeit Oy laivanvarustajana: Oy Finnlines Ltd ja Merivienti Oy vuosina 1947–1982* (Imatra: Enso-Gutzeit).
Karvonen, T., J. Vaiste and H. Hernesniemi (2008) *Suomen meriklusteri 2008* (Helsinki: Tekes).
Kaukiainen, Y. (1991) *Sailing into Twilight. Finnish shipping in an age of transport revolution, 1860–1914* (Helsinki: Suomen Historiallinen Seura).
——(1993) *A History of Finnish Shipping* (London and New York: Routledge).
—— (2006) 'Journey costs, terminal costs and ocean tramp freights: How the price of distance declined from the 1870s to 2000', *International Journal of Maritime History*, 18 (2), 17–64.

Kaukiainen, Y. (2008a) 'Growth, diversification and globalization: main trends in international shipping since 1850' in L. R. Fischer and E. Lange (eds), *International Merchant Shipping in the Nineteenth and Twentieth Centuries: The comparative dimension,* Research in Maritime History, no. 37 (St Johns, NL, IMEHA), 1–56.

——(2008b) *Ulos maailmaan. Suomalaisen merenkulun historia* (Helsinki: SKS).

——(2009) 'The container revolution and liner freights', *International Journal of Maritime History,* 21 (2), 43–74.

——(2010) 'Konttivallankumous ja Suomi' in J. Ojala, J. Eloranta and H. Roiko-Jokela (eds), *Monelta kantilta. Ilkka Nummelan juhlakirja* (Jyväskylä: Jyväskylän yliopisto).

Kaukiainen, Y. and P. Leino-Kaukiainen (1992) *Navigare necesse. Merenkulkulaitos 1917–1992* (Helsinki: Merenkulkuhallitus).

Kavussanos, M. G. and St. N. Marcoulis (2005) 'Cross-industry comparisons of stock returns in shipping, transportation and other industries', *Research in Transport Economics,* 12 (2), 107–42.

Klausen, K. K. (2010) 'Koncernledelse i det offentlige – nu også i kommunerne?', *Ledelse & Erhvervsøkonomi,* 75 (2), 7–24.

Klepper, S. (1996) 'Entry, exit, growth, and innovation over the product life cycle', *American Economic Review,* 86 (3), 562–83.

Knarvik, K. H. M. and F. Steen (1999) 'Self-reinforcing agglomerations? An empirical industry study', *Scandinavian Journal of Economics,* 101 (4), 515–32.

Knudsen, K. (1997) 'The economics of zero taxation of the world shipping industry', *Maritime Policy and Management,* 24 (1), 45–54.

Kuisma, M. (1997) *Kylmä sota, kuuma öljy. Neste, Suomi ja kaksi Eurooppaa* (Helsinki: WSOY).

—— (ed.) (2009) *Kriisi ja kumous. Metsäteollisuus ja maailmantalouden murros 1973–2008* (Helsinki: SKS).

Kumar, S. and J. Hoffmann (2002) 'Globalisation: the maritime nexus' in C. Grammenos (ed.), *The Handbook of Maritime Economics* (London: Lloyd's), 35–62.

Kurki, R. (1990) *Parlamentaarisen alusrekisteritoimikunnan mietintö. Betänkande av Parlamentariska fartygsregisterkommissionen* (Helsinki: Liikenneministeriö [Board of Transport]).

—— (2003) *Ålands sjöfartsarbetsgrupp delrapport* (Helsinki: Kommunikationsministeriet).

Kuuse, J. and K. Olsson (1997) *Sjöfart och sjöförsäkring under 125 år* (Göteborg: Sveriges Ångfartygs Assurans Förening).

Laine, J. (1986) 'Valtiovallan puheenvuoro' in J. Vainio (ed.) *Merenkulun tila ja tulevaisuus* (Turku: University of Turku).

Lange, O. (1995) *Logbog for Lauritzen 1884–1995: Historien om konsulen, hans sønner og Lauritzen Gruppen* (Copenhagen: Copenhagen Business School Press).

Larsson, B. (2000) *Svenska varor på svenska kölar: Staten, industrialiseringen och linjesjöfartens framväxt i Sverige 1890–1925* (Göteborg: Handelshögskolan vid Göteborgs Universitet).

Larsson, S. and J. Saving (1990) *Nordstjernan inifrån: 1890–1990* (Stockholm: Norstedt).

Lassen, D. D. and P. B. Sørensen (2002) 'Financing the Nordic welfare states: the challenge of globalization to taxation in the Nordic countries', *Report prepared for the Council of Nordic Ministers*.

Lastikka, P. (1983) *Finlands rederiföreningens historik. Särtryck: Finlands Rederiförening 1932–1982* (Helsinki), 166–217.

Lauring, K. (2008) *Containertrafik gennem 50 år – Container traffic for 50 years* (Elsinore: Handels- og Søfartsmuseet).

Lavie, D. (2006) 'Capability reconfiguration: an analysis of incumbent responses to technological change', *Academy of Management Review*, 31 (1), 153–74.

Lennerfors, T. T. (2009) *Stockholmsrederierna – Ägandet och nätverkens betydelse för tanksjöfartens utveckling i Stockholm 1980–2000* (Stockholm: Breakwater Publishing AB).

Levinson, M. (2006) *The Box: How the shipping container made the world smaller and the world economy bigger* (Princeton, NJ: Princeton University Press).

Lindgren, E., E. Stenberg and S. Villa (2008) *Stena – beskrivning av en Sfär* (Göteborg: BAS).

Lloyd's List (2011) Torm seeks to reverse its fortunes as it opens Brazil base, 14 January.

Lorange, P. (2005) *Shipping Company Strategies: Global management under turbulent conditions* (Amsterdam: Elsevier).

—— (2009) *Shipping Strategy: Innovating for success* (Cambridge: Cambridge University Press).

Lorange, P. and V. D. Norman (eds) (1973) 'Risk preference in Scandinavian shipping', *Applied Economics*, 5 (1973), 49–59.

Lovett, W. A. (1996) *US Shipping Policies and the World Market* (Westport, CT: Quorum Books).

Lund, C. (1995) Søgangen blev for stærk. A/S Det Dansk–Franske Dampskibsselskab 19. december 1902– 21. november 1979. *Handels- og Søfartsmuseets Årbog* (Elsinore: Handels- og Søfartsmuseet).

Lundgren, N. G. (1996) 'Bulk trade and maritime transport costs: the evolution of global markets', *Resources Policy*, 22 (1–2), 5–32.

Maddison, A. (2001) *The World Economy: A millennial perspective* (Paris: OECD).

——(2003) *The World Economy: Historical statistics* (Paris: OECD).

——(2008) *Historical Statistics of the World Economy, 1–2008 AD* (www.ggdc.net); this is an updated version of Maddison (2003).

Malmberg, T. and M. Stampehl (2007) *Femtio år med Silja* (Esbo: Tallink Silja).

Mansell, J. N. K. (2009) *Flag State Responsibility: Historical development and contemporary issues* (Heidelberg: Springer).

Martinussen, E. A. (1992) 'Cruise Shipping', *SNF Report 59/92* (Bergen: Stiftelsen for samfunns- og næringslivsforskning).

Mattson, A. (ed.) (1965) *Tre generationer på sju hav: Broströmskoncernen 1865–1965* (Göteborg: Broströmkoncernen).

Merenkulku.fi (2010) Databases at Merenkulku.fi website maintained by The Finnish Transport Agency and The Finnish Transport Safety Agency (Trafi).

Metaxas, B. N. (1985) *Flags of Convenience: A study of internationalisation* (London: Gower).

Mitroussi, K. (2003) 'Third-party ship management: the case of separation of ownership and management in the shipping context', *Maritime Policy and Management*, 30 (1), 77–90.

Mokyr, J. (2006) 'Preface: Successful small open economies and the importance of good institutions' in J. Ojala, J. Eloranta and J. Jalava (eds), *The Road to Prosperity: An economic history of Finland* (Helsinki: SKS).

Møller-Maersk, A. P. (1974–87) *Annual Report* (Copenhagen: A. P. Møller-Maersk).

——(2008–11) *Sustainability Report* (Copenhagen: A. P. Møller-Maersk).

—— (2009) *A. P. Møller-Mærsk: Årsrapport 2008* (Copenhagen: A. P. Møller-Maersk).

Møller, K. and H. Pade (1988) *Industriel Success* (København: Samfundslitteratur).

Murphy, H. and S. Tenold (2008) 'Strategies, market concentration and hegemony in chemical parcel tanker shipping, 1960–1985', *Business History*, 50 (3), 291–309.

Næss, E. D. (1984) *Kan Norge overleve som skipsfartsnasjon* (Bergen: SIØS).

Näringsdepartementet (2001) *Den svenska sjöfartspolitiken* (Stockholm: Näringsdepartementet).

Nerheim, G. and Gjerde, K. Ø. (1996) *Uglandrederiene: Verdensvirksomhet Med Lokale Røtter* (Grimstad: Andreas K.L. og Johan Jørgen Ugland).

Nightingale, B. (2005) 'Norway's headway', *Lloyd's Shipping Economist*, 28 (6), 7–9.

Norden (2009) *Annual report 2008* (Copenhagen: Norden).

——(2010a). *NORDEN purchases 3 product tankers*, press release, Copenhagen: D/S Norden, 20 January.

—— (2010b). *NORDEN purchases 2 product tankers*, press release, Copenhagen: D/S Norden, 19 April.

Norges Offentlige Utredninger (1980) Uteregistrering av skip og skipsfartens egenkapital, 45.

——(1983) Skipsfartens konkurranseevne, 7.

Norges Rederiforbund (2006) *Quarterly Information*, no. 2.

Norman, V. D. (1971) *Norwegian Shipping in the National Economy* (Bergen: Institute for Shipping Research).

—— (1981) 'Market strategies in bulk shipping' in E. Hope (ed.) *Studies in Shipping Economics – in honour of Professor Arnljot Strømme Svendsen* (Oslo: Bedriftsøkonomens Forlag), 13–28.

——(1982) 'Market strategies in bulk shipping', *Norwegian Maritime Research*, 10 (4), 26–36.

——(1999) 'Skipsfartskrisen etter 1973 – forløp og årsaker', *Sjøfartshistorisk Årbok 1998* (Bergen: Bergen Maritime Museum), 161–84.

——(2005) 'Norsk skipsfart – en næring vi må ta vare på?', unpublished memo, Bergen.

North, D. C. (1958) 'Ocean freight rates and economic development 1750–1913', *Journal of Economic History*, XVII, 537–55.

—— (1966) *The Economic Growth of the United States, 1790–1860* (New York: Norton).

Norwegian Shipping News, various issues.

O'Rourke, K. and J. G. Williamson (2002) 'When did globalisation begin?', *European Review of Economic History*, 6 (1), 23–50.

OECD, *Maritime Transport,* various issues, 1954–95.
——(2007) *Compensated Gross Ton (cgt) System 2007* (OECD: Paris).
Ohrelius, B. (1982) *Sjöfarten på Stockholm 1932–1982: Ångfartygs-befälhavare-sällskapet 1857–1982: minnesskrift vid sällskapets 125-årsjubileum* (Stockholm: Sällskapet ÅB).
Ojala, J. (2010) 'Työn tuottavuus merenkulussa 1710–2010' in K. Heimonen and H. Tervo (eds), *Työ, talous ja yliopisto. Jaakko Pehkonen 50 vuotta* (Jyväskylä: Jyväskylän yliopisto).
Ojala, L. and P. Saarto (1992) *Merenkulku kansantaloudessa* (Helsinki: Liikenneministeriö).
Økonomi- og Erhvervsministeriet (2006) *An Agenda for Growth* (Copenhagen: Ministry of Economic and Business Affairs).
Olofsson, P. G. (2000) 'Konkurs eller frivillig rekonstruktion? Rederiet Saléninvests finansiella kris, förhandlingarna, konkurs och tiden därefter' predoctoral thesis, Stockholm University.
Olsson, K. (1983) Från pansarbåtsvarv till tankfartygsvarv: de svenska storvarvens utveckling till exportindustri 1880–1936 (Göteborg: Svenska Varv AB).
—— (1996) Göteborgs Historia: Näringsliv och samhällsutveckling, vol. 3 (Stockholm: Nerenius and Santérus).
Osieke, E. (1979) 'Flags of Convenience vessels: Recent developments', *The American Journal of International Law,* 73 (4), 604–27.
Ot.prp. nr. 45 (1986–7) *Odeltingsproposisjon: Om lov om norsk internasjonalt skipsregister* (Norway: Parliament).
Paavonen, T. (2008) *Vapaakauppaintegraation kausi. Suomen suhde Länsi-Euroopan integraatioon FINN-EFTAsta EC-vapaakauppaan* (Helsinki: SKS).
Pade, H. (1991). *Vækst og dynamik i dansk erhvervsliv* (Copenhagen: Schultz).
Palmberg, J., B. Johansson and C. Karlsson (2006) *Den svenska sjöfartsnäringens ekonomiska och geografiska nätverk och kluster* (Jönköping: Internationella Handelshögskolan i Jönköping).
Panayides, P. M. (2003) 'Competitive strategies and organizational performance in ship management', *Maritime Policy and Management,* 30 (2), 123–40.
Panayides, P. M. and K. P. B. Cullinane (2002) 'The vertical disintegration of ship management: Choice criteria for third-party selection and evaluation', *Maritime Policy and Management,* 29 (1), 45–64.
Pedersen, O. K. (2008) *Institutional Competitiveness: How nations came to compete,* Working Paper no. 47 (Copenhagen: Copenhagen Business School, International Center for Business and Politics).
Pedraja, R. de la (1999) *Latin American Merchant Shipping in the Age of Global Competition* (Westport, CT: Greenwood Press).
Petersen, K. (1991) *Rederibranchen: Danmarks Internationale Konkurrenceevne* (ed. H. Pade) (Copenhagen: J. H. Schultz Information A/S).
Pihkala, E. (2007) 'Ulkomaankaupan kehitys ja sen arviointi' in J. Jalava, J. Eloranta and J. Ojala (eds), *Muutoksen merkit. Kvantitatiivisia perspektiivejä Suomen taloushistoriaan* (Helsinki: Tilastokeskus–Statistics Finland).
Pontoppidan, K. (1987) 'Nyt dansk skibsregister vil stoppe tonnage-flugten', *Morgenavisen Jyllands-Posten,* 30 September.
Porter, M. E. (1980) *Competitive Strategy: Techniques for analyzing industries and competitors* (New York: Free Press).

Porter, M. E. (1990) *The Competitive Advantage of Nations* (New York: Free Press).

Posner, M. V. (1961) 'International trade and technical change', *Oxford Economic Papers*, 13 (3), 323–41.

Poulsen, R. T. (2007) 'Liner shipping and technological innovation: Ostasiat and the container revolution, 1963–75', *Scandinavian Economic History Review*, 55, no. 2, 83–100.

—— (2010) 'The emergence of new organisational forms in liner shipping: Swedish liner shipping and international consortia, 1960–75', *Journal of Transport History*, 31 (1), 69–88.

——(2011) 'Shifts in the maritime labour market: drivers of demand for and supply of seafarers, ca. 1965–2008', *Proceedings of 9th North Sea History Conference* (Stavanger).

Poulsen, R. T. and H. Sornn-Friese (2011) 'Downfall delayed. Danish shipbuilding and industrial dislocation', *Business History*, 53 (4), 557–82.

Pylkkänen, A., T. Bergholm and K. Teräs (eds) (2002) *Satamillaan maa hengittää. Suomen satamaliiton historia 1923–2000* (Helsinki: Suomen satamaliitto).

Rasmussen, F. A., B. V. Rønne and H. C. Johansen (2000) *Dansk Søfarts Historie, vol. 6: 1920–1960. Damp og diesel* (Copenhagen: Gyldendal).

Ratcliffe, M. (1985) *Liquid Gold Ships: A history of the tanker 1859–1984* (London: Lloyd's of London Press).

Rederi AB Transatlantic (1988) *Årsredovisning 1987* (Göteborg: Rederi AB Transatlantic).

——(1989) *Årsredovisning 1988* (Göteborg: Rederi AB Transatlantic).

Rederi AB Gotland (2009) *Årsredovisning 2008: Rederi AB Gotland* (Visby: Rederi AB Gotland).

Rehnström, K. and L. Olsson (2003) *Svensk sjöfartsnärings innovationssystem: Igår, idag och imorgon* (Göteborg: Sjöfartens Analys Institut).

Rinman, T. (1956) *Handelsflotta och sjöfart: Sverige på världshaven* (Malmö: Allhems Förlag/Sveriges Redareförening).

——(1990) *Rederiet: Johnson Line under 100 år* (Göteborg: Rinman & Lindén).

Rinman, T. and R. Brodefors (1982) *Sjöfartens historia* (Göteborg: Rinman & Lindén).

Rochdale Committee (1970) Committee of Inquiry into Shipping, Report presented to Parliament by the President of the Board of Trade by Command of Her Majesty (London: HMSO).

SCB, 1960–2009. *Statistisk Årsbok för Sverige*, SOS/Sveriges Officiella Statistik.

Schumpeter, J. A. (1934) *The Theory of Economic Development: An inquiry into profits, capital, credit, interest and the business cycle* (Cambridge, MA: Harvard University Press).

——(1947) 'The creative response in economic history', *The Journal of Economic History*, VII, November (2), 149–59.

Seland, J. (1973) 'Comment on characteristics of ownership', in P. Lorange and V. D. Norman (eds), *Shipping Management* (Bergen: Institute for Shipping Research), 30–5.

Selkou, A. and M. Roe (2004) *Globalisation, Policy and Shipping. Fordism, Post-Fordism and the European Union Maritime Sector* (Cheltenham, UK and Northampton, USA: Edward Elgar).

Selvig, P. and L. C. Selvig (2000) *Yearbook of Scandinavian Shipowners and Ship Management Companies* (Sandvika: Imi).

Sickel, W. G. (1914) 'Pooling Agreements', *Annals of the American Academy of Political and Social Science*, 55, 144–54.
Sjöfartsverket (1998) *Den svenskflaggade handelsflottans konkurrenssituation* (Stockholm: Sjöfartsverket).
—— (2010) *Handlingsplan för ökad rekrytering av personal till sjöfartssektorn* (Norrköping: Sjöfartsverket).
Sjögren, H. (1999a) *Spelen i Saléninvest: Staten, bankerna, ägarna och ledningen 1973–97* (Stockholm: Ekerlids Förlag).
——(1999b) 'Shipping as gambling: governance mechanisms and the 1984 bankruptcy of Saléninvest', *Scandinavian Economic History Review*, 47 (1), 48–64.
—— (2008) 'Stockholms sjöfart i omvandling', in H. Lindgren and T. Petersson (eds) *Tillväxt & Tradition: Perspektiv på Stockholms moderna ekonomiska historia* (Stockholm: Stockholms stad).
Sjögren, H. , R. T. Poulsen and T. T. Lennerfors (submitted) 'The transformation of Swedish shipping, 1970–2010: markets, regulation, strategies and know-how', *Business History Review*.
Slack, B. and A. Frémont (2009) 'Fifty years of organisational change in container shipping: regional shift and the role of family firms', *GeoJournal*, 74 , 23–34.
Sletmo, G. K. (1989) 'Shipping's fourth wave: ship management and Vernon's trade cycles', *Maritime Policy and Management*, 16 (4), 293–303.
——(2001) 'The end of national shipping policy', *International Journal of Maritime Economics*, 3 (4), 333–50.
Sletmo, G. K. and S. Holste (1993) 'Shipping and the competitive advantage of nations: The role of international ship registers', *Maritime Policy and Management*, 20 (3), 243–55.
Søfartsstyrelsen (1999) *Det Blå Danmark 1999* (Copenhagen: Danish Maritime Authority).
—— (2003) *Søfartspolitisk vækststrategi. Kompetencer og vækst* (Copenhagen: Danish Maritime Authority).
——(2010) *Facts about Shipping 2011* (Copenhagen: Danish Maritime Authority).
Sornn-Friese, H. (2003) *Navigating Blue Denmark: The structural dynamics and evolution of the Danish maritime cluster* (Copenhagen: Danish Maritime Authority).
Sornn-Friese, H. and M. J. Iversen (2010) 'The Making of the Danish International Ship Register (DIS) - Foreshadowing of the Danish Maritime Cluster: A history of responsive policy to structural change in international shipping', unpublished manuscript.
—— (2011) 'Incentives, capability and opportunity: exploring the sources of Danish maritime leadership', *International Journal of Maritime History*, 23 (1), 193–220.
SOU (1998) *Svensk sjöfartsnäring hot och möjligheter* 129 (Stockholm Sveriges Offentliga Utredningar).
—— (2006) *Betänkande av Tonnageskatteutredningen* 20 (Stockholm Sveriges Offentliga Utredningar).
Soukola, T. (2003) Järjestö jäänmurtajana. Suomen merimiesunioni työmarkkinaosapuolena ja suomalaisten laivatyöntekijöiden turvallisuuden vankentajana 1944–1980 (Helsinki: Otava).
Spruyt, J. (1994) *Ship Management* (London: Lloyd's).

Stena AB (2009) *Stena AB Årsöversikt 2008* (Göteborg: Stena AB).
Stokes, P. (1997) *Ship Finance: Credit expansion and the boom–bust cycle* (London and Hong Kong: LLP) First edn 1992.
Stokseth, B. (1992) 'Open-hatch bulk shipping', *SNF Report 56/92* (Bergen: Stiftelsen for samfunns- og næringslivsforskning).
Stopford, M. (2009) *Maritime Economics*, 3rd edn (London: Routledge), 1st edn 1997.
Stortingsmelding (Report to Storting) no. 23 (1975–6), *Om sjøfolkenes forhold og skipsfartens plass i samfunnet* (Oslo).
——no. 52 (1980–1) *Om skipsfartsnæringen* (Oslo).
——no. 53 (1984–5) *Om skipsfartsnæringen* (Oslo).
——no. 31 (2003–04) *Vilje til vekst – for norsk skipsfart og de maritime næringer*
Stråth, B. (1987) *The Politics of De-industrialisation: The contraction of the West European shipbuilding industry* (London, New York and Sydney: Croom Helm).
Sturmey, S. G. (1965) 'National shipping policies', *The Journal of Industrial Economics*, 14 (1), 14–29.
——(1986) 'The code of conduct for liner conferences: A 1985 view (1)', *Maritime Policy and Management*, 13 (3), 185–221.
——(1975) 'A consideration of the ends and means of national shipping policies', in S. G. Sturmey, *Shipping Economics: Collected papers* (London: Macmillan).
Sundberg, G. (1998) Lundqvist rederierna 70 år.:Ångfartygs aktiebolaget Alfa. Rederiaktiebolaget Hildegaard (Mariehamn: Lundqvist rederierna).
Svendsen, A. E. (1992) 'Gas shipping', *SNF Report 19/92* (Bergen: Stiftelsen for samfunns- og næringslivsforskning).
Svensk Sjöfarts Tidning, Göteborg, various years.
Sveriges Redareförening (2005) *Sveriges Redareförenings Verksamhet: Sjöfartsåret 2004* (Göteborg: Sveriges Redareförening).
——(2007) *Sveriges Redareförenings Verksamhet: Sjöfartsåret 2006–2007* (Göteborg: Sveriges Redareförening).
——(2008) *Sveriges Redareförenings Verksamhet: Sjöfartsåret 2007–2008* (Göteborg: Sveriges Redareförening).
——(2009) *Sveriges Redareförenings Verksamhet: Sjöfartsåret 2008–2009* (Göteborg: Sveriges Redareförening).
——(2010) *Sjöfartsåret 2009–2010: Sveriges Redareförenings verksamhet* (Göteborg: Sveriges Redareförening).
Sveriges Redareförening and Lighthouse (2010) *Svensk Sjöfart Nyckeltal Januari 2010* (Göteborg: Sveriges Redareförening and Lighthouse).
Talley, W. K. (2000) 'Container shipping: impacts of a technological improvement', *Journal of Economic Issues*, 34 (4), 933–48.
Tenold, S. (2000) *Changes in the Distribution of the World Fleet, 1970–87* (Bergen: SIØS).
——(2001a) 'Saving a sector – but which one? The Norwegian Guarantee Institute for Ships and Drilling Vessels Ltd', *The International Journal of Maritime History*, 13 (1), 39–62.
——(2001b) *The Shipping Crisis of the 1970s: Causes, effects and implications for Norwegian shipping* (Bergen: Norges handelshøyskole).
——(2006) 'Tankers in trouble: Norwegian shipping and the crisis of the 1970s and 1980s', *Research in Maritime History*, no. 32 (St Johns, NL, IMEHA).

——(2008) 'Crisis? What crisis? – The expansion of Norwegian shipping in the interwar period' in L. U. Scholl and D. M. Williams (eds), *Crisis and Transition – Maritime Sectors in the North Sea Region – 1790–1940* (Bremen: Verlag H. M. Hauschild GmbH), 117–34.

——(2009a) 'Vernon's product life cycle and maritime innovation: Specialised shipping in Bergen, Norway, 1970–1987', *Business History* 51 (5), 770–86.

——(2009b) Bulk Shipping Market Turmoil? Been there, seen that: Lessons from the last crisis in the shipping sector. Paper presented at the 2009 conference of the International Association of Maritime Economists (IAME) in Copenhagen, June 24–26.

——(2009c) *Norwegian Investments in Specialised Shipping: An exploration of the formative period, 1960–1977* (Bergen: SNF).

——(2009d) 'Specialisation strategies in Norwegian shipping: A Vernon product cycle approach', *SNF Working Paper*, no. 20/09 (Bergen: SNF).

——(2010) 'So nice in niches – specialization strategies in Norwegian shipping 1960–77', *The International Journal of Maritime History*, 22 (1), 63–82.

Tenold, S. and H. W. Nordvik (1996) 'Coping with the international shipping crisis of the 1970s: A study of management responses in Norwegian oil tanker companies', *International Journal of Maritime History*, VIII, 33–69.

Teräs, K. (2002) 'Modernisoituvat satamat' in A. Pylkkänen, T. Bergholm and K. Teräs (eds), *Satamillaan maa hengittää. Suomen Satamaliiton historia 1923–2000* (Jyväskylä: Suomen Satamaliitto).

Thanopoulou, H. A. (1995) 'The growth of fleets registered in the newly-emerging maritime countries and maritime crises', *Maritime Policy and Management*, 22 (1), 51–62.

Thanopoulou, H. A. and J. Theotokas (2007) 'Small firms in a global industry: the case of Greek shipping (1974-2004)', *Economic Policy Studies*, July, 107–27.

Theotokas, I. (2007) 'On top of world shipping: Greek shipping companies' organization and management', *Research in Transportation Economics*, 21, 63–93.

Thorsøe, S., P. Simonsen, S. Krogh-Andersen, F. Frederichsen and H. Vaupel (1991) *DFDS 1866–1991: Ship development through 125 years – from paddle steamer to ro/ro ship* (Copenhagen: DFDS).

Thowsen, A. (2004) 'John Fredriksen', *Norsk Biografisk Leksikon* (Oslo: Kunnskapsforlaget).

Thowsen, A. and S. Tenold (2006) *Odfjell: The history of a shipping company* (Bergen: Odfjell ASA).

Todd, D. (1991) *Industrial Dislocation: The case of global shipbuilding* (London and New York: Routledge).

Tor Line (1985) *20 years Tor Line* (Göteborg: Tor Line).

Torm (various years) *Annual Report* (Copenhagen: Torm).

Tushman, M. L. and D. Anderson (1986) 'Technological discontinuities and organizational environments', *Administrative Science Quarterly*, 31 (3), 439–65.

Uggla, C. (2008), Man säljer inga julgranar på annandagen – en bok om Hans Werthén (Stockholm: Ekerlids).

UNCTAD, *Review of Maritime Transport*, various issues, 1971–2009.

Uola, M. (2001) Hollming 1945–2000. Sotakorvausveistämöstä monialakonserniksi (Rauma: Hollming).

Vadseth, K., B. Kolltveit and H. B. Butenschøn (2000) *Six Decades on the Seven Seas : A saga of value creation: The Anders Wilhelmsen Group 1939–1999* (Oslo: Andresen & Butenschøn).

Vainio, J. (ed.) (1986) Merenkulun tila ja tulevaisuus (kansalliset kehittämismahdollisuutemme). Turussa 7.–8.4.1986 pidetyn seminaarin esitelmät ja puheenvuorot (Turku : Turun yliopisto).

Vainio, J. and S. Kajander (2002) *Suomen merenkulun strategia. Ehdotus 2003–2012* (Helsinki : Liikenne- ja viestintäministeriö).

Vainio, J. and S. Kajander (2003) *Suomen merenkulun strategia* (Turku: Turun yliopisto).

van den Noord, P. (2000) 'The tax system in Norway: past reforms and future challenges', *OECD Economics Department Working Paper.*

Vernon, R. (1966) 'International investment and international trade in the product cycle', *Quarterly Journal of Economics*, 80 (2), 190–207.

Viitanen, M., T. Karvonen, J. Vaiste and H. Hernesniemi (2003) *Suomen meriklusteri* (Helsinki: Tekes).

Wasström, K. (2000) Finlands och EU:s sjöfartspolitik. Certificate in International Shipping and Commerce – miniatyravhandling (Turku: Turun yliopisto).

Wergeland, T. (1992) 'Norsk skipsfarts konkurranseevne', *SNF Report 50/92* (Bergen: Stiftelsen for samfunns- og næringslivsforskning).

Westphall, P. (1978) Aktieselskabet Det Østasiatiske Kompagni. The East Asiatic Company Limited. (Copenhagen: EAC).

Wijnolst, N. and T. Wergeland (1996) *Shipping* (Delft: Delft University Press).

Wijnolst, N. and T. Wergeland (2009) *Shipping Innovation* (Amsterdam: IOS Press).

Wijnolst, N., J. I. Jenssen and S. Sødal (2003) *European Maritime Clusters* (Rotterdam: Foundation Dutch Maritime Network/Agder Maritime Research Foundation).

Willoch, K. (1971) 'Norsk skipsfartspolitikk' in P. J. Bjerve and O. Myrvoll (eds), *Økonomi og Politikk* (Oslo: H. Aschehoug & Co.).

Yannopoulos, G. N. (1988) 'The economics of "flagging out"', *Journal of Transport Economics and Policy* (2), 197–207.

Zannetos, Z. S. (1966) The Theory of Oil Tankship Rates: An economic analysis of tankship operations (Cambridge, MA: MIT Press).

Index